A History of in Hanover:

Murder on Broadway

John F. Gallagher

Riverhaven Books

www.RiverhavenBooks.com

A History of Homicide in Hanover: Murder on Broadway
is a historical work; all materials referenced may be found in the
Bibliography and Notes sections at the end of this book.

Copyright© 2015 by John F. Gallagher

First printing

Parts of this book were originally published under the title
*Rum, A Tailor's Goose, and A Soap Box: Three Murderous Affairs
in the History of Hanover, Massachusetts* through Publish America.

Published in the United States by Riverhaven Books
www.RiverhavenBooks.com

ISBN: 978-1-937588-51-9

Printed in the United States of America
by Country Press, Lakeville, Massachusetts

Edited by Bob Haskell
Formatted by Stephanie Lynn Blackman
Whitman, MA

For my wife and children

Table of Contents

Acknowledgements

The author thanks the following organizations and individuals for their assistance:

Abington Historical Society, Dyer Memorial Library, Abington, MA; Ancestry.com; Archdiocese of Boston, Chancery Archives, Braintree, MA; Autumn Haag, research archivist, Massachusetts Archives, Boston, MA; Shelley B. Barber, Library/Archives assistant, Boston College, John J. Burns Library; Boston Public Library, Microtext Department, Boston, MA; Braintree Historical Society, James Fahey, Gilbert Bean Museum and Research Center, Braintree, MA; Carol Franzosa, Hanover Historical Society, Hanover, MA; Chinese Historical Society of New England, Boston, MA; Dedham Historical Society, Dedham, MA; Barbara Barker-Kemp, Judith Grecco, Friends of the Stetson House, Hanover, MA; Hanover Center Cemetery staff, Hanover, MA; Hanover Historical Society, Hanover, MA; John Curtis Free Library, Hanover, MA; Linda Beeler, head of reference, Thomas Crane Public Library, Quincy, MA; Massachusetts Bureau of Vital Records and Statistics, Boston, MA; Massachusetts Historical Society, Boston, MA; Jennifer Fauxsmith, research archivist, Massachusetts State Archives, Boston, MA; Mount Hope Cemetery staff, Boston, MA; Patrick and Heather Driscoll; Plymouth County Probate Court, Plymouth, MA; Plymouth County Registry of Deeds, Plymouth, MA; Plymouth Public Library, Plymouth, MA; Tom Chin, University of Massachusetts-Boston, Boston, MA; Weymouth Historical Society, Weymouth, MA; Weymouth Public Library, Weymouth, MA; Wing-kai To, PhD, professor of history, Bridgewater State University; Margaret Johnson, PhD, professor of psychology, Bridgewater State University; Lorraine McNally, Natick, MA; Patricia Orr, Plymouth, MA; Jacki Earp, Weymouth, Ma; Arthur Rogers, superintendent, Village Cemetery, Weymouth, MA; Dennis Moore, Buggy Barn Museum, Blanco, TX; Jeff Bridgers and Julie Stoner, Reference Section, Prints and Photographs [Division], Library of Congress, Washington, DC; Marvin D. Miller, "This Old Trunk," Hartford City, IN; Nancy E. Rexford, Northampton, MA; Cyrus L. Pray, Jr., Cedar Lane, TX; Catherine Harder-Bernier, Town Clerk, Hanover, MA.

The author especially thanks Bob Haskell, editor, Falmouth, MA, and Stephanie Blackman, publisher, Riverhaven Books, Whitman, MA.

Illustrations

Cover Hanover Center Cemetery – site of James Costley's unmarked grave – Furnished by the author

Rum

A Tailor's Goose

A Soap Box

Introduction

A sepia-toned photograph lies in the collection of the Hanover Historical Society in Hanover, Massachusetts. Taken at the turn of the twentieth century, the picture shows a modest, cape-style house nestled among trees of oak and pine and a row of neatly trimmed shrubs. Just outside the dwelling's front door, a sun-splashed rhododendron welcomes visitors with an imposing display of blossoms. Several well-kept outbuildings stand behind the house and a solitary cedar tree grows in a small field abutting the property. A stone wall in front borders a quiet, unpaved roadway dappled in shade. The pastoral beauty and tranquility the illustration strives to capture, however, is tainted by a disturbing message scrawled across its surface: "Three Irishmen Shot Here by Seth Perry in 1845."

In 1844, the Old Colony Railroad began building a rail line between Boston and Plymouth, and by 1845 work had reached the village of South Abington. On March 17, two brothers and a friend, all Irishmen and laborers on the project, decided to lay down their tools for the day to celebrate the feast of their patron saint, Saint Patrick, at a rum shanty on Broadway in South Hanover. An alcohol-fueled disagreement between the Irishmen, the shanty's keeper, and a local man ended in tragedy when violence erupted, two men were fatally shot, and a third was severely disfigured. The bloodshed aroused the passions of temperance proponents and law-abiding Hanover citizens who decried the violence and the immoral and abhorrent effects of intoxicating liquors.

Nearly thirty years later, and less than ten years after the devastation and sorrow of the Civil War, the body of a woman employed at the Howard House hotel on Broadway in Hanover's Four Corners village was found at the bottom of the Monatiquot River in East Braintree with a bullet wound in her head. State constables began an immediate investigation into the crime, focusing their attention on the Howard House's manager, a cunning and ambitious Canadian immigrant who believed he had planned and executed the perfect crime. Information and testimony offered by Hanover's residents helped police bring the victim's murderer to justice.

In 1904, Hanoverians were shocked and dismayed once again when a popular Chinese laundryman was found murdered in his shop on Broadway in Four Corners. His attacker, a recent immigrant from Prince Edward Island, tried to escape but was quickly apprehended after townspeople notified police of their suspicions.

Journey back in time as the author chronicles these crimes that afflicted Hanover during the nineteenth and early twentieth centuries. Contemporary newspaper accounts, civil and criminal records, town histories, census returns, vital records, church records, immigration files, archival manuscripts, prison records, and other documentary evidence are among the sources used to support a factual reconstruction of all three incidents.

Explore the everyday lives of Hanover's citizens, the social and moral issues of their time, and the impact each murder had on the community, the families of the victims, and the accused. Learn about the circumstances whereby the victims, all recent immigrants, came to America filled with dreams and aspirations they would never realize.

Foreword

Sir William Blackstone, a judge, jurist, and professor during the eighteenth century, established himself as the leading authority on common law and its principles. Blackstone's *Commentaries on the Laws of England*, published in four volumes between 1765 and 1769, provided the common law definition of murder as "when a person, of sound memory and discretion, unlawfully killeth any reasonable creature in being and under the king's peace, with malice aforethought, either expressed or implied."

Blackstone recognized that "all homicide is malicious, and of course amounts to murder," except in three situations – when homicide is justified by law; excused in cases of accident or self-defense; or "alleviated into manslaughter, by being either the involuntary consequence of some act, not strictly lawful, or if voluntary, occasioned by some sudden and sufficiently violent provocation."

Blackstone defined manslaughter as "the unlawful killing of another without malice, expressed or implied; which may be either voluntarily, upon a sudden heat, or involuntarily, but in the commission of some unlawful act."

~

Capital trials basically remained unchanged over the course of the nearly sixty years that transpired between the 1845 and 1904 murders, but important changes were made in trial procedure. In 1845, constitutional safeguards protected a defendant's liberty and afforded him every opportunity to establish his innocence. Article 12 of the Massachusetts Declaration of Rights guaranteed that a defendant in a capital trial had a right to a full explanation of the charges against him, a prohibition against self-incrimination, a right to confront witnesses against him, a right to legal counsel, and a right to a trial by jury. The court routinely appointed one senior and one junior counsel to represent capital defendants during a trial and an appeal.

The court guaranteed that the jury was randomly chosen and

impartial by allowing the defendant an unlimited number of peremptory challenges aimed at potential jurors. The court prohibited the use of peremptory challenges by prosecutors but did allow challenges for cause.

The defense was permitted a limited number of peremptory challenges based on no more than "sudden impressions and unaccountable prejudices we are apt to conceive upon the bare looks and gestures of another." The law, enacted in 1836, also permitted a defendant the right to challenge prospective jurors for cause in order to uncover and eliminate those who held biases against him, the prosecution, or the case. The law also required the trial judge to challenge a potential juror for cause to discover whether the person had "conscientious scruples or such opinion on the subject of capital punishment as to preclude him from finding a defendant guilty." This system of challenges allowed for the empanelment of a "death qualified" jury, or a jury in which capital punishment opponents had been purged.

In 1858, the Massachusetts legislature abandoned the common-law definition of murder and separated the crime into two degrees. Rather than deciding whether the defendant, if guilty, had committed murder or the lesser crime of manslaughter, the jury could determine what degree of murder the defendant had committed. If the crime did not fall into any of the degrees of murder established by law, the jury could then consider a verdict of manslaughter. First-degree murder was an offense committed with deliberately premeditated malice aforethought; or in the commission of, or attempt to commit, any crime punishable with death or imprisonment for life; or committed with extreme atrocity or cruelty. First-degree murder was punishable by death. Second-degree murder was defined as an offense that did not fit the definition of murder in the first degree and was punishable by life imprisonment.

In another important procedural change in 1866, legislation allowed defendants to testify on their own behalf. If the defendant did not testify, however, juries could make no presumptions about his or her guilt.

In 1869, new legislation allowed prosecutors a limited number of peremptory challenges in capital cases. The prosecutor could now challenge a prospective juror if he merely suspected the individual might acquit the defendant based on some real or supposed predisposition.

A revised statute in 1872 reduced the number of justices required at capital trials from three to two. Nineteen years later, Governor William Russell signed legislation that transferred jurisdiction for capital cases from the Supreme Judicial Court to the Superior Court and reestablished the three-judge panel. In 1894, this number was reduced to two or more judges, and to one judge in 1910.

~

Massachusetts businesses and government agencies practiced a six-day workweek in the nineteenth and early twentieth century. It was not uncommon for courts to hold sessions every day of the week except Sunday, a day of religious observance and leisure.

Courts conducted business on New Year's Day until November 1916, when Massachusetts enacted legislation following a public referendum recognizing the first day of January as a legal holiday. The first observance of the holiday was on Monday, January 1, 1917.

~

Significant changes also occurred in Massachusetts law enforcement. Local constables and special police maintained order and enforced the laws within suburban communities in the nineteenth century. Most were appointed annually or on an as-needed basis and were reinforced by sheriffs and deputy sheriffs within county jurisdictions. The governor appointed the county sheriffs, and the sheriffs appointed the deputies who served under their jurisdiction.

In 1865, Massachusetts enacted legislation to establish a statewide police organization comprised of about twenty deputy constables to supplement the law enforcement efforts of the cities, towns, and counties throughout the commonwealth. The governor appointed a chief constable to oversee their activities. The original mission of the state constabulary was to enforce crimes against public order and decency throughout the state.

A law enacted in 1871 replaced the chief constable with three police commissioners appointed by the governor and increased the force from twenty to seventy men. Three years later new legislation eliminated the three police commissioners and reinstated the office of chief constable.

Massachusetts abolished the constabulary in 1875 and established a state detective force limited to thirty men and directed by a chief detective appointed by the governor. The newly organized force was charged with a specific mandate: to aid the attorney general and all district attorneys and magistrates throughout the state in the investigation of criminal activity and in suppressing riots.

In 1879, the Massachusetts District Police, comprised of two men per prosecutorial district, replaced the state detective force. Governor Alexander Rice appointed Rufus Wade as the first chief and Governor John Bates named Joseph Shaw to lead the department after Wade's death in 1904. Seven prosecutorial districts existed at the time: Suffolk County was a district of its own; Middlesex County was in the Northern District; Essex County in the Eastern District; Norfolk and Plymouth Counties were in the Southeastern District; the Southern District encompassed the counties of Barnstable, Bristol, Nantucket, and Dukes; Worcester County was in the Middle District; Berkshire and Hampden Counties in the Western District; and Franklin and Hampshire Counties in the Northwestern District.

The primary responsibility of the district police was to assist the district attorneys in solving major cases and preserving and preparing evidence for the grand jury and subsequent trials. District police also provided criminal investigative services to local police jurisdictions, county medical examiners, the state's attorney general and treasurer, and all other state agencies with a specific request.

All personnel of the state constabulary, state detective force, and district police prior to 1884 were appointed by the governor after examination by a superior court justice. Chapter 320 of the Acts of 1884 established a Civil Service Commission, and the next year four men were the first appointed to the state force by virtue of a competitive civil service examination.

A candidate for the detective force of the district police was required to pass an examination testing his experience and qualifications in four areas. Veterans were given preference over nonveterans with the same score. The first part of the test assessed the candidate's writing skills by having him compose a letter to the civil service commissioners detailing his experience; the second part measured his mathematical skills; the third was a test of his ability to legibly and accurately copy a document; and the fourth tested his knowledge of crimes, criminal processes, legal papers, and court procedures in the prosecution of criminal cases.

~

These changes in the judicial, legislative, and executive branches of government evolved in the interest of safeguarding individual rights and guaranteeing due process of law. Officers of the law and officers of the court exercised strict and faithful compliance to these mandates as they investigated, prosecuted, defended, and adjudicated the individuals charged with the murders that so adversely impacted the peaceful town of Hanover, Massachusetts, during a span of six decades over a century ago.

Rum

I challenge any man who understands the nature of ardent spirit, and yet for the sake of gain continues to be engaged in the traffic, to show that he is not involved in the guilt of murder.

Lyman Beecher, 1845

Principal Characters

Victims:
Patrick Stapleton (?-1845)
James Stapleton (?-1845)
Pierce Dolan (?-?)

Accused:
Seth Perry (1793-1874)
   Samuel Baker Perry and Anne Bates married in Pembroke, Massachusetts, in 1786. The couple built a cape-style home the same year on Broadway near Cross Street in South Hanover and raised thirteen children. Their fifth and sixth children, twins Seth and John, were born in 1793. (The Perry home still stands at 1170 Broadway.) Seth married Melinda F. (Thayer) Cox of Hanson, Massachusetts, in 1828. Melinda's first husband, Seth Cox, died two years before in a drowning accident. The couple settled in a modest "shanty" a half mile from Seth's birthplace (Perry's shanty stood at the present site of 1359 Broadway). Melinda gave birth to three children – John Haveland in 1831, Caroline Howard in 1832, and Julia Ann in 1836.
Enos Bates (1810-1886)
   Bates was born in South Hanover, the only son of Enos Sr. and Lydia Tilden Bates. He and Seth Perry were first cousins.

Judges:
Lemuel Shaw (1781-1861), chief justice, Massachusetts Supreme Judicial Court
   Shaw was born in Barnstable, Massachusetts, in 1781, graduated from Harvard College in 1800, and was admitted to the Massachusetts bar in 1804. Massachusetts Governor Levi Lincoln appointed Shaw chief justice of the Massachusetts Supreme Judicial Court in 1830. Shaw received his law degree from Harvard in 1831.
   Shaw presided over the 1834 trial of anti-Catholic rioters who destroyed the Roman Catholic Ursuline convent in Charlestown. In that trial, the chief justice, according to superior court judge and Shaw biographer Frederic Hathaway Chase, "demonstrated that he could secure a fair trial in cases where bigotry in its bitterest form strove to

2

rear its head." Shaw refused to allow questions of a religious nature in any facet of the trial and ruled "that such matters were wholly irrelevant and collateral."

Among Shaw's many landmark cases was his 1836 ruling in *Commonwealth v. Aves* that "...an owner of a slave in another state where slavery is warranted by law, voluntarily bringing such slave into this state (Massachusetts), had no authority to detain him against his will, or to carry him out of the state against his consent, for the purpose of being held in slavery." Shaw based his decision upon the grounds that slavery was "contrary to natural right and could not exist in Massachusetts."

In 1844, Shaw would apply the doctrine of *Aves* in two other cases: *Commonwealth v. Potterfield* and *Commonwealth v. Fitzgerald*. Shaw ruled in both cases that a slave owner had no right to detain or carry out of Massachusetts a nonfugitive slave against his consent, even if the slave was brought into the state unintentionally.

In his 1900 *History of the Judiciary of Massachusetts,* longtime attorney William Thomas Davis described Shaw as "the incarnation of law and justice, and it was impossible to imagine him swayed by prejudice or popular clamor. He was obedient only to the dictates of an unerring judicial mind."

Charles A. Dewey (1793-1866), associate justice, Massachusetts Supreme Judicial Court

Dewey was a Williamstown, Massachusetts, native and an 1811 graduate of Williams College. He served as Hampshire County district attorney from 1830 until 1837 when Governor Edward Everett appointed him to the Supreme Judicial Court. Dewey would sit on the court's bench until 1866 and would write some fourteen hundred opinions. He would be regarded as a man with "...a large endowment of common sense. He understood better than most, the views, feelings, interests, and prejudices of common people, and his leading trait was his wise caution and foresight in the application of general principles."

Samuel Hubbard (1785-1847), associate justice, Massachusetts Supreme Judicial Court

Hubbard was born in Boston in 1785, graduated from Yale in 1802, and was admitted to the Massachusetts bar in 1806. Hubbard served intermittently as a Massachusetts state representative and state senator between 1816 and 1838. He was a member of the state convention called to amend the constitution following the separation of the state of Maine in 1820. He was a trustee of Phillips Andover Academy and sat on the corporate board of Dartmouth College. He cofounded the American Society for the Promotion of Temperance and was also president of the American Educational Society. Massachusetts Governor John Davis appointed him to the Supreme Judicial Court in 1842.

Prosecution:

John Henry Clifford (1809-1876), District Attorney, Southeastern District of Massachusetts

Clifford was born in Providence, Rhode Island, in 1809 and graduated from Brown University in 1827. He studied law under defense attorney Timothy Coffin, and he became a partner in Coffin's office after he was admitted to the Massachusetts bar in 1830.

Four years after the Perry case, Governor Nixon Briggs would appoint Clifford attorney general of Massachusetts. In that role, Clifford and District Attorney George Bemis would prosecute Harvard Medical School professor John Webster in the sensational Parkman murder trial of 1850. Webster murdered his colleague, Dr. George Parkman, and incinerated his remains in a lab furnace.

Clifford presented the government's closing argument at the Webster trial. Samuel Warren, British barrister, declared Clifford's performance unexcelled "...in close and conclusive reasoning, conveyed in a language equally elegant and forcible. Its effect, as a demonstration of the guilt of the accused, is fearful."

Clifford was elected governor in 1852 and served for one year. He declined his party's nomination for a second term, and Governor Emory Washburn reappointed him as the commonwealth's attorney general in 1854. Clifford stepped down four years later and resumed private legal practice.

Defense:

Timothy Gardner Coffin (1788-1854)

Coffin, a respected Bristol County lawyer, was born in 1788 on Nantucket Island of Quaker parentage. He attended Brown University and was admitted to the bar in 1811. He was a short, thickset man known for his wit and anecdotes.

In the *History of New Bedford and its Vicinity 1602-1892*, Coffin was described by Leonard Bolles Ellis as having "...the faculty of grasping every point in a case, on both his opponent's and client's side, and made use of them to the advantage of his cause. His arguments were full of force and he propounded questions and cross-questions with such rapidity and such variety that to evade his keen-witted perception was almost an impossibility."

Coffin had faced some formidable adversaries during his career, including Rufus Choate and Daniel Webster. Following a hard-fought case against Coffin on Nantucket, Webster was asked his opinion of his opponent. "He is the ablest lawyer in the United States. He is one I should prefer not to meet of all others I know of."

Perez Simmons (1811-1885)

Simmons, a Hanover native, attended Hanover district schools and Hanover Academy. Upon his graduation from Brown University in 1833 and after studying under Providence attorney Charles F. Tillinghast, Simmons was admitted to the bar in Rhode Island. He practiced law in Providence until 1843 when he returned to Hanover and was admitted to the Massachusetts bar.

Simmons was held in the highest regard by his colleagues, and "by his forgetfulness of self and indefatigable efforts on behalf of his clients, he marked himself as a faithful counselor and trustworthy lawyer." Simmons later held various political offices in Hanover, including selectman, state representative, and state senator.

Jury:
Samuel Thompson (1778-1851), farmer, Middleboro, jury foreman
Israel Briggs (1786-1855), farmer, Wareham
Benjamin Brown Jr. (1793-1871), ship caulker, Scituate
Peleg Bryant (1795-1875), yeoman, Kingston
Isaac C. Curtis (1811-1880), shoemaker, Pembroke
Thomas M. Hatch (1796-1880), carpenter, Abington
Newton Mitchell (1813-1865), farmer, Bridgewater
Joseph Northey (1794-1883), farmer, Scituate
Sydney Packard (1806-1878), shoe cutter, East Bridgewater
Seth Shurtleff (1803-1884), nail maker, Middleboro

Rotheus Washburn (1803-1870), cotton gin wright, Bridgewater
Nathan Whitman (1793-1862), farmer, East Bridgewater

Coroner:
Levi Curtis (1787-1853)

Physician:
Joseph Bassett Fobes (1814-1898)
  Fobes was born in Bridgewater, Massachusetts, and graduated from Harvard College in 1839. He had been a resident physician in Hanover since 1838. A man of medium height and burly build, "his visits were always very bustling and businesslike."

~~~

The Saint Patrick's Day shooting deaths of two Irish brothers, and the near-fatal wounding of another Irishman, shattered the placid, eastern Massachusetts town of Hanover in 1845.

Hanover was a community of nearly sixteen hundred souls. Two hundred seventy dwelling houses – modest cape-style cottages with end and center chimneys; hip-roofed, two-story residences; and homes featuring Georgian and Greek Revival architecture – were scattered across its pastoral countryside.

English colonists and their descendants had migrated from Plymouth and Duxbury two centuries before and had settled along the North River in what was then part of the town of Scituate in the Massachusetts Bay Colony. They were followed by others who settled beyond the river and in the eastern region of the town of Abington during the next seventy-five years. In 1727, the three hundred residents in those parts of Scituate and Abington petitioned the state legislature to set off eleven thousand acres – fifteen and a half square miles – of land and incorporate the area as the town of Hanover. The General Court and Lieutenant Governor William Dummer, who was also serving as acting governor, approved the petition on June 14, 1727, and Hanover was constituted as a separate township.

In the beginning, Hanover was primarily a farming community, but it soon expanded and thrived with new industries. Men built sawmills, gristmills, shingle mills, boxboard mills, and forges along the town's rivers and streams and used the water to power the machinery for processing grain and producing lumber, tacks, nails, iron bars, wagon axles, and locomotive cranks. Carriage makers, harness makers, wheelwrights, and plough makers also flourished as demand for products and services multiplied. Shoe manufacturing and shoe repair became an important source of income for many Hanover residents.

Along the North River, shipbuilding and the manufacture of cannons, cannonballs, and anchors flourished, especially during the American Revolution. Shipbuilding brought prosperity to the town but began a steady decline after the War of 1812 due to a lack of readily available

7

timber, the demand for larger ships, the river's inadequate capacity, and the advent of iron and steel ship construction.

Hanover's pioneers had deep religious convictions. The Congregationalists built the town's first meetinghouse in 1728. Episcopalians founded Saint Andrew's Church in the Four Corners village in 1811, and the Baptist Society erected its first church in North Hanover the following year.

Hanoverians recognized the importance and value of education and established the first "standing school" in 1730. The town appointed its first schoolmaster four years later. The Reverend Calvin Chaddock founded Hanover Academy in 1807 and educated students from Plymouth and Norfolk Counties in the arts, languages, "higher mathematics," navigation, and surveying.

~

The Hanover community, like so many others throughout the commonwealth and the country during the early nineteenth century, embraced the precepts of temperance. A united front swept the nation as advocates assailed the evil of drink and the attending consequences of greed, violence, and sloth.

Hanover's citizens voted to prohibit the sale and consumption of spirituous liquors on May 3, 1830. The bylaw revoked existing licenses that permitted sale and consumption by retailers and innkeepers on their premises and barred selectmen from issuing new licenses for the same purpose.

On November 4, 1835, the Massachusetts General Court and Governor John Davis enacted legislation to control the sale of alcohol and regulate licensed houses. A person found in violation of the statute was subject to a maximum fine of one hundred dollars.

In his *A Historical Sketch of the Town of Hanover, Massachusetts*, published in 1853, John Stetson Barry pointed out some of the positive changes that had evolved within the Hanover community and elsewhere, citing "the thriftiness of our villages; the decrease of native pauperism; the general sobriety of the people; the absence of loungers at the bar-

8

room of the tavern, or at the grocery on rainy days…" Efforts to promote sobriety must continue, he wrote, so "all who are made in the image of God, shall stand erect in their manhood, not victims of passion, or slaves of appetite; but walking the earth in the exercise of those nobler qualities, which distinguish us from the brutes, and which ally us to the angels."

Barry acknowledged "…that until within a comparatively recent period, spirituous liquors were a common beverage of all classes in the community, and were freely sold and freely used in every town in this State." He cautioned that the temperance cause had "attained but a measurable triumph" within the past twenty or thirty years. Proponents, he insisted, must continue their efforts to "check the tide which threatened to overwhelm."

Despite the efforts of lawmakers, town officials, and local constables to limit the illicit sale and use of intoxicating liquors, offenders persisted in dispensing alcohol without a license, supplying a demand that, regardless of temperance efforts, continued unabated.

~

About 1835, a dispute arose between Hanover resident Seth Perry and Hanover selectmen. Perry had hired a nurse to care for his wife before she gave birth to their third child, Julia Ann. The nurse, who was also pregnant, gave birth to her own child while living under Perry's roof. Unmarried and destitute, she imposed upon Perry for support. His situation now made worse, Perry turned to his siblings for help in caring for his four-year-old son, John, and his three-year-old daughter, Caroline.

No almshouse existed in Hanover at the time, but the town provided for the poor and agreed to pay Perry reasonable compensation to care for the woman and her child for an undetermined period. Later, when Perry presented his expenses at town meeting, selectmen objected to the amount. Perry insisted upon full compensation and, in a fit of temper, threatened the officials by stating, "…if the bill were not paid, that the town should suffer the consequences." Impervious to Perry's warning, the selectmen refused to reimburse him and "stand the consequences."

9

Perry sued the town but later withdrew the lawsuit when he realized he couldn't afford the litigation fees. He returned to the selectmen, claimed that his uncompensated support for the nurse and her child had left him unable to support his own family, and demanded that the town provide him with assistance. Selectmen suspected that Perry was not destitute and that his appeal was motivated by spite "for the purpose of putting the town to cost." Nevertheless, they agreed to subsidize him and employed Perry "…with the view of making him contribute by his labor to the support of his family while it was a charge upon it." Perry agreed to the arrangement, but when the town sent him on work assignments, he refused to perform the tasks, and selectmen withdrew the subsidy. Angered by their action, Perry vowed "he would make up the balance of his losses by selling rum."

In 1842, Hanover town officials twice brought Perry before the criminal court in Plymouth for violating the liquor laws. Local constables filed complaints against Perry for unlawfully selling spirituous liquors without a license on June 1 and December 1. Following a hearing, the court found Perry guilty and ordered him to pay a fine of twenty dollars and court costs on each count. The punishment did little to deter Perry. After paying the fines and costs, he returned to his shanty and resumed his illegal activities.

~

Nearly a million Irish people left their homeland between 1815 and 1845, and another million fled during the Great Famine between 1845 and 1852. Their arrival in foreign cities was not always welcomed. In Boston, the undernourished and unemployed Irish poured into the city, some finding shelter in overcrowded tenements, some existing in "shanties." They needed food, housing, clothing, and health care – expensive commodities – the cost of which was suddenly thrust upon a resentful, established society.

An ugly atmosphere of anti-Irish and anti-Catholic sentiment enveloped Boston. As Irish numbers multiplied, fear and hatred increased among Bostonians who perceived them as "idle, thriftless, poor, intemperate, and barbarian," little more than "wild bison" ready to leap over the fences that usually restrained the "civilized domestic cattle."

Attacks upon the doctrines of Roman Catholicism by Anglo-Saxon Protestants began in the 1820s and 1830s. In 1834, an angry mob burned a Catholic convent in Charlestown. The crusade against Rome continued into the 1840s, 1850s, and beyond, according to historian Thomas O'Connor in his book, *The Boston Irish: A Political History*, as "so-called native Americans denounced the 'blasphemy' of Roman Catholic doctrine, the 'immorality' of the Roman religion, the 'idolatry' of the sacraments, the 'cruelty' of the priests and the 'subversive' nature of papal authority."

In *The American Irish, A Political and Social Portrait*, author William V. Shannon viewed anti-Catholic and, by extension, anti-Irish animosity by the native population, as "an available, respectable pretext..." What natives, especially in the lower-middle and working class, truly resented was the Irish threat to jobs. According to Shannon, "The Irish workingman in the next block and not the Pope in Rome was the real enemy."

Despite this climate of opposition, Patrick and James Stapleton, Pierce Dolan, and other Irishmen arrived at an auspicious time in America's history. The country was in the midst of an industrial expansion that demanded significant labor resources. To entice Irish laborers, recruiting centers in Ireland and Boston offered "meat three times a day, plenty of bread and vegetables, with a reasonable allowance of liquor, and eight, ten, or twelve dollars a month for wages." Penniless and without skills, Irish immigrants seized on the opportunity and provided the grueling labor needed to build the canals, roads, bridges, and railways of America's rapidly expanding transportation system.

Although "track construction work was among the least prestigious, most dangerous, and most demanding unskilled work of the nineteenth century," according to Barbara Driscoll in her book, *The Tracks North: The Railroad Bracero Program of World War II*, the Stapleton brothers,

11

Dolan, and many other Irishmen hired on with the Old Colony Railroad when construction began on the line from Boston to Plymouth. They cleared the right of way, laid the gravel for the rail bed, lugged the crossties and rails into place, and hammered the spikes into the tie plates and ties to secure the rails to the bed.

The work was oppressive and exhausting. Edward Wakin points out in his book, *Enter the Irish-American*, that conditions were so harsh a common expression heard among the workers was "there's an Irishman buried under every railroad tie."

In 1843, about a thousand Irish laborers and their families arrived in Concord to build the Boston to Fitchburg rail line. According to William Barksdale Maynard in *Walden Pond: a history*, "The men were paid fifty cents a day for their labor, 'dark to dark' – up to sixteen hours straight, to the horror of liberal-minded Concordians."

~

During the 1830s and 1840s in New England, railroads emerged as an alternative to the old stage lines and post roads the general public and businesses relied upon for travel and commerce. In Massachusetts, the Old Colony Railroad Company received a charter on March 16, 1844, to build and operate a railroad from Boston to Plymouth. The charter authorized the construction of a thirty-eight-mile line from the Old Colony depot at Albany and Beach Streets, through Dorchester, across Dorchester Bay and the Neponset River through Quincy and Braintree, near South Weymouth, and through Abington, Hanson, and Kingston.

~

By the spring of 1845, construction had reached the village of South Abington in what is known today as the town of Whitman.

On a chilly Monday, March 17, a group of Irish laborers on the project decided at midmorning to lay down their tools and celebrate the feast of their patron saint, Saint Patrick. Pierce Dolan, Patrick Stapleton, Michael Kelly, John Crahan, John Connor, Shea, Doherty, Cummings, Callahan, and Barrett left the work site in a horse-drawn wagon and made their way to a notorious, illicit "grog shop" in Hanover.

The Irishmen pulled up to the groggery on Broadway near Center Street at ten o'clock. Set back about twenty-five feet from the roadway,

The scene of the crime - 1359 Broadway

it was a crude one-room shanty with a loft, an attached shed, and a single fireplace. They were met inside by the owner, Seth Perry, who was alone. A fifty-two-year-old man of medium height and stocky build, Perry had piercing blue eyes, brown hair, a dark complexion, and a reputation in the community as a corrupt, violent man. Townspeople had heard him claim that he kept about a dozen guns loaded in a back apartment of the shanty and that he expected some day or other "to see his yard stained with blood."

An hour after the celebrants arrived, Perry's cousin, Enos Bates, entered the shop. Bates, a "very stout" blacksmith and stonecutter with "sandy whiskers," was thirty-five and lived with his widowed mother on Center Street, less than a mile from Perry's shanty.

Perry poured liberally, and the Irishmen, as reported by the *Old Colony Memorial*, "…were soon able by a pretty free appliance of strong drink to get themselves a good deal excited…" The raucous celebration continued into the late afternoon.

At about four o'clock, James Stapleton, Patrick's brother, and

Jeremiah McCarty, Dennis Lynch, Michael Walsh, and several other coworkers arrived at Perry's shanty. Inside, they spotted Patrick Stapleton and Pierce Dolan sprawled in a couple of chairs, inebriated and unconscious. Others were milling about, smoking from clay pipes, glasses of rum and gin in their hands. Everyone roared when Walsh and Lynch doused the two sleeping men with a pitcher of water. Patrick cursed at first but quickly came to his senses and demanded another drink. Dolan, unperturbed, staggered to the other side of the room and passed out on the floor.

Perry poured glasses for the newcomers and the revelry continued. More than fourteen men were now gathered inside the cramped, smoke-filled room.

Enos Bates sidled up to Lynch and James Stapleton and struck up a conversation. A mutual dislike developed instantly between Bates and Stapleton.

"Whatever James Stapleton said, Bates argued against it," Lynch later recalled.

Patrick Stapleton burst into song and Perry told him to stop, but Patrick ignored him and sang louder. Bates walked over to Patrick and repeated Perry's order. When the rest of the crowd began to protest, Perry and Bates ordered everyone out. The Stapletons and Dolan refused to leave.

"There isn't any man good enough for me in the country," Bates blustered. "I can handle any man, Irish or Yankee."

Patrick rushed Perry and a violent struggle landed both men on the floor. When Bates interceded and took hold of Patrick, James rushed to his brother's aid.

"They took hold of each other and wrestled, and James Stapleton pulled Bates among the brushwood in the corner [of the shop]. He pulled Bates twice among the brush in the corner," Lynch recollected.

Perry rose and stumbled to the other side of the room, and Patrick turned his attention to Bates. Pierce Dolan, who had passed out in front of the fireplace, heard the commotion and entered the fray. The rest of the Irishmen made a hasty exit and headed toward the road as the fight spilled out of the shanty and into the yard. Suddenly, a musket report and a cloud of dense, blue, sulfur smoke filled the air.

"They were all out before I got out," Lynch remembered. "Perry was standing at the middle door, with his back towards me, when I passed out by him. Of those who had gone out before I did, some were opposite the front door, and some were in the road. I was only two or three steps [from the shop] when the shot passed my ear."

Lynch started to run. When he looked back he saw Patrick Stapleton stand and clutch his breast, then fall flat on his face. James Stapleton scurried to his brother's side. A well of tears filled his eyes as he embraced Patrick's lifeless body. He looked up and saw Perry standing in the doorway with a murderous look. He was holding a second weapon, a double-barreled shotgun. In a rage, James rushed him and Perry fired a shot from one barrel into his chest, killing him instantly. The Irishmen in the roadway scattered, and Bates and Dolan got up and ran. Perry took aim, fired the other barrel at Dolan, and shattered his jaw. Dolan fell to the ground, unconscious, as Bates made good his escape.

Perry sprinted two hundred yards across the road to the home of his brother, Perez, and remained out of sight. From there, he made his way to Albert White's house. He later went to the home of Joshua Mann and then to Haviland Torrey's store at Hanover Four Corners.

William Reed, Benjamin Hall, Joshua Smith, Melzar Sprague, and other neighbors rushed to the shanty after hearing the volleys. They were horrified by the carnage. The sprawled, motionless bodies of James and Patrick Stapleton lay no more than thirty feet from the shanty. They found Dolan with a gruesome wound to his face about fifty yards farther.

A crowd gathered around the shanty as word of the tragedy spread from house to house. Town constables and other officials arrived to take control and determine what had happened. Many of the Irish witnesses who had fled made their way back to the scene and gathered in the roadway about a hundred yards away.

Within the hour, Plymouth County coroner Levi Curtis joined

Hanover selectman Albert White at Perry's shanty, and the two men appointed a jury of inquest. White directed a group of men to deliver the bodies of Patrick and James Stapleton to the home of his cousin, Benjamin White, a third of a mile away across Teague's Bridge in the neighboring town of Hanson. Other men transported Dolan in a separate wagon to the same location so that Dr. Joseph Fobes of Hanover, who had responded to White's home at the request of Levi Curtis, could treat his wound.

~

Four to five hundred outraged Hanover residents gathered at Perry's shanty that evening and threatened to demolish it. Perry had never returned to the shanty and remained in hiding. An anonymous eyewitness described the scene in a letter to the editor of the *Massachusetts Temperance Standard*.

"On [constables] searching the house after the event there were found seven muskets, all of which were loaded, except the two discharged at the men. There was also a most plentiful supply of spirits, essences, etc., barrels and bottles and runlets of rum, brandy, wine, etc. The multitude gathered to witness the spectacle could hardly be repressed from burning the house, and were only restrained by having the barrels and bottles put out, which they broke to pieces as fast as they came in reach."

As authorities struggled to control the crowd at Perry's shanty, the coroner and Dr. Fobes performed autopsies on the remains of Patrick and James Stapleton at Benjamin White's. When Curtis and Fobes disrobed the two corpses, they found more than one hundred dollars in James's trousers. Curtis later tried to ascertain next of kin for proper disposition of the property, but when his inquiries produced no useful information, he transferred the property to the custody of Old Colony Railroad administrators.

The next morning, Tuesday, March 18, Curtis reconvened the inquest inside Perry's shanty. Constables had failed to locate Perry overnight, so Curtis began the inquest in his absence. Since the death of his wife, Perry and his children had lived in the next-door home of his brother, Levi, although Perry occasionally cooked and ate meals inside the shanty while conducting his illicit business. None of Perry's three children were present in the shanty when the murders took place.

As the inquest progressed and jurors listened to testimony, laborers from the Old Colony Railroad gathered at Benjamin White's, placed the bodies of Patrick and James Stapleton in wooden coffins and onto a wagon, and began the solemn journey to Saint Mary's Church in West Quincy, the only Catholic church within miles. Following a funeral Mass celebrated by the Reverend Bernard Carraher, the church sexton and the Stapletons' coworkers committed the brothers to pauper's graves in the churchyard.

The coroner's inquest concluded just after noon, but before it ended, Pierce Dolan, who was still recovering from his wound, was brought in to testify. When Dolan saw Enos Bates, who was in custody, he charged at him but was restrained before he reached Bates.

The jury deliberated on the evidence presented and issued a warrant for Seth Perry's arrest. Jurors found Bates not responsible and released him.

The search for Perry ended at ten o'clock the same evening when Benjamin Bowker and other constables found him about a mile away from his shanty at the Hanover home of Judson Bates on Broadway. Perry submitted to his arrest without protest and was taken to Plymouth Jail, a granite structure built in 1819 and located behind the Plymouth County Courthouse in Court Square. He entered a not-guilty plea before a magistrate at the Plymouth court the following morning. The proceedings attracted an overflow crowd and required a contingent of constables from throughout the county to maintain order. When the hearing concluded, the magistrate remanded Perry without bail to await trial.

~

Within days of the Saint Patrick's Day shootings, word of the bloodshed reached communities throughout the region. Newspapers drew attention to the sorrowful events with headlines such as, "Deadly

Affray at Hanover," "Rum and Murder," and "Shocking Outrages."

Temperance advocates met at Faneuil Hall in Boston on Thursday evening, March 20, to discuss the "melancholy events of murder, on Monday last, by liquor." The group denounced the murder of the two men in Hanover "by a keeper of a grog-shanty or rum-shanty, named Perry," asserting that the event had afforded "another most melancholy proof of the effects of the liquor business, as causing crime, murder, pauperism, and great evils to the community." In support of their disdain for the sale of intoxicating drinks, the attendees, in unanimous resolutions, "once more enter our solemn protest against liquor-selling, as an immorality that ought not to continue." Further, "that we will 'cry aloud and spare not,' till the people compel the grog-shanty, saloon, and all places selling strong drinks, to change their business."

On March 22, 1845, the *Old Colony Memorial* published an article about the killings and alleged that a dozen Irishmen, all intoxicated, had caused a disturbance at Perry's "grog shop." Perry had reportedly refused to serve them any more liquor, had ordered them from his shop, and had shot several men following a scuffle.

A week after the *Old Colony Memorial*'s account of the shooting, Charles Dyer, a forty-nine-year-old Hanover tack manufacturer, wrote to the newspaper's editor to rectify inaccuracies he found in the article. Dyer was one of several jurors who had heard evidence at the coroner's inquest the day after the incident. He was a temperance advocate and a vocal opponent of Perry's illicit rum dealing.

According to Dyer, testimony at the inquest revealed that Seth Perry had never refused anyone a drink but had poured freely; not all of those present were inebriated but instead were "sober men, pledged teetotalers."

Dyer expressed confidence in the testimony presented at the inquest. "In justice to the witnesses in this affair," he wrote, "I must say I never saw men appear better, and manifest a more commendable temper, and desire to tell the facts just as they occurred."

~

Two days after the Stapletons died, Joseph Beal of Kingston, an auditor for the Old Colony Railroad, appeared at Plymouth County Probate Court and petitioned Judge Aaron Hobart to appoint him as administrator for the brothers' estates.

Beal declared under oath that Patrick and James Stapleton of Abington, Massachusetts, were aliens, had died intestate, and had left no heirs or relatives in Massachusetts to inherit their assets under the laws of the commonwealth.

Judge Hobart appointed Beal as administrator of the goods and estates of James and Patrick Stapleton on May 6. The court ordered Beal to make and return a "true inventory of all the real estate and all the goods, chattels, rights, and credits of the deceased" within three months. The court further ordered that Beal "render upon oath, a true account of his administration" within one year.

Beal presented his inventory to the probate court three months later. He ascertained that the two brothers had no property other than the $114.20 in cash found by coroner Curtis in James Stapleton's trousers at the autopsy. Beal divided the sum and ascribed $57.20 to James Stapleton and $57 to Patrick Stapleton.

It was not until February 15, 1847, that the probate court judge allowed Beal's petitions of administration for the Stapletons' estates. Disbursement of funds to Levi Curtis, E. Gilmore, the *Old Colony Memorial* newspaper, the Middleboro Probate Court, and a stipend to Beal for services rendered as administrator of the estates depleted the assets.

~

A grand jury held in Plymouth at the Court of Common Pleas on Monday, April 14, 1845, indicted Seth Perry on two counts of murder and one count of assault with intent to kill. Perry was brought before Justice Luther Stearns Cushing and entered a plea of not guilty. Cushing remanded Perry without bail and continued his case until Tuesday, May 13, 1845, for arraignment before the Supreme Judicial Court. Perry entered a not-guilty plea on that date. The court scheduled Perry's trial for Tuesday, June 17, 1845, and ordered that he remain held without bail.

~

As scheduled, the Supreme Judicial Court convened in Plymouth at the Plymouth County Courthouse on June 17. One hundred fifty spectators, mostly women, filled the gallery in the back of the courtroom.

The 1820 courthouse, a two-story red brick Georgian-style structure, stood in Plymouth's Court Square. The façade included tall, rectangular windows in arched brick recesses and a statue of the goddess of justice in a centered niche.

A central entrance covered by a portico led to the first-floor offices of the clerk of court, the register of deeds and probate, and a jury room. A spacious courtroom with gallery seating, jury rooms, and a law library were on the upper floor. The rectangular windows on either side of the courtroom provided sufficient light until dusk, when the court generally adjourned.

Chief Justice Lemuel Shaw

As prescribed by law, three justices of the Supreme Judicial Court – Chief Justice Lemuel Shaw, Associate Justice Charles Dewey, and Associate Justice Samuel Hubbard – presided at the trial. Attorneys Timothy Coffin and Perez Simmons represented the defendant, and District Attorney John Clifford represented the commonwealth.

Before the trial began, defense counselors Coffin and Simmons interviewed Perry, questioned witnesses, and reviewed physical evidence to determine the appropriate strategy for his defense. From the outset, Perry had made it known among friends and neighbors that he remembered being beaten but did not recall shooting anyone. The lawyers knew it would be impossible to deny that Perry had shot the three men, given the number of witnesses to the incident, so they focused on two theories. First, that Perry, in the "heat of passion," brought about by incitement, had acted in self-defense. Second, that he was not legally responsible for his actions due to "temporary insanity."

To prove temporary insanity, Coffin and Simmons needed expert testimony from a respected psychiatric expert. They consulted Dr. Samuel Woodward, superintendent of the Massachusetts State Lunatic Hospital in Worcester. Woodward was considered a nineteenth-century pioneer in American psychiatric care, and his hospital, the first public one in America for the care of the criminally and "pauper" insane, was reported to be "a phenomenal success in the recovery of patients once considered incurable." Woodward had testified in other criminal trials on the validity of a temporary insanity condition as a defense.

As for the prosecution, DA Clifford had to show that Seth Perry killed with "malice aforethought" in order to prove a charge of first-degree murder under common law.

Court officers led Seth Perry into the courtroom at 1:50 p.m. A *Boston Post* reporter described Perry's physical appearance as "a sickly hue, but it is also marked with deep and broad lines, which indicate the past indulgence of the fiercest passions which war against the soul."

Chief Justice Shaw and Associate Justices Dewey and Hubbard took their places on the bench five minutes later and called the court to order. Before the jury selection process began, DA Clifford and defense attorney Coffin jointly petitioned the court to try Perry for the murders of Patrick and James Stapleton together because they believed the facts surrounding their deaths were the same. The court denied the request, stating "it would be safer, in a case of life and death, not to depart from the usual course of trying but one such indictment at a time," and instructed both attorneys to proceed solely with the indictment against Perry for the murder of Patrick Stapleton.

Jury empanelment began, and after eighteen peremptory challenges by the defense and no challenges for cause by the prosecution, twelve jurors were selected. The jury included Samuel Thompson, Israel Briggs, Benjamin Brown Jr., Peleg Bryant, Isaac Curtis, Thomas Hatch, Newton Mitchell, Joseph Northey, Sydney Packard, Seth Shurtleff, Rotheus Washburn, and Nathan Whitman. The average age was forty-five years; the youngest juror, thirty; the oldest, sixty-six. Chief Justice Shaw

21

appointed Samuel Thompson as jury foreman.

Perry's attorneys had made every effort to avoid empaneling a Hanover resident lest he had knowledge of the defendant's reputation in the community and harbored animosity against Perry for any past transgressions.

The court clerk read the indictment against Perry for killing Patrick Stapleton. DA Clifford then presented his opening statement.

Clifford told the court that on the afternoon of March 17, 1845, Patrick Stapleton, along with several of his friends, visited the illicit rum shanty of Seth Perry in Hanover. In the afternoon, a dispute and struggle between Patrick Stapleton and Enos Bates, "an assistant to Perry in the business of his establishment," led to the murder of Stapleton by Perry

outside the shanty. According to Clifford, Perry took deliberate aim at Patrick and killed him, then turned his gun on Patrick's brother, James, and killed him. Perry also fired at Pierce Dolan, a friend of the Stapletons, and wounded him.

Clifford told the court that Perry always kept a number of loaded guns inside his shanty and that after the shootings Perry "expressed neither surprise nor resentment; but coolly locked up his shanty and went to a magistrate with the pretended complaint against the companions of

District Attorney
John Henry Clifford

the deceased making a disturbance at his place."

Clifford called thirty-year-old Dr. Joseph Fobes to the witness stand. Fobes testified that he had examined Patrick Stapleton's body at the home of Benjamin White in Hanson on March 17 and determined that a gunshot had caused his death. Fobes conjectured that the deceased must have been in a stooping or bent posture and to the left of the person who fired at him. The musket ball entered near Stapleton's collarbone on the left side, traversed through his lungs, and came out on the right side of his back.

Clifford tried to introduce testimony regarding the wounds to James

Stapleton, but Attorney Coffin objected. The court sustained Coffin's objection and ruled that the prosecution had not laid a proper foundation for the introduction of evidence relative to Fobes's examination of James Stapleton.

Fobes was excused following his direct examination and without cross-examination by the defense. Attorney Coffin reserved the right to recall Fobes later in the trial.

Clifford next called Joshua Smith of Hanson, a fifty-two-year-old farmer and surveyor, to verify the accuracy of a sketch of the murder scene Smith had prepared. After the sketch was marked as evidence, Smith referred to it to explain how he had documented the positions of the bodies in relation to Perry's shanty. According to Smith, James Stapleton was shot eight feet from the door of the shanty, Patrick thirty feet away, and Dolan one hundred and ninety-eight feet. Smith indicated that Perry's shanty was located about twenty-six feet from the road that led from Hanover to Hanson.

Smith was excused when the defense declined cross-examination.

Melzar Sprague, a fifty-year-old machinist from Hanson who lived about a half mile from Perry's shanty, next took the stand. Sprague told the court that he went over to Perry's shanty at about sundown after hearing about the shootings and saw the bodies on the ground. James Stapleton was lying on his back about ten feet from the shanty with his feet pointing toward the shanty door, and Patrick Stapleton was on his face, about thirty-two feet from the door. Sprague testified that a group of men carried the bodies to Benjamin White's house, a short distance across Teague's Bridge in Hanson. Sprague reported that, in White's house, he saw a gunshot wound on James Stapleton's breast and the impression of a rifle muzzle just above the hole made by the ball.

Sprague further testified that, on his way to White's house, he saw Pierce Dolan sitting in a wagon in front of Hanover selectman Albert White's house on Center Street holding a bandage to his face. Sprague followed the wagon's driver from Albert White's to Benjamin White's house where Dolan received treatment.

"Did you return to Perry's shanty at any point afterward?" asked DA Clifford.

"Yes, I went back the same evening and inspected the interior where I found a recently-fired double-barreled shotgun inside the door."

"What else did you see?"

"The room was in disarray, and there were spots of blood on some birch wood logs kept by the fireplace. There were barrels, kegs, and bottles of new rum and cherry rum inside the shanty as well as several other guns."

"Your honor," Coffin interjected. "The defense objects to the witness's testimony as to the contents of the vessels."

"Objection overruled," Chief Justice Shaw said. "The court will allow it."

Sprague identified a double-barreled gun shown to him by DA Clifford as the same weapon he had seen at Perry's shanty. He also identified a second gun he had seen at the shanty and stated that it too appeared to have been fired recently.

The defense had no questions, and Sprague was excused.

Clifford next summoned Jeremiah McCarty, one of the Old Colony Railroad laborers who had visited Perry's rum shanty on March 17. McCarty testified that in the afternoon he and another railroad man named Walsh had left South Abington for Perry's shanty. He found Dolan, Patrick Stapleton, and Irishmen Shea, Cummings, Kelly, Crane, and Connor, "Mr. Bates," and Seth Perry inside. As McCarty entered, he saw Dolan and Patrick Stapleton asleep in chairs. Walsh and another Irishman woke both men up with a splash of water. McCarty testified that Perry had offered him a drink, which he refused because he was a teetotaler.

McCarty said that at some point James Stapleton arrived at the shanty. Shortly thereafter, James and Enos Bates began to argue. That led to a fight in which Bates pinned James to the floor. James called to his brother Patrick to help him, and Patrick pushed Bates off his brother. Hesitant to enter the fray, McCarty said he chose to leave the shanty with several others and started back to South Abington; that he was a short distance from the shanty when he heard the sound of gunshots; but that he could not see who was shooting.

"Have you named everyone who was inside the shanty when you arrived?" asked Attorney Coffin.

"Yes, as best as I can remember," McCarty replied.

"Did any leave the shanty before you?"

"Three of them, Connor, Kelly, and Crahan, went out before I did."

"Was everyone inside drinking?"

"Some of them were drinking. Not all. I saw Bates drinking."

Dennis Lynch was the government's next witness and testified that he had arrived at Perry's shanty in the afternoon with McCarty, James Stapleton, and others. Lynch found Pierce Dolan, Patrick Stapleton, and other Irishmen, as well as Bates and Perry inside the shanty. Lynch took a drink from Perry and was talking with Enos Bates when James Stapleton joined the conversation and an argument ensued.

"Whatever James Stapleton said, Bates argued against it," Lynch testified. "They took hold of each other and wrestled, and James Stapleton pulled Bates among the brushwood in the corner. He pulled Bates twice among the brush in the corner."

"What happened next?" the district attorney asked.

"When James and Bates took hold the second time, Perry told them they had best go out, and they all went out. They were all out before I got out. Perry was standing at the middle door, with his back towards me, when I passed out by him. Of those who had gone out before I did, some were opposite the front door, and some were in the road. I was only two or three steps when the shot passed my ear."

"What did you do?"

"As soon as I heard the shot, I made a run. I looked round, saw Patrick Stapleton make a jump, and fall right on his face, in great distress of mind. I was getting over the fence when the second shot was fired. After I got over the fence I heard a third shot. There was a longer time between the second and third shots than between the first and second. I kept right on."

"Did you see who fired the shots?" asked Clifford.

"I did not see who fired, and did not look to see," Lynch replied. "I did not know but I might get hit."

On cross-examination, Lynch admitted he had "drank some that day." He swore it was James Stapleton, not Patrick, who was involved in the fracas with Bates and explained that he was the last person to leave the shanty because he was farthest from the doorway, lighting his pipe at the fireplace, when Perry ordered everyone from the premises.

At the defense's prompting, Lynch described the scene when he first entered the shanty.

"When I went into the house, Patrick was sitting on a chair, with his head down, as if he would be dropping asleep. James Stapleton was in my party, and went in with us."

"Had James Stapleton been to the shanty earlier in the afternoon?" Attorney Simmons asked.

"He was not there that afternoon till we were there," Lynch replied.

Lynch's responses were hurried and difficult to decipher because of his thick brogue. He was asked again and again during his testimony to repeat his statements.

"Did you see Patrick Stapleton involved in a struggle?"

"I did not see Patrick take hold of anybody."

"Did you see Connor clutch Perry by the throat?"

"I did not," Lynch answered.

Justice Shaw excused Lynch from the stand, and the government called Pierce Dolan. Dolan had recovered from his wounds but still had difficulty recalling details about the day in question. Dolan remembered he had gone to Perry's shanty with Cummings, Callaghan, and others, but he wasn't sure if it was in the morning or afternoon. After having several drinks at Perry's, he passed his bottle to Patrick Stapleton and fell asleep in front of the fireplace. A noise woke him, and he saw some scuffling.

"I don't recollect what happened then till I went out into the yard, and there I saw Patrick Stapleton fall," Dolan testified. "The next thing I saw was another of them down. I then ran across the road and into the field, and turning my head round, I saw just at the corner of the house a man whom I took to be Perry, with a gun in his hand; and as I turned to go on again, I received a ball just under my right cheekbone."

"What happened next?" asked the district attorney.

"The next thing I recollect I was getting out of a wagon. The bullet was extracted that night from my left cheek, in the same house that the bodies of James and Patrick were laid out."

"Are you sure it was Perry who fired the shot that struck you?"

"The man had the gun partly raised when I turned my head round in the field. I had seen Perry about all day, and I thought the man I saw was him," Dolan answered.

Dolan admitted during cross-examination that he was intoxicated at the time of the incident, but he couldn't remember how much he had drunk. He had difficulty recalling what happened inside the shanty and couldn't remember who was there, except to say that at some point, his friend Callaghan had taken hold of two guns and Perry told him they were loaded.

"Do you remember anyone saying to you, 'I thought you would have killed those two boys, Perry and Bates; and if you hadn't been shot you would have done it'?" Attorney Simmons asked.

"I don't know that any man ever said that to me," Dolan answered. "I have said, 'I know there was a row there, but I don't know whether I was in it or not.' This was the answer I gave when people asked me if I was in a row that day at Perry's."

Clifford had no questions on redirect and informed the court he had finished with the witness. The jurors filed out, and court was adjourned for the day.

~

On Friday morning, June 18, the prosecution resumed examining witnesses. By this point in the trial Clifford had established that James had died and that Pierce Dolan had been wounded on the day in question.

Clifford recalled Dr. Fobes and asked him to describe the wounds found on both men. Fobes explained that a fatal ball had entered James Stapleton's left breast and passed directly through and then out his back. Another ball had shattered Dolan's lower jaw and rested in the fleshy part of his left cheek. Fobes removed the ball, which had been flattened, from Dolan's cheek. Clifford presented the ball for the jury's inspection.

The defense did not cross-examine the doctor, and Clifford called Enos Bates to the stand. Bates testified that he had gone to Perry's shanty at about 11:00 a.m. on the day in question. Patrick Stapleton, Pierce Dolan, and five others were there when he arrived. Bates said he remained at the shanty until the shooting occurred, but he wasn't sure what time that happened.

Chief Justice Shaw interrupted Clifford's examination and asked Bates why he had gone to Perry's on March 17.

"I was going by, stopped in, and stayed some hours," Bates answered.

"Did you have anything to drink?" asked Shaw.

"I drank once or twice, but I won't be positive," said Bates.

"How did the affray start?" Clifford asked.

"One of them, Patrick Stapleton, made some noise and Perry told him to keep still several times. After that I told him to keep quiet, or persuaded him not to make so much noise. By that they did not like it, and began to clinch me and Mr. Perry."

"When you say 'they,' who do you mean?"

"There was no trouble between James Stapleton and Perry; there was a scuffle between Patrick Stapleton and Perry. [I] cannot tell whether both or either fell on the floor, but I saw them on the floor."

Bates was unsure who fell first but said he did not see any blows exchanged by the two men. He said he was "scuffling" with Dolan.

"He clinched me and the scrubbish [*sic*] we had rather raised or angered the Irishmen. Then we went out doors, the two Stapletons, Pierce Dolan, and myself scrabbling along the way."

"When did you hear the first shot?" Clifford asked.

"How long it was before the first gun was fired, I could not tell. When the first gun was fired part of us were down and part up. The effect of the first shot was that it broke up the scurry, and Patrick Stapleton was shot."

"What happened next?"

"As soon as I got up, Perry stood in the door with a gun in his hand. I was frightened and went away. I went as quick as I could. I ran away a few minutes before the next shot."

The district attorney asked Bates if he was angry with the Irishmen.

"I do not know as I was much mad. It appeared as though the Stapletons were mad," Bates replied.

Attorney Coffin cross-examined Bates and asked his opinion of the Irishmen's sobriety. He said that the Irishmen had drunk enough. Bates repeated the version of the fight inside the shanty that he had given on direct testimony but added that he believed James Stapleton had thrown him upon a heap of brush in the corner of the room. He said Patrick came to James's assistance and that there were blows between him and the two brothers. He didn't recall Dolan striking him but said that Dolan was part of the melee and was engaged with him as they went outside the shanty.

Coffin asked Bates what the Irishmen were saying to him as they were assaulting him and if he considered the attack serious. Bates couldn't remember what was said, but he felt his life was in grave danger. He denied seeing either of the Stapletons choking Perry and never noticed any bruises on Perry. He also denied seeing any of the combatants in possession of a club.

Coffin inquired about Perry's guns. Bates testified that Perry was in the habit of keeping loaded guns in his entryway. He said Perry routinely shot at geese flying overhead during the spring and fall.

When asked by Coffin if he had seen either of the Stapletons fall, Bates stated he had not. He recalled that one or two minutes had expired between the first and second shots. He said that James Stapleton went toward the door where Perry was standing after the first shot and that he didn't know which way Dolan had fled.

29

DA Clifford was troubled by Bates's testimony. His account of the struggle inside the shanty clearly conflicted with the testimony of previous witnesses and statements Bates had offered during the coroner's inquest. He asked for an opportunity to impeach Bates's credibility. Chief Justice Shaw took note of Clifford's objection and informed him that he would take his request under advisement.

Bates resumed his testimony, and after several additional questions Defense Attorney Coffin informed the court that he had finished examining the witness. Before excusing Bates from the stand, Shaw asked him if he had personal knowledge about the defendant's usual place of residence. Bates told the judge that Perry generally lodged with his brother, who lived next door, but that he sometimes cooked his meals in the shanty. He described the shanty as having one room with an attached shed and said it had served as a home for Perry and his wife until she died.

The chief justice excused Bates and called a recess to give himself time to clarify whether Perry actually lived in the shanty. At that time, under English common law, a man had a right to protect his home from attack – "a man's home is considered his castle." If a man is attacked inside his home by someone who is there illegally, he has a right to defend himself. If he killed the person or persons who had attacked him inside his home, the law considered the killing justifiable homicide. This law, also known as the "Castle Doctrine," is still in effect in most states throughout America today.

When court resumed in the afternoon, Shaw granted Clifford's request to introduce evidence that would show that Bates had changed his testimony. Clifford called David Oldham to the stand and asked him about statements Bates had made during the inquest. But before Oldham could reply, the chief justice ruled that "his testimony would not fall within the limits prescribed by the court." Clifford didn't pursue the matter any further, and the court excused Oldham.

John Connor was the prosecution's next witness. He testified that he had been at Perry's shanty with Michael Kelly and John Crahan between four and five o'clock on the afternoon of the shooting. He said that Bates, Perry, the Stapletons, and seven other railroad men were inside when they arrived. He saw an argument between James Stapleton and Enos Bates, each bragging that he was a better man than the other. He also heard Bates declare "there wasn't any man good enough for him in the country," and that he could "handle any man, Irish or Yankee."

Connor said he took a drink at the shanty but found it distasteful and threw it on the floor. He left with Kelly and Crahan, and just as they stepped outside Connor heard a clamor and turned to see the two Stapletons and Bates struggling in the doorway.

"As they came out of the door, James, I think, fell down partly, and the other two fell over him in the doorway. Then they all got up, and then Bates got both of them down in front of the door, about ten feet from the door. Then they tackled Bates and got him down," Connor testified.

"Did you see Dolan at that time?"

"Yes, Dolan was also involved in the affray."

"What happened then?" the district attorney asked.

"I next heard a noise from the house, as if somebody was moving something. I saw Perry coming down the ladder from the loft. The ladder was nearly up and down, going up from the left of the entry, inside, as you go into the door. He was within two or three rounds of the floor, and he jumped or fell the remaining distance. But he came down on his feet on the floor," Connor said.

"There were guns standing in the entry, by the casing of the door, and some inside in the room," he continued. "There were [*sic*] a pair of small pistols hanging up in the room."

"When Perry reached the floor he had a musket in his hand. He had it in his hands when I first saw him on the ladder. The moment his feet reached the floor, he put his gun up to his face and discharged it. I turned my head to see if he had hit anything, and saw Patrick staggering, with his right hand up to his breast. He walked forward I should think nearly a rod, and fell upon his face."

"What did you do next?" Clifford asked the witness.

31

"I then turned and run, or walked away, I don't know which. When I got off a little ways, I heard another discharge. It turned my head at the report and then continued to get out of the way. I had lost sight of the house when I heard the third shot," said Connor.

"Were the shots fired one after the other in rapid succession?" asked Clifford.

"I don't think there was so much time between the second and third shot as there was between the first and second."

During cross-examination by Attorney Coffin, Connor, much to the chagrin of the government, disclosed a fact that supported Coffin's theory of self-defense. Coffin asked Connor to describe in more detail the scuffle he had seen outside Perry's door. Connor told the court that Patrick Stapleton was bending down beside Bates and that James Stapleton was also over Bates and that Bates was striking at both men. He did not know if Patrick Stapleton was striking or holding Bates.

"Cummings was mixed up in the scuffle outside at first," Connor testified. "He had a birch stick of wood, which he was holding over Bates, and struck him once with it before the first gun was fired."

Coffin smiled and returned to his table. DA Clifford had no questions for Connor on redirect and Chief Justice Shaw excused him.

The district attorney intended to impress upon the jury Perry's propensity for violence with his next three witnesses.

Clifford called Thomas Manan of Pembroke who testified that he passed Perry's shanty twice on the day of the shooting. He said he saw a man asleep in the afternoon and that Bates and Perry and two other men had come out to look at him.

"Did you stop at the shanty?" asked the prosecutor.

"I went into the house. Perry, Bates, and two men who had a wagon, were talking over the law scrape that Perry was going to have and laughing about it. They hoped he would come out bright, wished Perry good-bye, and said they hoped to find him still there when they should come that way again."

"Who else was inside the shanty?"

32

"There were a number of persons sitting back, quiet. One man was sitting alone, singing."

"What did you mean by a 'law scrape'?" asked Clifford.

"I understood the law scrape was a liquor case that was coming on. I thought it was an appeal case," Manan replied.

The defense had no questions for Manan, and he was excused. Clifford recalled John Connor.

"Do you remember what Perry was wearing when he fired the shots?" Clifford asked.

"Perry had a green dress [*sic*] on, and brown pants," answered Connor.

When Coffin indicated he had no questions, Clifford called Haviland Torrey, a fifty-three-year-old merchant with a store at Hanover's Four Corners, to testify about Perry's actions after the shootings. Torrey told the court that Perry appeared at his store at "about candle-light" and asked for Alexander Wood, Torrey's business partner and a Plymouth County justice of the peace. Perry wanted a warrant for the arrest of five Irishmen who had assaulted him. Torrey told Perry that Wood was confined to bed with an illness and was not available.

"Did Perry tell you what happened?" Clifford asked the witness.

"Yes," replied Torrey. "Perry said that the Irishmen came to his place early in the day and wanted some rum, and that he told them that he had no rum for them; that they came in the afternoon with reinforcements, and said that he had some rum. They said it was Saint Patrick's Day and that they would have it. He said he refused them again, and then they fell afoul of him and beat him; that they got him outdoors and pounded him against the house, but did not get him down, and said that Enos ran. I asked him if he knew the names of the Irishmen who had assaulted him, and he replied that it would spoil a new pen to write them, they were so hard. He said he got out of his shop, locked it, and had the key in his pocket. He did not state that he had done anything to the Irishmen. I did not hear of the homicide till half an hour after he left the shop."

Benjamin Bowker, the government's next witness, testified that he assisted others in the arrest of Perry at about ten o'clock the night after the shooting. He said that Perry was at the home of Judson Bates, about a mile from Perry's shanty, and that Perry was wearing an "oldish" green jacket when he was arrested.

On cross-examination by Attorney Coffin, Bowker explained that when he asked Perry to go with him to see "Squire" White, a justice of the peace and Hanover selectman, Perry readily agreed and told him he wanted to see White too. Bowker noted that Perry was bruised and had a blackened left eye with a cut over it. He was covered with blood.

Defense counsel also questioned Bowker about an incident during the coroner's inquest the day after the shooting at Perry's shanty. Bowker told the court that Dolan, although shot in the face, was brought into the inquest to testify and when he saw Enos Bates, who was in temporary and informal custody of two citizens, Dolan tried to rush him but was restrained before he reached Bates.

"What did Dolan say at that time, if anything?" Coffin asked.

"He said he wished they had finished him," Bowker answered.

Bowker said he went to Perry's shanty after the shooting and found six guns. Coffin displayed a double-barreled gun and a brass gun. Bowker identified both and said they were two of the guns he had seen at the shanty. He said he found a drop of blood on each weapon and dirt on the muzzle of the brass gun.

Coffin finished cross-examining Bowker by asking if he had seen signs of a struggle inside the shanty. Bowker said he had noticed birch sticks and other kindling scattered all over the floor. DA Clifford indicated he had no questions on redirect, and Bowker was excused.

Clifford hoped to offer additional evidence of Perry's propensity for violence with his next witness. William Winslow, a fifty-seven-year-old farmer from South Scituate (Norwell) testified that he had encountered the defendant during the first week of March as he passed Perry's shanty while riding to South Bridgewater. Perry asked for a ride to Thomas Hobart's. Perry climbed on Winslow's wagon and struck up a conversation. Perry said he had a good many enemies in Hanover; that

Melzar Hatch was one of them and that he suspected Hatch of leading the efforts to prosecute him for his illicit sale of rum. He told Winslow that Hatch had better beware, as Perry kept "hounds." Perry then showed Winslow a pistol and said that Hatch "…might hear them (the pistols) growl; that he had given them their breakfast that morning."

Clifford called another witness to verify Perry's familiarity and skill with firearms. Thomas Damon, a thirty-five-year-old carpenter from Hanover, testified that he visited Perry a week before the shootings and Perry offered to sell him a gun. Damon inspected a double-barreled gun and a brass gun, both similar to the guns in evidence. Perry boasted about his proficiency with the weapons and showed Damon a board he and his brother had used as a target and how he had beaten his brother in a match.

On cross-examination, Damon explained that he went to Perry's shanty just after the shootings and noted blood in the entryway. He also saw blood on brush and wood inside the shanty as well as two or three drops on a cleaver. He found evidence of blood on the rear of the building, as if a wounded person had leaned against it.

Charles Dyer, the tack manufacturer who had contested the *Old Colony Memorial* newspaper's accuracy about the Saint Patrick's Day events, next testified about a conversation he had with Seth Perry about a year before. Perry wanted to know why he and other townspeople, particularly Hatch, complained about his rum selling.

"I told him he was mistaken," Dyer testified. "But I also told him that a brother-in-law had bought rum off him, and made a bad use of it, and I asked him not to sell him anymore. I would complain of him, singlehanded and alone, and shouldn't trouble Mr. Hatch or anybody else about it."

"How did Perry respond?" asked the district attorney.

"He asked me if I knew he had growlers loaded. I told him I heard the report that he carried them. He then asked me if I was not afraid of him. I told him that I was not, as I had never injured him, had always treated him kindly, and was still ready to treat him so. I told him I should never go across the field for fear of falling in with him on the road."

When Coffin indicated he had no questions for Dyer, DA Clifford informed the court that the government's evidence was "all in."

~

Defense Attorney Perez Simmons stood to present his opening

statement when court reconvened after a brief recess. Before he informed the jury of his theory of what happened on the day in question, Simmons addressed "an excitement which had existed against the prisoner – an excitement which had carried some of the most conspicuous members of the community to the extent of destroying the prisoner's property, after he had been committed to jail. Among those who had sacked his shanty were men who had been foremost in prosecuting the prisoner for violating license laws."

Perez Simmons, Esq.

Simmons told the jury that four days before Perry's trial began temperance advocates held a convention at Perry's shanty, complete with speeches and bands that paraded around the property playing a death march. The presence of the "unexampled crowds of spectators" at the courthouse was evidence of the excitement caused by these events, Simmons said, suggesting that public opinion was against his client and that Perry might not receive a fair trial because of it.

Simmons then turned his attention to the state's case against his client. He found it absurd that the state would try to convince the jury that Perry, unprovoked by threats or assault, had arbitrarily shot dead two of his customers and wounded a third.

"No juror possessed of any experience in human nature could possibly believe this," Simmons railed. "Nor would [a juror] be able to comprehend how the guns could ever have been called into use on the fatal afternoon until they heard the evidence for the defense."

Simmons told the jury that the defense intended to prove that Perry never fired his weapons until after he and Enos Bates had nearly been

36

beaten to death by the Stapletons and their companions. The fight outside Perry's shanty was a continuation of the fight inside with Bates, Perry's assistant, who was being set upon by "ten intoxicated and exasperated Irishmen." Perry, in defense of Bates and his house and home, did what any man would do under the circumstances and did so justifiably and without malice. Simmons also commented on the testimony given by the prosecution's witnesses, stating that their versions in court differed significantly from what they had been heard to say before the trial.

Simmons called his first witness. Sixteen-year-old Perez Perry, Seth's nephew, lived across the road about two hundred yards east of the defendant's shanty. Perez testified that he heard two shots on the day of the incident and from his bedroom window saw ten or twelve men running from his uncle's place. He then recalled seeing his uncle running toward his house about four or five minutes later, blood streaming from his face, a cut on his forehead, and his eye bruised. After he washed his face, his uncle left the house and went towards Albert White's place, then to Mr. Hall's and other places, returning to the house soon after.

Sixty-year-old William Reed, the next witness for the defense, told the court he saw Seth Perry at Albert White's at about 5:00 p.m. on the evening of the shooting with blood on his clothes, his forehead cut, and his eye half closed and blackened. At 5:35 p.m., Perry told Reed he was going to Joshua Mann's, and they parted company.

Attorney Simmons asked Reed if he had visited the scene of the shooting. Reed said he had and had seen the bodies of the Stapletons lying near Perry's shanty. About a month later, Reed testified, he returned to Perry's shanty and saw dried blood on the floor at the entryway and on the woodwork inside.

Simmons inquired about Perry's use of firearms, and Reed told the court that Perry kept guns for sale and barter and occasionally participated in target shooting with neighbors.

Simmons asked Reed a question to substantiate that Perry was defending house and home on the day of the tragedy. Reed said he knew Perry to use his shanty as his dwelling house.

In another question to refute the testimony of Pierce Dolan, Simmons asked Reed if he had any conversation with Dolan after the shooting. Reed said he spoke with Dolan the same night and Dolan told him that he didn't know who shot him and didn't know where he was when he was shot.

Benjamin Hall, age thirty-six, lived in Reed's house and testified that he had seen Perry on the night of the shooting and saw wounds on his face and blood on his clothes. He also said he had seen bloodstains in the entryway to Perry's shanty and elsewhere. He thought that Perry was excited, but not intoxicated, on the night of the shooting when he saw him.

Simmons called Joshua Mann, a forty-eight-year-old Hanover farmer, and asked him if he had seen Perry just after the shooting.

"I saw Perry in the road near his shanty but could barely recognize him because of his bruised and bloody condition," Mann testified.

"Did he appear intoxicated to you?"

"No, he did not, but he was agitated and in a tremor."

Mann said he went into Perry's shanty later the same night with a lantern and saw that the interior was in disarray. Mann also testified that he was at Benjamin White's house on the day of the shooting and had seen Dolan there. Enos Bates showed up outside the house, and when Dolan saw him, Dolan said, "Keep him out of my sight," then kicked at Bates and started toward him, but was stopped when two men stepped in between them.

Andrew Bates, a thirty-one-year-old shoemaker from Hanson, also testified about his observations of Perry's condition on the night of the shootings. He told the court that Perry was a gun dealer and that he and Perry sometimes went "gunning" together.

Martin Prince, a forty-five-year-old laborer from Hanson, said he gave Seth Perry a ride in his wagon to the Four Corners sometime after the shooting on March 17. They stopped at Oren Josselyn's store where Prince said he helped Perry clean up and "washed his head in spirits."

After Prince stepped down, the defense called Oren Josselyn, a state representative and the Hanover town clerk. Josselyn corroborated Prince's account.

Ethan Perry, a farmer who had known Seth Perry for more than thirty years, was the defense's seventh witness to testify about the defendant's physical appearance on the night of the shooting. The witness said that he went to Perry's shanty and inspected the interior the morning after the tragedy. He saw bloodstains on the wood pile near the fireplace and on the floor and found what he described as two "very heavy bludgeons." A crack in one contained a tuft of hair.

Simmons, as a prelude to the testimony of Dr. Woodward that he intended to introduce the following day, asked Ethan Perry to tell the court about a bizarre incident that had occurred many years before.

"I have known Perry upwards of thirty years. He was deranged once," the witness testified. "When I was quite a small boy, he came with his father to our house. He got the prayer book and sat back in the room. He then took up a [door] hinge and put it round my grandfather's neck, and my father and his shut him up in a bedroom."

After a brief cross-examination by the district attorney, Perry was excused, and Chief Justice Shaw announced an adjournment until eight o'clock the next morning.

~

The defense called four more witnesses beginning at 8:00 a.m. Thursday, June 19, to prove that the Irishmen had victimized the defendant and placed him in fear of his life. Joshua Studley Jr., Lebbeus Stockbridge, John Dwelley, and Allen Clapp all testified to Seth Perry's bruised and bloodied appearance on March 17.

Returning to the defendant's mental condition and hoping to lay a foundation for the introduction of his expert witness, Dr. Samuel Woodward, Simmons called Benjamin White to take the stand. White's home near Teague's Bridge in Hanson was where the bodies of Patrick and James Stapleton and the wounded Dolan had been taken.

White stated he had known the defendant for over forty years. He testified that when Seth was sixteen years old, he was deranged.

"He went round the streets, bareheaded, drumming on a tin pail," White said.

White didn't know if Perry used intoxicating liquors at that time, but he knew Perry to be in the habit of drinking later on.

Dr. Samuel Woodward of the Worcester Lunatic Hospital took the stand next. Simmons asked Woodward what effect a blow to Perry's head would have on the brain. Before the doctor could respond, however, Chief Justice Shaw ruled that the defense had failed to lay a proper foundation for such a question and prohibited any further examination of the witness. Woodward was excused, and Simmons moved on.

The defense next called a witness to discredit the previous testimony of government witness John Connor, who said he had seen Perry descend from a loft with a gun in his hand. John Crahan, who was at Perry's on March 17, testified that he left Perry's place after being there only a few minutes. He was on the road in front of Perry's place when the shooting began and was not in a position to see the shanty's entrance. He said that Connor was on the opposite side of the road and somewhat closer to the shanty from where he was standing and "might" have been able to see Perry in the doorway.

On cross-examination, Crahan said he had not seen a disturbance inside the shanty when he was there. He did see Bates and the two Stapletons scuffling outside, but he was some distance away and couldn't tell who was on top.

DA Clifford recalled Charles Dyer to confirm Connor's ability to see Perry in the shanty doorway. Dyer testified that the door to Perry's shanty was hung on the right post and opened inward. He believed a person in the road could easily see someone going up or down the ladder inside the entryway.

The defense moved to impeach Dyer by questioning him about his participation in the destruction of Perry's shanty and property on the night of the shooting and about his animosity toward Perry for selling rum. The court sustained an objection by the district attorney and ruled the questions as immaterial and inadmissible.

The defense called Judson Bates to the stand. He testified that he had seen blood on Perry's shirt and face shortly after the shooting. He said Perry had dined at his house at about nine o'clock the following evening and that constables had arrived and arrested Perry an hour later.

Dr. Winslow Warren, a fifty-year-old physician from Plymouth, told the court that he examined Perry at Plymouth Jail on March 19. Warren said a bruise over Perry's left eye extended to his forehead. The doctor denied seeing any evidence of a significant facial laceration.

The government recalled Dr. Fobes and asked him about treating Pierce Dolan. Fobes said he examined Dolan two or three days after he had extracted the ball from his jaw on the day of the shooting. Dolan was delirious with fever and his face was swollen. Fobes prescribed a treatment and recommended rest.

The defense had no questions for Fobes, and when the physician stepped down, Attorney Coffin informed the court that the defense had concluded its case. The court called a brief recess after which Coffin delivered his closing argument.

Timothy Coffin closed for the defense with a discussion of the law as it pertained to murder and manslaughter. He contended that the government had failed to prove the defendant had acted with malice, a crucial element of the indictment. He cited the inconsistency of testimonies by the Irish witnesses who were present at the defendant's shanty on the day of the shootings.

"Their object had been to fix the firing upon Perry," Coffin maintained, "and then, supposing that if it should come out that he was acting in self-defense, the killing of their friends and countrymen would go unavenged. They had all agreed to testify that there had been no fighting in the house, and that no one had in any manner molested Perry."

The defense had presented incontrovertible evidence, Coffin maintained, to show that a large, hostile group had gathered in the shanty; that Perry had sustained physical injury; that bloodstains were found inside the shanty; that Perry and Enos Bates had tried to evict Patrick Stapleton when he caused a disturbance; that Patrick Stapleton had assaulted Perry; that Enos Bates had gone to Perry's aid.

"Here," Coffin declared, "commenced a desperate fight between two against ten – a degree of odds which justified a resort to the nearest weapons at hand. When the fight carried out into the road and Perry saw his friend down with three men upon him and one striking at him with a birch stick, he might well fear that they would first kill him, and then turn upon himself, and therefore was excusable in firing in such an extreme emergency."

Coffin argued that after Perry had shot Patrick Stapleton, James Stapleton rushed him. Perry didn't fire at first, Coffin contended, but tried to poke James with the muzzle of the gun to keep him at bay. James persisted and left Perry with no choice but to fire upon him. Coffin concluded his summation with a plea for a verdict of not guilty and returned to his seat at the defense table.

Chief Justice Shaw motioned to the district attorney. Clifford rose and opened his closing argument by describing the defendant as "of a brooding, vindictive, and lawless disposition, [who] had familiarized his mind to the idea of inflicting summary vengeance on those who might offend him."

Clifford questioned Perry's use of firearms to resolve the conflict. Rather than threatening the men fighting with Bates or firing a warning shot to break up the struggle, Perry, "having no respect for human life, deliberately fired upon the deceased, one after the other, with as much indifference as if they were nothing more than so many noxious animals." Clifford argued that Perry's only reason for shooting the fleeing Dolan was to eliminate him as a witness to the killings.

Clifford commented on Dr. Warren's testimony, pointing out that the physician had not seen any serious injury to Perry. Since there was no evidence to show how Perry might have received the marks observed by witnesses, the jury was left with only one conclusion – that Perry's injuries were self-inflicted. How else could Perry disprove that he had shot three men in cold blood? He had to show that he had acted in self-defense, so he bruised his own eye, daubed the floor and birch sticks and his face and clothing with blood, and went to the home of nearly every friend and neighbor to exhibit himself.

The district attorney reminded jurors of Haviland Torrey's testimony and how Perry, feigning injury, had attempted to seek warrants against the Irishmen for assault.

"When he went to see a magistrate, under the pretense of being an injured man, his whole story was false throughout," Clifford alleged. "He said he would not sell rum to the Irishmen; that they then became angry and got hold of him, but did not get him down; and that Bates had run away. But not one word did he say about the Irishmen who had been killed. In fact, he supposed he had killed all three, at whom he had fired, and that no witness existed to convict him with their murder."

Before concluding his argument, Clifford appealed to the jurors to set aside any religious or ethnic prejudices they might hold against the victims and asked that they rely only on the facts as presented during trial.

Chief Justice Shaw delivered the charge to the jury and explained the general principles of the law in cases of homicide. He then turned his attention to the evidence and instructed the jury to ignore any references to insanity as a defense.

In 1843, an English court established the standard for insanity in the McNaughton case. McNaughton had shot and killed the British prime minister's secretary and was acquitted "by reason of insanity." The "McNaughton rule" created a presumption of sanity unless the defense proved "at the time of committing the act the accused was laboring under such a defect of reason, from disease of the mind, as not to know the nature and quality of the act he was doing, or if he did know it, that he did not know what he was doing was wrong." The rule became the standard for insanity in the United States and is still the standard in some states today.

A year before Seth Perry's trial, Chief Justice Shaw had presided over the Abner Rogers murder trial. Rogers had murdered the Charlestown State Prison's warden, Charles Lincoln. Dr. Isaac Ray,

43

American founder of forensic psychiatry, whose work was cited in the McNaughton case, testified for the defense and claimed that Rogers could differentiate between right and wrong but was driven by an "irresistible impulse" to murder the warden. According to Ray, Rogers believed that what he had done was right because of his mental state.

Rogers's attorney, George Bemis, pleaded with the jury to abandon the "common opinion" that a plea of not guilty by reason of insanity was nothing more than a clever excuse for getting away with murder. The prosecutor in the case argued that medical opinion should not be trusted and that the methods used by so-called experts could not lead to the truth.

Shaw had relied on Ray's expert opinion during his charge to the jury in the Rogers case. If the defense had proven that the defendant's mind was, in fact, diseased, the jury must then consider "whether the disease existed to so high a degree, that for the time being it overwhelmed the reason, conscience and judgment, and whether the prisoner acted from an irresistible impulse." Simply put, Shaw wanted the jury to decide whether Rogers's criminal actions were the result of his mental disease or if Rogers was overwhelmed by emotion, deterring him from making a rational decision. The jury found Rogers not guilty by reason of insanity.

In Perry's case, Shaw instructed the jury that the defendant's actions did not meet the "irresistible impulse" standard. Shaw believed that Perry possessed a sound mind and acted with uncontrolled emotion when he fired at Patrick Stapleton.

He dismissed the defense's theory that the killings were justified, based on self-defense, and explained the legal aspects of a man's right to defend his own home. He explained the difference between murder and manslaughter and asked the jury to consider whether Perry's acts were done in "the 'heat of blood,' and if so, he is guilty of manslaughter and not homicide."

Shaw recognized that the testimony presented by many of the witnesses was vague, and he attributed it to their state of intoxication during the incident. But if the testimony convinced the jury that there had been a fight inside the shanty and that the struggle outside the shanty was a continuation of this fight, it was their burden to determine whether such circumstances would likely cause "heat of blood, which in the eye of the law extenuates even an unlawful killing, and reduces it to manslaughter."

~

The jurors retired to deliberate at 8:00 p.m., and two hours later the foreman informed the court they had reached a verdict. District Attorney Clifford and Attorneys Coffin and Simmons took their places at the bar as deputies led Seth Perry to the prisoner's dock. Chief Justice Shaw and the two associate justices entered the room, stepped to the bench, and called for the jury.

"Gentlemen of the jury, have you agreed upon a verdict?" Shaw asked.

"We have, your honor," replied jury foreman Samuel Thompson as he rose from his seat.

"Gentlemen, look upon the prisoner. Prisoner, rise and look upon the jury," Shaw instructed.

"What is your verdict?"

"We find the prisoner, Seth Perry, not guilty of murder, but guilty of manslaughter," Thompson declared.

Perry and his attorneys showed no reaction and quietly took their seats. After the court clerk recorded the verdict, DA Clifford asked the court to delay sentencing until the next morning.

Clifford did not want to proceed with a trial against Perry for the murder of James Stapleton for several reasons. First, the trial would come at great expense to the commonwealth. Second, the prosecution had exposed its entire case and had laid bare its weaknesses during the first trial. A second trial could result in a similar conviction or, worse, an acquittal. Clifford's only alternative for assuring a conviction was to discuss a plea bargain with Perry and his counsel.

The next morning, Friday, June 20, after conferring with Clifford, defense Attorney Coffin notified the court that the defendant would retract his plea of not guilty of the murder of James Stapleton if the district attorney entered a *nolle prosequi* ("we shall no longer prosecute") as to the allegation of "malice aforethought" and reduce the commonwealth's charge against Perry to manslaughter. Clifford informed the court that he agreed with Coffin's stipulation.

Perry was brought before the court, and Clifford entered a motion to dismiss the charge for the murder of James Stapleton. When Chief Justice Shaw granted the motion, Perry retracted his plea of not guilty of murder and pled guilty to manslaughter.

The district attorney also entered a *nolle prosequi* on the indictment of assault with intent to kill Pierce Dolan, and the charge was dismissed.

~

On June 21, 1845, a *Boston Courier* correspondent reacted to the jury's verdict against Seth Perry. He disagreed with the jury's finding and wrote that Chief Justice Shaw's charge had persuaded the jurors to arrive at a manslaughter conviction. The correspondent offered his opinion that Shaw had left them "free to finding as they did, upon the ground that Perry and Bates might be considered one party in the affray, and the Irishmen the other, and that the act was committed in the heat of blood, occasioned thereby." The correspondent again emphasized that although he believed "Perry was undoubtedly somewhat abused by the Irishmen during the day," he witnessed "no direct proof of the fact."

"The great and increasing reluctance, in this community, to capital punishment, has, undoubtedly, much influence in cases of this kind." His dismay with the verdict and his reference to "cases of this kind" suggests that the writer perceived an element of ambivalence among juries to convict and execute those accused of murder. His opinion was valid because a movement to overturn the state's right to impose capital punishment was gaining momentum at that time.

The hesitation by juries to convict defendants of crimes punishable by death is evidenced by the outcome of trials conducted between 1835 and 1849 when twenty-one men were tried for murder and only five were convicted. Three had their sentences commuted to life in prison, and two were hanged. Jurors acquitted eight men, and another eight, including Seth Perry, were convicted of the lesser crime of manslaughter.

About 1830, a crusade to gain public support for abolishing capital punishment in Massachusetts began with Robert Rantoul Jr., a Harvard College graduate and a lawyer. Rantoul was born in Beverly in 1805 and was admitted to the Middlesex bar in 1831. He was elected as a state representative for Gloucester in 1834. During his term, he introduced legislation to abolish the death penalty, but the bill never passed.

Rantoul believed that the government had no legal right to take the life of another. He insisted that the United States Constitution and the laws of Massachusetts prohibited capital punishment. He contended that man no longer lived in an uncivilized, savage society and had the power to "affect the general progress of society" and the freedom "to use knowledge, reason and reflection to change any law, including that 'remnant of feudal barbarity,' the death penalty."

Rantoul also maintained that the death penalty was not a deterrent to crime, nor did it provide "the best protection for society." Rantoul insisted that the death penalty "diminished the 'natural sensibility of man for the sufferings of his fellow man' and generally promoted 'cruelty and a disregard of life.'"

Rantoul questioned those who rationalized capital punishment on religious grounds. He admitted that the Old Testament justified the death penalty, but he believed that the circumstances of that time did not apply in today's society. He believed an enlightened and pragmatic society should not base the laws of punishment on revenge but on the Christian precept of "Thou shalt not kill."

In a further indication that public debate about capital punishment was changing attitudes and values during that period, Massachusetts voters elected a Democratic governor in 1840 who was a proponent for eliminating the death penalty. The candidate, Marcus Morton, based his platform of abolishing capital punishment on arguments proposed by Rantoul.

Charles Spear, a Universalist minister, became New England's foremost proponent for abolishing capital punishment when he published his *Essays on the Punishment of Death* in 1844. Spear firmly believed in the benevolence of God, freedom of the will, and the salvation of all men. According to Spear, these three principles "would overcome every existing evil." He suggested that "...all criminals, including murderers, could, and should, be reformed."

In 1845, Rantoul, Spear, and other Boston reformers initiated a campaign to dissuade capital punishment proponents and place political pressure on elected officials to eliminate the death penalty by organizing the Massachusetts Society for the Abolition of Capital Punishment. In the same year, the society published the first issue of *Hangman*, a weekly newspaper that supported the organized campaign against the death penalty through essays, meeting announcements, news about the plight of convicted murders, and calls to action including circulating petitions for commuting sentences.

~

If it was not a reluctance to impose capital punishment, what other factors may have influenced the jury's decision to acquit Seth Perry of a murder charge? Did the social atmosphere that existed at this juncture in American history influence the outcome of the trial? Is it possible that prejudice against the Irish clouded the minds of judges, jurors, and attorneys in this case, preventing a fair and impartial judgment of the facts? Established society resented the growing population of immigrants and considered them the lowest of classes. Yankees freely voiced public criticism and directed their hate and bias toward foreigners in general and Irish Catholics in particular.

In his 2008 book *Murder and the Death Penalty in Massachusetts*, Boston College history professor Alan Rogers commented on the influence of racial bias and ethnic hatred in capital trials. He observed that "A community's social and political imperatives and its values and biases affect the way in which justice is defined and administered." One can only hope that the evidence spoke for itself, neutrality and candor prevailed during deliberations, and open-minded jurors returned a dispassionate verdict.

~

The court sentenced Perry to ten years in the state prison at Charlestown for the death of Patrick Stapleton and ordered that he serve the first three days of his sentence in solitary confinement. He was sentenced to an additional three years, to be served on and after the first sentence, for the death of James Stapleton.

After sentencing, deputy sheriffs transported Perry, handcuffed and with heavy irons on his ankles, from Plymouth to the prison in Charlestown (on the site of present-day Bunker Hill Community College). The officers placed Perry in the custody of prison officials on June 28, 1845.

The formidable granite fortress on Lynde's Point in Charlestown, Massachusetts, was completed at a cost of $170,000 ($47 million today) and opened on December 12, 1805. The prison was two hundred feet long and forty-four feet wide. A central section, sixty-six feet long by twenty-eight feet wide and five stories high, contained rooms for prison officials as well as a kitchen in the basement and a chapel and hospital in the top story. Wings on each side of the central section were four stories high with twenty-eight cells on the first story, thirty cells on the second. Each cell measured eight by eleven feet. On the third and fourth stories were thirty-two larger cells, each eleven by seventeen feet.

A stone wall, fifteen feet high, five feet thick at the bottom and three feet thick at the top, surrounded the nearly ninety-eight thousand square foot prison yard which was diligently watched by guards who peered through the windows of wooden watch boxes perched atop the walls. Officials believed the prison to be impenetrable, fireproof, and impossible to undermine.

The north wing was completed in 1828 and consisted of 142 cells, each one three and a half by seven feet and seven feet high with doors of wrought iron. The south wing was added in 1850 and contained one hundred and fifty cells on five tiers. Four coal stoves in each building kept the occupants warm. Windows on the sides and ends of the

49

buildings as well as skylight windows, all secured with iron gratings, allowed sufficient light during the daytime, and at night oil lamps provided lighting until 1853, when gas lighting was installed.

The prison held 287 inmates when Perry was brought there in 1845. He was one of three convicts between the ages of fifty and sixty and one of ten men who were serving time for manslaughter.

A turnkey and watchman led Perry to the arch inside the solitary section of the prison, searched and stripped him, cut his hair short, and shaved off his whiskers. Perry was then provided with a pair of thick pantaloons, a thick jacket, a pair of thin pantaloons, a thin jacket, two pairs of shoes, three shirts, two blankets, and a cap. Jackets, pants, and cap were half blue and half red and made of coarse cloth. The turnkey assigned him convict number 3880 and entered his physical description into the prison's commitment register: fifty-two years of age; five feet six and a half inches tall; blue eyes; brown hair; dark complexion; large wen on the back of his head; two colored moles on his right breast; two small scars on the middle of his back, and a large scar on his left knee.

In accordance with his sentence, Perry spent the first three days at the prison in idle, solitary confinement. He was confined to a ground-floor cell, eight by eleven feet, which was furnished with a straw bed, a pillow and blanket, a wooden chair, and a "slop bucket."

A watchman provided Perry with daily rations of bread and water. Air and light entered the windowless cell through openings, two feet high and four inches wide, high on the wall. This brief, harrowing confinement served two purposes: to introduce the inmate to the stark reality of prison life; and to give the inmate a preview of how severe his punishment would be if he failed to follow prison rules.

The turnkey transferred Perry to a new cell when his time in solitary concluded. The new cell contained an iron bedstead with a palm leaf mattress and pillow with cotton sheets, pillowslip, blankets, and spread. The bed was turned up against the cell wall when not in use. The cell was also outfitted with a slop bucket, a small table and a stool, a shelf, a pamphlet outlining the prison's rules, a Bible, a catalogue of books in the prison library, a bottle of vinegar, pepper, salt, and a knife, fork, and spoon.

In his book, *Prison Discipline in America*, Francis Calley Gray reported that "the prison at Charlestown resembles a great manual-labor school." The prison's warden in 1845, Frederick Robinson, assigned convicts as stonecutters, shoemakers, cabinet makers, tailors, blacksmiths, brush makers, whitesmiths, and tin workers, and required them to work in silence. Order was strictly maintained in the workspace, and supervisors quickly reported violations to the warden.

All of the prisoners were held in solitary confinement at night and began work at sunrise in the summer and at first light in the winter. They worked for about an hour before they were allowed breakfast, which they took back to their cells and ate in solitude. After forty-five minutes, guards led them to the prison chapel for ten to fifteen minutes of worship. The prisoners were then escorted back to their work shanties.

The prisoners proceeded to the "cook-room" at 12:30 p.m., received their midday meals, and went to their cells, again to eat in solitude. They were allowed forty-five minutes, although in the summer, during periods of extreme heat, they were given an hour. They returned to work and toiled until about 6:00 p.m. when guards led them to the chapel to sing and read scripture. After services, the prisoners collected their dinners and retired to their cells for the evening. This schedule remained constant every day of the week except Sunday, which was set aside for rest and reflection. The midday meals typically consisted of boiled beef and potatoes, and for supper, mush and molasses with rye bread or Indian bread and rye coffee. Other meals included broth, bread, potatoes, soups made of fox heads and offal, hasty pudding made from Indian meal, salt pork, and pea or bean porridge.

A "master of the shanty" supervised the inmates during the course of the day. When a master observed a rule infraction, he took the offender to the warden. The warden would hear the master's complaint, give the offender an opportunity to explain or defend his action, and hand out a punishment if necessary. A first or minor offense usually resulted in a warning and chastisement after the offender promised to behave.

For more serious or repeat offenses, the warden banished the offender to solitary confinement with meager rations of food. The warden also meted out floggings which never exceeded ten lashes for each offense. He authorized floggings for forty-five convicts from 1843-47. The warden ordered a total of 242 lashes during those years. One prisoner received fifty lashes intermittently.

There is no indication that prison officials ever disciplined Seth Perry, nor are there any reports that he was involved in any violent confrontations with fellow inmates during his incarceration.

Along with punishment for rules infractions came some privileges for prisoners. Prison authorities gave each inmate time to exercise, once in the morning and once in the afternoon, and always alone. Prisoners were shaved twice a week, and their hair was cut every three months. Inmates were permitted to bathe once a week in a tidal basin secured by gates in the northwest section of the prison yard, except in the winter, "…when the bathing is regulated by the physician," due to extreme temperatures and the risk to the prisoners' health.

The warden granted permission for some of the inmates to maintain gardens near their workspace. They could tend to two-foot square boxes of soil containing "tomatoes, lettuce, cucumbers, onions and other vegetables for their own use." He also authorized time for Sunday religious services and evening prayers in the prison's chapel. Some inmates were allowed to play their own musical instruments during the services and could practice every Saturday for an hour. Time for reading and writing was also permitted, and a slate and pencil were furnished to each inmate so he might learn to "write and cipher." Inmates were also given access to the prison's small library. These privileges, however, could be taken away instantly if a prisoner broke one of the rules.

Upon discharge, a convict received one pair of socks, one pair of shoes, one pocket handkerchief, one shirt, one pair of pants, one coat, and five dollars. He also received legal counsel and employment assistance from the Boston Society in Aid of Discharged Convicts.

~

In 1846, John Ross Dix published a collection of observations, *Local Loiterings in the Vicinity of Boston, by a Looker On.* During a visit to the state prison in Charlestown, Dix encountered Seth Perry and provided a graphic account of his description and demeanor.

Dix and Warden Robinson walked through the prison yard and into a spacious shed where convicts, wearing red and blue prison clothing, were engaged in masonry work. As he passed them, Dix "could observe furtive glances, and ferocious looks, and sullen scowls," and wondered what prevented the men, armed with hammers, from attacking him or the prison guards.

Dix and the warden passed on into the next work shanty where men convicted of more serious crimes, including murder, were assigned. As they entered that shanty, the warden pointed out a man making kegs for white lead. Dix described the man as being about sixty years old, with gray hair and "an athletic form." The warden informed Dix that the man "had killed two men and almost massacred another."

"Seeing that he was an object of attention, he paused amidst his work, and turning round looked me full in the face, and so repulsive a countenance I have very rarely seen," Dix wrote. "The grotesque prison cap which he wore was stuck on the summit of his head, and the point of it standing up over his forehead, and the two side pieces of the rim projecting over his ears, somewhat like horns, made him look not unlike the pictures of Mephistopheles in Retsch's *Outlines of Faust*. His eyes were very large, of a light color, and impudently diabolical in their expression; he had a small nose, a large mouth, and a pointed chin. Altogether he looked the very incarnation of evil."

Dix was appalled as Perry stood "unabashed, unconfounded [*sic*], and apparently as unconcerned as if the blood of his brethren had not gone up to God, with a cry of vengeance." As Dix turned to leave the shanty, he looked back and saw Perry's head "resting on a stone, his great gray eyes staring at me, his lips compressed, and his brow knit up as if in defiance. He looked perfectly frightful. If ever there was a heart which

53

could or would not repent, it must, I think, have been the one which had the breast of that hardened-looking old man."

~

Prison officials credited Seth Perry with time served in Plymouth Jail and released him on April 24, 1858. He had served his thirteen years. Perry returned to Hanover and stayed with his family and friends until that November when he purchased an acre and a quarter of land on Broadway in South Hanover from his brother, Cephas, for one dollar. The parcel was located between property owned by Cephas and another brother, Levi, and was known locally as Sand Hill. Perry built a small dwelling and lived in seclusion. He was found dead in his home, at eighty-one, on November 25, 1874. Bernard Damon, Hanover's town clerk, recorded Perry's cause of death as "old age."

Perry's family cared for his three minor children while he was in prison. They lived for a time with Perry's sister and brother-in-law, Wealthy and Albert Stetson. Perry's two daughters were married in Hanover five years before his release. His oldest daughter, Caroline, married Nathan Turner, of Hanson, Massachusetts, in the spring of 1853. Perry's other daughter, Julia, married James Turner, a distant relative to Nathan, of Hanover, that fall. Julia died in 1870 in Hanover. Caroline died in Danvers, Massachusetts, in 1902.

Four days after the Confederates opened fire on Fort Sumter in April 1861, Perry's son, John, enlisted in the Fourth Regiment, Massachusetts Volunteer Infantry. He later served in the Seventh Regiment. He deserted at Yorktown, Virginia, on August 16, 1862, but returned to duty and served until October 31, 1862, when he died of unknown causes at Hampton, Virginia.

Seth Perry died intestate. Edward Perry filed an application at the Plymouth Probate Court on December 9, 1874, to administer his estate. Edward, a second cousin to Seth, was a justice of the peace and an influential businessman in Hanover. The court appointed Edward as administrator on December 13 and ordered an inventory of Seth Perry's estate, which Edward filed the following day.

Perry's property in Hanover was appraised at $150 and his personal estate was valued at $745. The personal estate included $600 in cash, a silver watch, household furniture, tools, and three guns. His heirs received $735 after the property was auctioned off and his debts were paid.

~

Enos Bates inherited the family farm on Center Street when his mother died in 1852. He tended the farm and plied trades as a shoemaker and stonemason. He also leased out living space on the farm to John and Mercy Larkum and their four children to supplement his income.

At the outbreak of the Civil War, John Larkum and his eldest son, John Jr., enlisted in the 18th Regiment, Massachusetts Volunteer Infantry. The son survived the war, but the father did not. He died on April 14, 1862, at Lookout Point, Maryland, and was buried at Arlington National Cemetery.

His widow, Mercy Larkum, gave birth to an illegitimate child, Minnie Leland Larkum, on June 21, 1863. Bates married Mercy at the First Congregational Church in Hanover fourteen months later. The couple had three children: Enos Lincoln, Rosa May, and Charles. Rosa May and Charles died in infancy before 1870. Enos Lincoln married Cora Perkins in 1897 and died in Weymouth in 1944.

Enos Bates died in Hanover on May 9, 1886, at seventy-six. Like Perry, he died of "old age." His wife and children laid him to rest in the Hanover Center Cemetery.

Enos also died without a will. On August 23, 1886, Plymouth Probate Court judge Jesse E. Keith appointed Jedediah Dwelley, a Hanover selectman and Plymouth County commissioner, as administrator of Enos Bates's estate on August 23, 1886. Dwelley informed the court that Bates had left a widow, Mercy, and two children, Enos Lincoln Bates and Minnie Leland (Larkum) Bates, all of Hanover.

Enos's real estate was appraised at $1,850. The estate included a house, a stable, and a shanty on a seven-acre lot and an additional nineteen and three-quarter acres of swampland. Enos's personal estate, including household furniture, a buggy, a covered wagon, a sleigh, an oxcart, a horse, hay, lumber, and tools was assessed at $318. The balance was divided among Enos's wife and two children.

Mercy Bates was seventy-four when she died in Hanover on February 16, 1899, reportedly of hepatitis. She was buried beside her husband in Center Cemetery.

A Tailor's Goose

Nor is there any law more just, than that he who has plotted death shall perish by his own plot.

Ovid – Ars Amatoria (I, 655)

Principal Characters

Victim:
Julia Hawkes (about 1835-1874)

Accused:
James Henry Costley (about 1835-1875)

Judges:
John Wells (1819-1875), associate justice, Massachusetts Supreme
Judicial Court
> Wells was born in Rowe, Massachusetts, in 1819 and graduated from
> Williams College in 1838. He studied at Harvard Law School and was
> admitted to the Franklin County bar in 1841. Governor Nathaniel
> Banks appointed him judge of probate and insolvency for Hampden
> County in 1858, and Governor Alexander Bullock elevated him to
> associate justice of the Massachusetts Supreme Judicial Court in 1866.

Charles Devens (1820-1891), associate justice, Massachusetts Supreme
Judicial Court
> Devens was born in Charlestown, Massachusetts, and graduated
> from Harvard College in 1838. He was admitted to the Franklin County
> bar in 1841 and later represented the same county in the state senate.
> Devens served in the Union Army during the Civil War and was
> engaged in some of the war's most significant battles. He was wounded
> at the Battle of Fair Oaks and again at Chancellorsville. He was
> brevetted to major general in 1865 and was mustered out in 1866.
>
> Governor Bullock appointed him as an associate justice of the
> superior court the following year, and Governor Washburn elevated
> him to associate justice of the Supreme Judicial Court in 1873. Devens
> and Chief Justice Horace Gray presided over the murder trial of Mark
> Boothby that October. Boothby was found guilty of second-degree
> murder in the shooting death of his wife and was sentenced to life in
> prison.
>
> Devens would leave the bench in 1877 to serve as attorney general
> of the United States under President Rutherford B. Hayes. Devens

returned to Massachusetts at the end of Hayes's term and was reappointed to the Supreme Judicial Court by Governor John Long.

Prosecution:

Charles Russell Train (1817-1885), Massachusetts Attorney General

Train was born in Framingham, Massachusetts, graduated from Brown University in 1837, studied law in Cambridge, and was admitted to the Suffolk County bar in 1841. He held various political offices between 1847 and 1871 and became Attorney General of Massachusetts in 1872.

His first important trial as attorney general was his prosecution of Leavitt Alley in 1873 for the murder and dismemberment of Abijah Ellis, whose body parts were found floating in the Charles River in two separate barrels. Alley was acquitted. (Judge Wells presided at the trial.)

Train would later prosecute the Boston "boy fiend," Jesse Pomeroy, a sociopath who maimed and tortured seven children and murdered two more. Pomeroy was found guilty and sentenced to solitary confinement for life.

Asa French (1829-1903), District Attorney, Southeastern District of Massachusetts (Norfolk and Plymouth Counties)

French was born in Braintree, Massachusetts, and graduated from Yale in 1851. He received a bachelor of laws degree from Harvard Law School in 1853. After he was admitted to the bar in the Supreme Court of New York in 1853, French returned to Boston where he set up a practice. Massachusetts Governor William Claflin appointed him as district attorney for Norfolk and Plymouth Counties in 1870.

In 1871, French prosecuted John Moran for the murder of Constable Charles Packard in Stoughton. Moran was found guilty of second-degree murder and received a life sentence.

James Costley was the second person prosecuted for a capital offense by Train and French in 1874. William Sturtevant bludgeoned to death his two great-uncles and a housekeeper in Halifax, Massachusetts, that February. A June 29 trial before the Supreme Judicial Court at Plymouth, with Judges Wells and Ames presiding, resulted in Sturtevant's conviction and a sentence of death by hanging. Sturtevant's execution was scheduled for May 7, 1875.

Defense:

Horace Cheney (1844-1876)

Born in Parsonsfield, Maine, the son of Oren Cheney, founder of Bates College, Cheney graduated from Bowdoin College in 1865 and received his juris doctor from Harvard Law School in 1868. Before setting up his own law practice, Cheney was an assistant district attorney in Suffolk County for a short time. Attorney General Charles Train, upon Cheney's death, wrote: "He was an enthusiast in his love of the profession, a fine legal scholar, and seemed to me to possess all the elements required to ensure success as a *nisi prius* lawyer. He (if one may be allowed the expression) was faithful and indefatigable to a fault."

Baylies Sanford (1825-1875)

Sanford was born in Dennis, Massachusetts, studied at Amherst Academy, and graduated from Amherst College in 1845. He was admitted to the Massachusetts bar in 1851 and practiced law in Taunton until 1859 when Governor Nathaniel Banks appointed him as district attorney for the Southern District of Massachusetts. He resigned from his position and left Massachusetts in 1860 to practice law in New York City. He returned to Massachusetts in 1869.

Jury:

Ebenezer F. Talbot (1814-1882), Norwood, carpet manufacturer, jury foreman

Adam McIntosh (1825-1880), Canton, farmer

Southworth Alden (1825-1890), Stoughton, house painter

David A. Conant (1837-1900), Needham, carpenter

Olney J. Chilson (1827-1890), Bellingham, farmer

Francis Bacon (1821-1905), Dover, farmer

Nathaniel Sheldon (1814-1884), Wrentham, farmer

William Rooney (1818-1901), Brookline, laborer

Walter B. Bartlett, (1851-1943) Hyde Park, piano tuner

Henry W. Smith (1832-1896), Walpole, twine maker

James Trefrey (1819-1901), Dedham, auctioneer

James Coombs (1833-1920), Medway, grocer

Investigators:

Hollis Pinkham (1836-1905)

Pinkham was a Pittsfield, New Hampshire, native. He enlisted in 1861 in the Massachusetts First Cavalry Regiment and was mustered out in 1865 as a first lieutenant and the regimental quartermaster of the Second Cavalry Regiment. He joined the Massachusetts State Constabulary in 1872.

Chase Philbrick (1823-1893)

Philbrick was born in Sanbornton, New Hampshire. He served in the Fifteenth Massachusetts Volunteer Infantry and was wounded at the Battle of Fredericksburg, Virginia, in 1862. He was honorably discharged from the same regiment as a lieutenant colonel in 1863. He became Lawrence city marshal after the war, a position he held until 1871, when was appointed to the state constabulary.

Napoleon Bonaparte Furnald (1828-1914)

A native of Quincy, Massachusetts, Furnald was a furniture dealer until Governor William Washburn appointed him to the state constabulary in 1872.

Coroner:

George Washington White (1819-1899)

Physicians:

Francis Flint Forsaith (1824-1894)

A New Hampshire native, Forsaith was a graduate of Dartmouth College and Vermont University.

Granville Wilson Tinkham (1848-1911)

Tinkham was born in North Bridgewater, Massachusetts, and graduated from Harvard University Medical School in 1871.

~~~

At eleven thirty on the clear, bright Sunday morning of May 24, 1874, two Weymouth men strolled onto the walkway of the Quincy Avenue toll bridge. The bridge, locally called Whitmarsh's after the keeper who lived at one end, overlooked the Monatiquot River and connected Washington Square (now referred to as Weymouth Landing) with East Braintree.

The two men stopped on the bridge and looked down into the gently flowing river as worshipers passed behind them on their way home from services at Union Church in Weymouth Landing. One of the men, thirty-three-year-old Alexander White, suddenly noticed what appeared to be a human form in the water. He nudged his companion, twenty-seven-year-old David Pelleran, and frantically drew his attention to what he saw submerged below.

Whitmarsh's Bridge

"There's a foot in the water!" White cried.

"You've got the jim-jams!" retorted Pelleran.

But as he peered more closely, Pelleran saw two legs protruding above the water line, swaying with the current. White shouted to others gathered on the riverbank below. John Bates, a boot maker, and Thomas South, a blacksmith, heard the cries and ran to help. Bates and a man named Leach jumped into a boat and paddled toward the body. A curious crowd had amassed during the commotion and watched as Bates and Leach secured the body with a boat hook and, struggling with the ominous load against the current, slowly rowed back to shore.

As Bates, South, Leach, and several other men pulled the body to shore, the steadily growing crowd saw that it was a woman clothed in a dress. With the exception of the legs from the knees down, her body was completely covered in mud. Her head was wrapped with a carriage robe, double folded and tied tightly with a manila rope looped three or four times around her neck. The robe had a red, white, and black-striped lining on one side and a solid red lining on the reverse.

A second rope tied to her neck was attached to a linseed gunnysack. The men opened the sack and discovered a twenty-four-pound tailor's goose, a heavy flatiron used to smooth out wrinkled fabric. The goose was marked with the numerals 88. The weight of the tailor's goose had held the woman's head and shoulders down to the river's bed, but as her body decomposed, the accumulation of gases in the body cavity had raised her torso and lower extremities to the surface.

The men left the body on the shore until the arrival of Norfolk County coroner and deputy sheriff George White and Samuel Curtis, a Weymouth Landing undertaker. White, who also held positions as town constable and postmaster, instructed Bates, South, and others to carry the body to a fish shanty about thirty feet away.

After a cursory examination of the corpse inside the shanty, White had Bates and South carry it a hundred yards to the Union Fire Company No. 1 engine house in East Braintree (located on present-day Allen Street). White sent Bates to the nearest telegraph office to contact state police, and Constable Napoleon Furnald of Quincy arrived a short time later and launched an investigation.

At the engine house, White removed the rope and carriage robe and saw the distorted facial features of a woman about thirty-five years old, five feet tall, with dark hair, dark complexion, and a broad forehead. Neither man recognized the woman. She was clad in a black and brown striped dress with a black alpaca overskirt, a felt skirt, a flannel underskirt, and ribbed hose. On her right foot she wore a size three, low-cut shoe, commonly known as a "Newport tie." Her left foot was shoeless. An impression on the third finger of her left hand suggested a missing ring, and on her right ear she wore a jade earring shaped as a ten-pointed star.

The two men also observed something even more ominous, an apparent gunshot wound on the right side of the woman's head. Since

A tailor's goose

there were no punctures in the carriage robe, the men surmised that someone had shot her before placing the robe over her head. The second rope, tied around her neck and connected on the other end to the gunnysack, was imbedded so deeply into her flesh that Curtis had to carefully cut it to remove it. White and Curtis agreed that she had been submerged in the water for a week or more.

The two men removed the woman's clothing and packed her body in ice. Curtis gently cleansed the woman's face and covered her from the neck down with a sheet. Several hundred townspeople passed through the engine house in the hope that someone could identify her, but no one had ever seen the woman before.

White immediately convened an inquest and empaneled a jury to investigate the woman's death. Under Massachusetts law, the coroner possessed the same power as a judicial officer and was authorized to compel the attendance of jurors and any person he believed had knowledge of the death he was investigating. The jurors' verdict carried the same weight as a grand jury indictment and empowered the coroner to issue a warrant for the arrest of an accused person unless the individual was already in custody. In that case, the law required a grand jury indictment before trial proceedings against the accused could begin.

White appointed Elias Richards, Albion Hall, Henry Gardner, Phillips Curtis, Dr. Alexander Nye, and Thomas South to the jury. After brief testimony and a view of the body, White adjourned until 2:00 p.m. on Tuesday, May 26. He then called local physicians Francis Forsaith and Granville Tinkham to conduct an autopsy.

Constable Furnald telegraphed state police headquarters in Boston and requested additional resources to assist in the homicide investigation. Chief Constable George Boynton ordered every available officer of the state constabulary's seventy deputy constables to the scene. Boynton himself responded with Detectives Daniel Jones and Thomas Bagley and directed a canvass of the area for witnesses and a search of the crime scene for further evidence.

Word about the gruesome discovery spread quickly, and newspaper correspondents rushed to the scene to conduct a canvass of their own. The story appeared on the front pages the next day and included witness statements and a detailed description of the victim and her clothing.

~

Doctors Forsaith and Tinkham performed the autopsy inside the engine house late that afternoon. The doctors described the deceased as a thirty-five to forty-year-old, well-developed woman. There was no evidence of rigor mortis, suggesting that she had been dead for four days or more. They noted black marks under her eyes and an abrasion about a half inch above one eye, as well as bruises on her abdomen.

Forsaith inserted a probe into the right side of the woman's skull and found that a bullet had passed diagonally through her brain and fractured the skull on the opposite side. He removed the upper portion of the skull and dissected the brain. As he did so, a flattened pistol ball fell from the skull's membrane. Both doctors agreed that the woman had carried a child at one time but was not pregnant when she died.

The doctors ruled out the possibility that the victim was still alive when she entered the water. A drowning victim characteristically displays a frothy mixture of water, air, and mucus about the nose and throat. The same frothy mixture appears in the victim's windpipe and lungs and water is found in the throat and stomach. The lungs are spongy, swollen, and soft to the touch. None of these symptoms were present. Forsaith and Tinkham concluded that the pistol wound had caused the woman's death and that she was dead before she entered the river. They estimated that she had died approximately ten days before.

After the autopsy, Samuel Curtis took custody of the body and brought it to his undertaking establishment in Washington Square. He asked Ephraim Chamberlain, a photographer with an office nearby, to take pictures of the woman's features. Curtis then preliminarily prepared the body, placed it in a coffin, and deposited it in a receiving tomb at Village Cemetery in Weymouth Landing.

~

Jane Randall Smith, a resident of Wollaston Heights in Quincy, read an account of the Monatiquot River incident in a Boston newspaper on Monday evening, May 26, recognized the description of the woman's clothing, and contacted Samuel Curtis. Smith, accompanied by her sister, Margaret Garibaldi, met with Curtis and state constables at Curtis's office the next morning. Smith informed them that the newspaper description of the deceased's clothing closely matched the attire of her friend, Julia A. Hawkes. Curtis showed Smith the garments, and she confirmed that they belonged to Julia.

When Smith and her sister described Julia's features and mentioned that Julia had two false teeth on one side of her jaw, Curtis asked if they'd accompany him to view the body. The two women assented and Curtis, the state constables, and Dr. Alexander Nye, a Weymouth Landing dentist and inquest juror, escorted them by carriage to the receiving tomb at the cemetery. Sunshine poured into the darkened recess when Curtis opened the double doors of the tomb. Curtis guided the bier supporting Julia's pine coffin to the middle of the ten by twenty-foot chamber and removed the lid. Smith and Garibaldi gasped as they looked upon Julia's grotesque corpse.

"Yes, that's Julia," Smith sobbed as her sister embraced her.

Dr. Nye offered Smith his handkerchief and gently ushered the two women out of the tomb as Curtis replaced the coffin lid.

Upon their return to Curtis's office, Smith told the men she had first met Julia in 1853 at the Medford House, an inn and tavern in Medford, Massachusetts. She and Julia worked together in the Medford House kitchen and quickly became friends. Julia left Medford about 1854, according to Smith, and held several positions in hotels and private homes in the Boston area until the summer of 1873 when she accepted a job offer from a man named Costley, the manager of a hotel in Hanover.

Smith told the men that Julia remained at the Hanover hotel until April 30, 1874, when the hotel closed, and visited her in Wollaston on Tuesday, May 5. Smith said she had seen a considerable amount of money in Julia's pocketbook while she was there. On Friday, May 8, Julia boarded an 11:00 a.m. train for Boston. Smith had not seen Julia since then.

Over the next several days, others came forward to identify Julia's body at the receiving tomb. They included Smith's sister, Johanna Randall of Boston; Annie White of Newton, a former resident of the Howard House; and Michael Flanagan, a friend of Julia's from Boston's South End.

According to Jane Smith, Julia Hawkes was of French descent and was born Julia Brazeau about 1835 in or near Saint John, New

Brunswick. She married and gave birth to one child. Upon the death of her husband, Julia left Saint John and sought employment to support the child, who was left in the care of grandparents. Smith did not know the names of the grandparents, nor was she able to identify any other kin in Canada or the United States. Officials pursued other channels to locate family members, but failed. Julia's body was released to undertaker Samuel Curtis who arranged for her interment at Village Cemetery.

Julia Hawkes

Julia left her friend, Jane Randall Smith, at the Medford House in 1854 and went to Brookline, Massachusetts, where Isaac Rich, a wealthy fish merchant and one of the founders of what would become Boston University, engaged her as a domestic servant in his home. By 1860, she had left Rich and taken a position at the Mont Vernon House hotel in Mont Vernon, New Hampshire, where she reconnected with Smith, who worked there as a cook.

Julia left Mont Vernon around 1865 to become a housekeeper at the Daniel B. Stedman home in the Savin Hill section of Dorchester, Massachusetts. Stedman had amassed a fortune in the crockery and glass business and owned an impressive mansion overlooking Dorchester Bay. Stedman had released Julia in 1872 after his business was destroyed in the Great Boston Fire.

In November 1872, Jonathan Ingersoll Bowditch, a successful trader and merchant, employed Julia as a domestic at his estate on Moss Hill in Jamaica Plain, Massachusetts. Julia remained with Bowditch until August 1873 when James Henry Costley hired her as a cook at the Howard House.

Julia maintained her friendship with Jane Smith and Smith's family, the Randalls, during her twenty years in the Boston area. Julia boarded with the Randalls, who regarded her as a member of their family, whenever she was unemployed.

Julia opened a savings account at the Union Institution for Savings on Bedford Street in Boston in 1872. She made six deposits between July 3, 1872, and October 15, 1873. She withdrew $268.05 and closed her account on April 3, 1874. Jane Smith's sister, Deborah Randall, who lived on Oxford Street about a block from the bank, occasionally deposited money on Julia's behalf. Randall told police that Julia had consulted her about the prospects of buying a home in Hanover, but Randall had dissuaded Julia from pursuing that idea.

~

Coroner George White summoned jurors on Tuesday, May 26, and continued the inquest into Julia Hawkes's death. At the conclusion of the proceeding, White adjourned and ordered jurors to reconvene on June 4 for a final review of the evidence.

On the same day, after interviewing Jane Smith and her sister, Margaret Garibaldi, at Curtis's undertaking establishment, state detectives Hollis Pinkham and Chase Philbrick and state constable

Napoleon Furnald rode trains from Weymouth Landing and then from

North Abington to Hanover to confront the man named James Costley.

The officers disembarked at the Hanover depot at about 1:00 p.m. and engaged an open carriage at Howland's stable for the short trip to the village. Along the way, they saw two women, Harriet McLaughlin and Adeline Lindsay, standing outside a home on Broadway and stopped to ask if they knew Julia Hawkes or James Costley. McLaughlin told them that she knew both and had spoken to Costley not more than an hour before. She directed the men to the Howard House hotel on the northwest corner of Broadway and Washington Streets.

State Constable Napoleon Furnald

Much had changed in Hanover since the deaths of the Stapleton brothers in 1845. Four Corners village, located at the intersection of Washington Street and Broadway, was about three miles northeast of Seth Perry's former grog shop. It was a popular stopover on the stagecoach line as far back as the late eighteenth and early nineteenth centuries. Its hotels and taverns had accommodated and entertained such notables as Paul Revere and Daniel Webster.

One of the first hotels in the village opened in 1797 when David Kingman converted his private residence into an inn and tavern. The premises changed hands five times over the next seven decades. Franklin Howard, a tailor, purchased the lodging house, then called the Hanover House, from Elijah Barstow in 1870, renamed it the Howard House, and employed James Costley as a hostler to care for the horses of visiting guests. Howard leased the hotel to Costley for an annual rate of $475 in November 1872. Costley became the hotel's manager.

Costley was packing a trunk in a room at the rear of the hotel when Pinkham, Philbrick, and Furnald arrived. The three men later described Costley as thirty-five to forty years old, five feet eight inches tall, with a muscular build and dark complexion. He had a moustache and goatee.

After introductions, the officers asked Costley if he knew Julia Hawkes. He said he did and informed them that Julia had worked at the hotel until it closed on April 30. When asked if Julia had left any trunks at the hotel, Costley said no, she had gone "down east" to visit some friends, and at Julia's request he had shipped her trunks to Boston.

Philbrick questioned Costley about his whereabouts during the previous month. Costley told him that he went to Boston by train on Saturday, May 2, and returned to Hanover on May 4. He revisited Boston on May 6 and happened to encounter Julia Hawkes on Beach Street. He told Philbrick that he gave Julia the claim checks for the trunks he had shipped for her.

State Detective Chase Philbrick

The officers observed the hotel's unkempt condition. Pinkham brought this to Costley's attention, and Costley explained that the hotel hadn't been cleaned since Hawkes had left. He added that a furniture auction he had held at the hotel on May 1 had only exacerbated conditions.

Exploring the hotel more closely, the officers came upon a room in which traces of what appeared to be blood were evident on the walls, the door, and the door latch. There were stains on the carpeted floor and a bloodstained towel in one corner. When Pinkham questioned Costley about the stains, he wouldn't give a satisfactory reply and quickly changed the subject.

The officers found a pair of women's rubber overshoes in another small room. They surmised that the shoes had belonged to Julia Hawkes. The shoes were caked with mud that was still moist. Near the overshoes on a table the officers found three handkerchiefs, one embossed with the initials J. H. C.

The evidence against Costley began to mount as the search progressed. Constable Furnald lit a candle and explored a dark recess under a ladder leading to the attic. He found a length of clothesline, consistent in appearance with the ropes found around Hawkes's neck. The rope's end was freshly cut.

Near the end of the search, Costley asked the officers, "I suppose you're here in regard to the body found at Weymouth?"

"We shall have to take you into custody," Philbrick answered.

"Very well, gentlemen," Costley coolly replied, "but I should like to have got away on the four o'clock train."

The officers searched him and found a wallet containing $238 wrapped in a paper band marked Union Institution for Savings. They discovered a pistol cartridge, a set of keys, and a pocketknife in his pockets. They found another cartridge in the room. Pinkham asked Costley if he owned a pistol. Costley said he had bought one in Boston but had given it as a gift to his fiancée, Sarah Cushing of Hanover. He said the cartridge was one of several the officers might find around the hotel and that the proprietor, Franklin Howard, had brought them home from the service after the war.

James Henry Costley

Detective Pinkham and Constable Furnald searched Costley's trunk and found two letters addressed to Costley and one letter addressed to Thomas I. Thomas, two pocket handkerchiefs, a hand stamp used for postal markings, and a bottle of ink. When Detective Philbrick took custody of the letters, Costley said he wanted them back because they were personal and written by his fiancée. Philbrick assured him that if the letters were not important or material to the case he was investigating, he would ensure that no improper use would be made of them.

After they completed their search, Pinkham, Philbrick, and Furnald secured the hotel with Costley's keys and escorted him to the Hanover depot where they boarded the North Abington-bound train for a connection to Plymouth. On arrival, the detectives confined him to a cell at Plymouth Jail on suspicion of murder pending an arraignment in Plymouth County Court the following day.

71

~

Pinkham and Furnald appeared at the Plymouth County Courthouse for Costley's arraignment on Wednesday, May 27. Court officers brought Costley before Justice Arthur Lord to answer a charge of murder. Costley entered a plea of not guilty, Judge Lord continued the case until 11:00 a.m. Friday, June 5, and remanded Costley to Plymouth Jail without bail.

The Howard House

After leaving the court, Pinkham and Furnald returned to the Howard House to search for evidence. The officers inspected a shed attached to a barn in the back of the hotel and found a tailor's goose on a dusty shelf. The goose, marked with the numerals 88, perfectly matched the one in the gunnysack tied to Julia Hawkes's neck. The officers noticed an imprint in the dust next to the goose. The imprint was consistent with the dimensions of the goose they had found.

In the same shed, the officers also found a linseed gunnysack consistent in appearance and texture to the sack that had contained the tailor's goose found at East Braintree. The officers later learned that railroad officials had recently employed a man to repair the roof at the nearby Hanover railway station. The man, referred to as "Brackett," had boarded at the Howard House during the course of his work. Brackett had carried the sand and gravel for making the repairs in gunnysacks similar to the sack found at the hotel. Police investigated Brackett's activities at the time of the murder and eliminated him as a suspect.

The officers searched the hotel again and, in a stovepipe hole in the kitchen chimney, discovered an envelope with a recent Boston postmark that was addressed to Costley. The envelope contained four pistol cartridges that matched those found on Costley the day before. The bullets in the cartridges were the same caliber as the bullet found imbedded in Hawkes's brain.

Village Cemetery,
Weymouth,
Massachusetts

They reentered the room where they had seen the bloodstains. Pinkham retrieved the bloodstained towel, cut a sample from the discolored floor carpet, and packaged both items for microscopic examination.

The officers seized the trunk Costley had started to pack the day before and took it with the other evidence back to Chief Boynton's office at state police headquarters in Boston.

~

On Thursday, May 28, Chief Constable Boynton, Detectives Pinkham and Philbrick, and Constable Furnald visited Costley in Plymouth Jail. The four men questioned him without the presence of counsel and tried, in vain, to get a confession from him. Costley expressed sympathy about Julia Hawkes's death but denied any involvement.

In an effort to establish his whereabouts prior to the discovery of Hawkes's body, Boynton asked Costley if he owned a horse. Costley replied that he had owned several but had sold them when he auctioned off his hotel property on May 1.

Boynton went over Costley's May 26 statement and asked him to elaborate on his May 6 encounter with Hawkes on Beach Street in Boston. Costley repeated the account he had given to Pinkham, Philbrick, and Furnald at the Howard House. How did he get to Boston, Boynton asked Costley. By train, Costley replied. In answer to another question by Boynton, Costley denied having rented a horse or team at any time between May 1 and May 24.

Boynton asked Costley if he owned any carriage robes. Yes, he had owned three or four but had sold them to a peddler, Costley answered. Pinkham showed Costley the robe taken from the victim's body. "That's my robe," Costley said. But he quickly retracted his statement and remarked, "No, that don't look quite like mine. The stripes are different."

Pinkham produced the gunnysack found at the hotel and asked Costley if he recognized it. Costley said he had seen similar sacks at the hotel and told Pinkham that a man named Brackett had done some roofing on his hotel and had left them there.

Probing further into his movements, the officers asked Costley if he had traveled to Boston at any time after seeing Hawkes on May 6. Costley said he had taken a train to the city on two other occasions. On the first occasion he had stayed at a hotel called the Jefferson House at 18 North Street on May 9 and 10 and had returned to Hanover on Monday, May 11, Costley related. He recalled registering his name at the hotel. He said he had returned to Boston on May 16 and taken a train to New York City. He stayed at the Metropolitan Hotel until Tuesday, May 19, and returned to Hanover.

Costley refused to answer any further questions. As the investigators prepared to leave, Boynton couldn't resist saying one last thing to Costley. "If you had succeeded in anchoring that woman's feet as well as you did her head, you would be all right."

"I have nothing further to say," Costley retorted.

~

As Costley languished in jail, Pinkham, Philbrick, and Furnald remained hard at work verifying Costley's statements. Chief Constable Boynton assigned other detectives and constables to interview friends of Julia Hawkes to ascertain her movements leading up to the day of her death.

Furnald went to Four Corners to interview people who knew Costley and learned that many people liked and respected him. Most expressed confidence that the police had arrested the wrong man and that the trial would result in Costley's vindication.

Furnald also learned that a local photographer, James Williams, lived near Four Corners and had taken portraits of both Costley and Julia Hawkes. Furnald found Williams at his home on River Street in South Scituate (later Norwell). Williams confirmed that he knew Costley and Hawkes and had taken photographs of the pair. Williams found the glass negatives and made two prints for Furnald.

Furnald determined that Costley had first arrived in Hanover about 1870 and found work on Abner Stetson's farm in South Scituate. Before that, Costley had traveled around the country with the Thayer, Noyes and Company Great United States Circus as a teamster and a watchman for the ticket wagon. By August 1870, Franklin Howard, owner of the Howard House, had hired Costley as a hostler in the hotel's stable. Before long, Costley was working inside the hotel as a waiter and bartender. Howard agreed to lease the hotel to Costley in November 1872, and Costley assumed the hotel's management.

Costley was active socially and had become a member of the Phoenix Masonic Lodge, located at Four Corners. Furnald heard that he had met and become engaged to Sarah Cushing, the daughter of John Cushing, a wealthy sea captain. The thirty-eight-year-old woman lived with her mother on Church Street in Four Corners and had inherited a substantial amount of property when her father died in 1871. Furnald visited the house on Church Street and interviewed Cushing. She confirmed her engagement to Costley and refused to believe that he was guilty of the murder – or any crime, for that matter. She told Furnald that she was deeply in love with Costley and was determined to marry him.

As his investigation in Four Corners continued, Furnald heard about a suspicious death that had occurred at the Howard House the previous December. Townspeople suggested that Love Congdon, a thirty-five-year-old divorcee from Hyannis and a hotel employee, had welcomed the attentions of Costley and eventually had an affair with him.

On December 28, 1873, Congdon retired for the evening at the hotel and was found dead in her bedroom the next morning. Her sudden demise raised questions because she had displayed no indications of illness or discomfort the night before.

Eben Waterman, a Plymouth County coroner and justice of the peace in Hanover, summoned a jury and held an inquest into Congdon's death. Julia Hawkes and James Costley were among the witnesses who were called to testify. Jurors questioned Costley about his knowledge of the circumstances surrounding the death. Hawkes, then a cook at the hotel, corroborated Costley's testimony. Townspeople in Hanover believed that Hawkes's testimony had allayed suspicion about the death and had thwarted a postmortem examination of Congdon's body. Residents told Furnald that Hawkes had "shed tears copiously and otherwise acted very strangely" after her testimony.

The jury rendered a verdict that "death had been caused by poison administered by her own or another's hand." Hanover town clerk Bernard Damon recorded Congdon's cause of death as "colic," a condition of acute abdominal pain caused by lead poisoning.

Residents found it odd that Waterman had closed the case so quickly. Many suspected that Costley and Hawkes knew much more about the death, and some were convinced that Costley had poisoned Congdon.

~

Constable Furnald contacted his counterparts in Plymouth County and discovered that deputy constables George Pratt and Uriah McCoy had cited Costley on more than one occasion for illegally providing liquor on the hotel premises. Costley apparently carried on a large "bottle trade" on the premises.

During one search of the hotel, police discovered a device designed to dispense liquor surreptitiously. Costley had placed a large barrel filled with spirits on a staging between the hotel stable and a shed. He inserted a tube into the barrel, ran the tube beneath the ground and behind partitions, and threaded it through the hotel's exterior wall and under a broad shelf in the pantry. The tube was inserted into a pipe with a stopcock and a nozzle small enough to fit inside a bottle. Costley had cut a hole in the countertop above the shelf. Coming just flush with the countertop was the handle of the stopcock and the nozzle.

Costley cut an off-center hole in the bottom of a pail and filled it with white beans. He placed the pail on the countertop so it would cover the hole in the counter above the stopcock but prevent it from releasing the beans. If an unsuspecting or unauthorized person lifted the pail, the beans would fall from the bottom. This would naturally cause the person to hastily put down the pail. However, people familiar with the setup would gently push the pail to one side along the shelf, disclose the stopcock without disturbing the beans, and pour the liquor from the nozzle.

Furnald delved into Costley's assertion that he did not own a horse and had not rented a horse and carriage around the time of the murder. On May 29, he canvassed stables in Hanover, Weymouth, Braintree, and Quincy and could not find anyone who could verify that Costley had owned a horse or rented a team.

Furnald interviewed nineteen-year-old Mary McCurdy, a former employee at the Howard House, at her Hanover home. She told Furnald that she had first met Julia Hawkes in August 1873 when Julia came to work at the Howard House. On the afternoon of April 30, 1874, McCurdy noticed Julia at the Hanover depot with two trunks and watched as she boarded a four o'clock train. McCurdy never saw her again.

While Furnald continued his investigation in Hanover, state detectives Christopher Bailey and Chase Philbrick were busy tracing Julia Hawkes's whereabouts just before her death. The two men went to Jane Smith's home in Quincy where Smith retold the circumstances of Julia's visit on May 5.

The two detectives left Quincy and proceeded to the home of Daniel Stedman in the Savin Hill section of Dorchester. Stedman had employed Hawkes for seven years as a maid and cook in his household. The lady of the house, Miriam Stedman, greeted the detectives at the door and invited them inside. As they interviewed Mrs. Stedman, it quickly became evident that she and Hawkes had enjoyed a close relationship. Stedman told them that Julia had called at the house on Monday, May 11, and had left the same day. She never saw Julia again.

Stedman stated that a deep bond of affection had developed between her and Julia during Julia's years in the household and that Julia had frequently confided in her. She disclosed that Julia had entrusted her financial affairs to Stedman, including leaving her passbook in Stedman's care. Stedman produced Julia's Union Institution for Savings passbook, and Philbrick noted that Hawkes had withdrawn $268.05 on April 3, 1874. This was nearly the same amount as the packet of bills bound in a Union Institution for Savings paper band that James Costley had possessed when he was arrested. Philbrick took custody of the passbook and later verified Hawkes's account activity through Union bank records.

When they left the Stedman house, the two detectives split up. Bailey went to 109 Albany Street, Boston, to interview Michael Flanagan, one of the witnesses who had identified Hawkes's body. Philbrick returned to police headquarters with the newest evidence. Flanagan told Bailey he had known Julia Hawkes for eight or nine years and that the last time he had seen her was on May 11 when she stopped by his home to visit his mother.

Bailey went to the Randall home on Oxford Street in Boston's garment district to interview Deborah and Johanna Randall. He determined that on Tuesday, May 12, Mrs. Hawkes had visited the two women and had spent the greater part of the day there. Deborah Randall told Bailey that Julia had seemed dejected and anxious, not her usual buoyant and happy self. Julia mentioned that Costley had asked her to accompany him to Oregon where he intended to get a fresh start and open his own hotel. In the meantime, he had arranged temporary employment for her in Weymouth Landing. She said she was boarding at a "friend's house" at 63 Camden Street in Boston's South End until Costley completed his plans.

Julia left the Randall house on an errand and did not return. Neither Deborah nor Johanna had seen or spoken to Julia since then.

Bailey then proceeded to 63 Camden Street and met the proprietor, Mary Day, the wife of Boston police officer James Day. Day confirmed that Hawkes had boarded there for nearly two weeks. She said that a man named James Costley had appeared at her door on Monday, April 27, and had asked to engage a room for a lady friend until June 1. He told Day that the woman had lost her position and room at her last place of employment and needed accommodations until she could secure a new situation. He explained to Day that the woman had friends in Boston but that she didn't want to reveal her whereabouts to them, at least temporarily.

Day asked Costley for a form of reference before she would agree to his request. Costley produced a flyer advertising the auction at the Howard House on May 1 and told her that he was the manager of the hotel and a legitimate businessman. Satisfied, Day handed Costley a room key after he had paid her a one-week advance of two dollars for the room. Before he left, Costley said that because the room was at the top of a long flight of stairs, he would warn his lady friend to leave her larger trunks behind and bring a few things in a small carrying case. Day said that the lady friend, Julia Hawkes, arrived on May 1 with the key and a small trunk and stayed until May 13. Day hadn't seen her since then.

Day said that Costley returned to the boardinghouse at about 10:00 a.m. the next day, May 14. He had the key to Julia's room and told Day he had come for Julia's belongings. Day accompanied him to the room and helped him pack a small bag. She found a bottle of hair oil on a bureau and gave it to Costley for packing. He told Day it wasn't necessary, stating, "Oh, no, she won't want that." Day also found a nightdress. Costley told her not to bother with it. She pressed Costley to take the item. Finally, Costley said, "Well if you insist on it, put it in." He then left the house with Julia's effects.

Day told Detective Bailey that Hawkes had befriended another boarder during her stay. Minnie Arbuckle had vacated her room on May 15 and given Day a forwarding address in Chicago before she left. When Bailey contacted her in Chicago, Arbuckle told him that she had first met Julia on May 2 at the rooming house on Camden Street. She recalled that James Costley had visited Julia in her room three times between May 2 and May 13.

On May 13, Arbuckle and Julia left their rooms on Camden Street to stroll along Washington Street to Chester Park in Boston's South End. Arbuckle remembered that Julia wore a bonnet and cloak, a brown and black skirt, and Newport tie shoes. Julia told Arbuckle that she was going to Weymouth Landing that evening for several months. Julia said she was

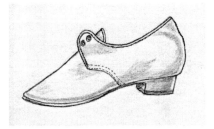

Newport tie shoe, 1870s

leaving her belongings behind and asked Arbuckle to give them to Costley if he came for them. They parted company at about 5:15 p.m. It was the last time Arbuckle saw Julia. Police never accounted for a cloak or bonnet during the days after Julia's body was discovered.

~

Investigators gathered at police headquarters to compare notes and review the case. Based on Costley's movements within Boston, they decided to concentrate their efforts on locating a livery near Camden Street or the hotel where Costley claimed he had stayed. After interviews with several stable owners, the detectives finally located a livery at 9 Van Rensselaer Place where stablemen confirmed that Costley had hired a team. Riedell's Stable was located around the corner from the Creighton House, 245 Tremont Street, where detectives later determined Costley had rented a room on May 9 while in the company of a woman. Costley signed the hotel register as "J. H. Costello and wife, Duxbury, Mass." Police suspected that Julia Hawkes was the woman who had accompanied Costley that evening.

This information discredited a statement that Costley had made during the interview with police at Plymouth Jail on May 28. Costley told investigators he had stayed at the Jefferson House on May 9 and 10.

On May 30, 1874, Detective Pinkham interviewed the stable owner, James A. Riedell, as well as Riedell's employees, Joseph Neas, Frank Wills, and James Spillane. Pinkham showed the men the photograph of Costley that Constable Furnald had received from James Williams. All four immediately recognized Costley as the man who had hired a horse and buggy at the stable on two occasions. Riedell told Pinkham that the man in the photograph had identified himself as James Costley and that he had hired a bay horse and piano box buggy on May 9, saying he wanted to take the team to Weymouth Landing. Riedell said Costley returned with the team at about midnight and left two valises with stableman Joseph Neas. He told Neas he would return for the valises in several days. Neas and Wills told Pinkham they had lifted the valises and that one seemed unusually heavy.

At about 6:30 p.m. on Wednesday, May 13, Costley returned to the livery alone and reclaimed the two valises. He requested another rig and

made a point of asking for a steady horse. He told Riedell he intended to take the buggy to Weymouth Landing and expected to return about midnight. Riedell harnessed a dark bay horse to a square box buggy for Costley. As stable foreman Frank Wills placed the heavier of the two valises into the buggy, he asked Costley, "What have you got in here, gold?"

A square box buggy

"I wish it was," Costley replied. Wills loaded the second valise, and Costley drove away just before 7:00 p.m.

81

Costley returned the horse and buggy to the stable an hour after midnight on Thursday. Stableman James Spillane began to clean out the buggy at five o'clock and found a lady's shoe and a new claw hammer on the floor. Spillane gave them to Riedell, and the livery owner turned both articles over to Pinkham. The detective noted that the shoe, made for a left foot, bore striking similarities to the one found on the murdered woman's right foot when her body was recovered. He also observed that the hammer was new and wrapped in paper from the Thomas B. Barnes Hardware Store in Boston.

Pinkham visited the Barnes store and spoke with the manager, Justin Harris. Harris identified the hammer as one sold in his store, but he could not tell Pinkham who had purchased it. Pinkham noticed a variety of firearms on display at the store and asked Harris if he had sold a .22-caliber pistol recently. Harris checked his inventory list and found the sale of a .22-caliber pistol on April 27 but no record of the purchaser's name. When Pinkham showed him the picture of Costley, Harris could not positively identify him.

~

The inquest into the death of Julia Hawkes continued on June 4, 1874. At the conclusion of testimony, the coroner, George White, instructed jurors about the laws of the commonwealth and dismissed them to deliberate upon the facts presented.

The next day, deputy sheriffs ushered Costley into the Plymouth County Courthouse. A large crowd of onlookers had gathered outside hoping to get a glimpse of the prisoner.

Costley appeared with counsel before Justice Arthur Lord in the second-floor courtroom at 11:00 a.m. The government requested a one-week continuance on the matter after Costley entered a not-guilty plea. Counsel for the defense made no objections, and Judge Lord continued the case until 11:00 a.m. Saturday, June 13.

District Attorney Asa French expected a decision from the coroner's jury within days and did not want to proceed with his case until the inquest was concluded. He needed more time for his investigators to collect evidence, and an opportunity to consult with the state's attorney general, Charles Train, who, as was customary at the time, would co-prosecute the case at trial.

District Attorney
Asa French

French already knew that investigators no longer believed that Costley had committed the murder at Hanover in Plymouth County. He planned to prosecute Costley in Norfolk County, where the body was found. That would necessitate dismissing the complaint against Costley in Plymouth County and issuing a new complaint in Norfolk County.

French was informed that the coroner's jury reached a verdict on Saturday, June 6. "That the said Julia Hawkes came to her death on the night of the thirteenth of May last past, by means of a pistol ball willfully discharged from a pistol through her brain; and the jurors further say that upon the evidence before them they believe that James Henry Costley of Hanover is guilty of the murder of the said Julia Hawkes." The jurors also believed that Costley had committed the murder somewhere between Braintree and Weymouth in Norfolk County.

Costley appeared before Judge Lord at the Plymouth court in the probate session on June 13. Jailor captain A. K. Harmon brought Costley into the crowded courtroom and placed him in the open iron cage that served as the dock. Detectives Pinkham and Philbrick were seated outside the bar enclosure in the first row.

The government requested that Lord dismiss the complaint against Costley. Lord granted the request and discharged Costley. People watched in bewilderment as Harmon released Costley from the dock. What the onlookers didn't know was that detectives Pinkham and Philbrick had sought an arrest warrant for Costley from Judge Everett Bumpus at the Eastern Norfolk District Court in Quincy. Pinkham intercepted Costley before he left the courtroom, put his hand on his shoulder, and said, "Mr. Costley, in the name of the commonwealth and by virtue of this warrant I arrest you on the charge of murder and shall proceed to take you to Norfolk County." According to a *Weymouth Gazette* reporter, "Costley's eyes dropped and his face showed mental discomposure."

The officers escorted Costley by train to Quincy where they turned him over to sheriff's deputies at the courthouse. Judge Bumpus entered the courtroom, and the clerk read the complaint against Costley who was represented by former Bristol County district attorney Baylies Sanford. Costley listened attentively, and when asked if he was guilty or not guilty of the charge against him, firmly replied that he was innocent. Sanford waived any further examination, and Judge Bumpus, at the request of DA French, committed Costley to the Norfolk County Jail at Dedham pending the action of the Norfolk County grand jury.

~

By 1850, a steadily increasing criminal population compelled Norfolk County officials to demolish part of the 1818 Dedham Jail and the entire 1832 house of corrections to build an adequate facility on the same one-acre site. Completed in 1851 on Village Avenue, the new Dedham Jail was a granite and brick fortress with a central, octagonal building and attached wings on the north, east, and west sides. According to a *Boston Post* reporter, it appeared "more like a young ladies' seminary rather than a prison" with its surrounding green lawn and shady trees. Large, Gothic Revival-style, arched windows allowed maximum lighting inside the building during the day, and gas lamps lit the interior at night. The central building contained the guardroom, kitchen, laundry, hospital, and chapel. A hot-air furnace and several stoves in the basement heated the building, and a tank under the roof supplied water. Jailers in the guardroom had an unobstructed view of every door of the 112 cells, all eight feet square.

The grand jury returned an indictment against James Henry Costley on September 10, 1874. He was charged with committing the crime of murder on May 13, 1874, in Braintree and using a pistol, the ball of which entered Julia Hawkes's head and caused a mortal wound. Judge George Putnam, acknowledging the indictment, referred the case to the

Massachusetts Supreme Judicial Court for trial.

Although the evidence presented to the grand jury was sufficient for an indictment, the case was circumstantial. The district attorney would require strong evidence if he hoped to secure a conviction.

State detectives continued investigating Costley and his movements before and after the murder of Hawkes on May 13. Investigators learned that Costley had taken a room at the Jefferson House, 18 North Street, Boston, between 1:00 and 2:00 a.m. on May 14, shortly after returning the horse and buggy to Riedell's Stable. Hotel manager Joseph Flatley produced the hotel register and pointed to a signature by "John H. Costley, Hanover." Flatley identified the picture of James H. Costley as the man who had registered using the first name "John."

This evidence clearly refuted Costley's May 28 statement at Plymouth Jail that he had been at the Jefferson House on May 9 and 10 and had returned to Hanover on May 11. It also proved he had lied when he told Chief Boynton that he had not been in Boston between May 11 and 16.

Detectives were in a quandary as to the whereabouts of Hawkes's two russet-colored trunks that Costley had allegedly shipped on her behalf. A witness had seen her with the trunks at the Hanover depot on April 30. The witness said that Hawkes had left for Boston on the 4:00 p.m. train.

A Saratoga trunk

Detectives went to the Old Colony Railroad depot in Boston where they met Charles Everdean, baggage master. Everdean told them he had received two russet-colored Saratoga trunks from Hanover on May 4. Everdean released the trunks to expressman Daniel Lynch, who presented the two claim checks on May 14.

Police located Lynch at his stand at the corner of Court and Brattle Streets. Lynch told the officers he went to the Old Colony depot on May 14 after being engaged by Peter Warner of Dow's Stable, 20-22 Portland

Street. Warner gave Lynch two claim checks and asked him to pick up two trunks at the depot and bring them back to the stable. Lynch retrieved the trunks and returned them to Warner.

When the officers spoke with Warner at Dow's, they learned that Costley had visited the stable on the morning of May 14. Warner told them that Costley appeared with two claim checks, which he gave to Warner, and asked Warner to have someone pick up the two trunks at the Old Colony depot, bring them back to the stable, and store them until Costley returned for them. Warner then hired Lynch to retrieve the trunks.

Warner released the trunks to Cornelius Sullivan, another expressman, on May 16. Police contacted Sullivan, and he told them that James Costley had approached him at about 6:00 p.m. on May 16 and asked him to pick up two trunks at Dow's and transport them to the Boston and Albany depot. Sullivan said Costley went to the stable with him. They loaded the trunks on his wagon and rode to the depot. During the ride, Costley told Sullivan he was taking a train to New York that night. Sullivan unloaded the trunks at the depot, and Costley took them inside. Sullivan never mentioned a black valise, but police later suspected that Costley had placed the valise containing the robe, the tailor's goose, and the rope inside one of the trunks after he entered the depot.

~

Prosecutors considered several motives for the murder of Julia Hawkes but settled on the two they felt were the most plausible.

The first motive centered on the death of Love Congdon. Although officials lacked evidence to prove that Congdon's death in December 1873 was a homicide, questions still lingered. Attorney General Train and District Attorney French speculated that her demise had been at the hands of Costley. Perhaps Hawkes had some knowledge of the crime that would implicate Costley who feared she would expose him.

A second theory was that Costley had promised to marry Hawkes but had reconsidered when he recognized the pecuniary advantages of marrying the wealthy Sarah Cushing. Hawkes's refusal to break the engagement placed her in a perilous position. Costley was determined to marry Cushing, and Hawkes stood in his way. Only by eliminating Hawkes could Costley realize his selfish interests.

Train and French believed this motive was the most plausible. They believed Costley had taken Hawkes from the South End boarding house to Weymouth, a distance of about eleven miles, and had stopped at a secluded site where, under the cover of darkness, he coaxed her from the buggy and shot her. Police found no blood in the buggy Costley had hired, leading them to believe that Costley covered Hawkes's head with the carriage robe, tied the rope and tailor's goose around her neck, loaded her body back into the buggy, and then drove to the bridge in East Braintree to dispose of it. Although there were no witnesses to the crime, both prosecutors felt that the circumstantial evidence gathered by investigators provided more than enough proof for a first-degree murder conviction against Costley.

~

When the trial convened on Monday, December 28, 1874, the prosecution was prepared to present the case before the Supreme Judicial Court at the Norfolk County Courthouse in Dedham with the testimony of sixty witnesses and numerous evidentiary exhibits. It was the first special session of the Supreme Judicial Court ever held in Norfolk County.

Attorneys Baylies Sanford and Horace Cheney represented the defendant. They would call fourteen witnesses, including three physicians to refute the testimony of the prosecution's medical experts.

Sheriff's deputies removed Costley from his cell at Dedham Jail and marched him along the narrow streets to the courthouse. It was unseasonably warm and a light rain was falling as curious onlookers watched the men parade beneath leafless elm and sycamore trees. The prisoner and his guards marched through the Old Village Cemetery, past stately white colonial homes and the towering steeple of the First Church in Dedham. They ascended the broad stairs of the courthouse, and once inside the courtroom, the deputies placed Costley in the prisoner's dock, a cage of fancy wrought-iron latticework located eight feet from the jury box. A deputy removed Costley's handcuffs and locked the cage.

The elegant, white granite courthouse was built in 1827 in Greek Revival style. A ten-foot pediment supported by four granite pillars projected from the main building. A Roman-style dome and wings were added to either side of the original building in 1863. The imposing courtroom, with its high ceiling, ornate walnut benches, and white terra cotta walls, was overflowing with spectators when Associate Justices John Wells and Charles Devens entered at about ten o'clock.

Attorney General Train and District Attorney French immediately moved for trial.

Jury empanelment was the court's first order of business. When defense counsel, the prosecution, and the court completed their challenges, the twelve jurors took their places in the jury box. Among the jurors were four farmers, a house painter, a carpenter, a laborer, a piano tuner, a twine maker, an auctioneer, and a grocer. The court appointed Ebenezer Talbot, a sixty-one-year-old carpet manufacturer from Norwood, as jury foreman.

Judge Wells dismissed the jury and, after they had filed out, Defense Attorney Cheney moved that the court quash the state's indictment because "there was insufficient allegation in the indictment that the offense was committed within the commonwealth of Massachusetts; an absence of allegation that the pistol wound therein, as to the weapon with which the homicide was committed, was held by the defendant at the time of the commission of the offense in his hand or hands; and that the indictment was therefore informal and sufficiently void."

Associate
Justice John Wells

In response, Attorney General Train moved that both Braintree and Hanover were in the commonwealth of Massachusetts and that the omission to state that the pistol was held in the hand of the defendant was not material. Justice Wells overruled Cheney's motion.

Before hearing testimony, the court ordered that all witnesses remain sequestered outside the courtroom until called to testify. No witness was allowed to overhear the testimony of another, nor was a witness allowed to discuss his or her testimony with other witnesses. Judge Wells then called for the jury and, after the jurors were seated, instructed District Attorney French to proceed with his opening statement. French summarized the details of the case, and the court recessed until 1:00 p.m.

During the afternoon session, French called Alexander White, Thomas South, and John Bates to describe the circumstances under which they had found the victim's body on May 24. Undertaker Samuel Curtis testified that he first saw Hawkes's body on the riverbank. He and others removed the body to a nearby shed and then to the engine house. He removed the clothing, packed the body in ice, and covered it with a sheet. Coroner George White then testified about the condition of the body and the results of his examination.

Doctors Francis Forsaith and Granville Tinkham were the commonwealth's next witnesses, and they revealed the details of the autopsy they had performed. The district attorney produced several articles of clothing, and each witness identified them as clothing they had seen on the deceased the day her body was recovered. The articles were marked as commonwealth exhibits.

DA French showed Forsaith an anatomical skull and asked him to indicate the location of the wounds found on Hawkes's head during the autopsy. After he had done so, the court, at the district attorney's request, admitted the skull into evidence and marked it as an exhibit.

Forsaith told the court that he had found no external marks of violence on the deceased other than wounds on the right and left sides of her head. When he probed the wound from the right side of the head he found that the pistol ball had passed through the brain to the left side of her head and had fractured the skull, bending the bones out.

"As we were removing portions of the brain, the ball fell out in a flattened, bruised condition," Forsaith continued. "There was blood in the brain, indicating that the ball had ruptured one of the arteries and produced hemorrhage of the brain." In Forsaith's professional opinion, the wound caused the woman's death.

On cross-examination, Attorney Cheney picked up the skull from the exhibit table and asked Forsaith to point out once more the spot where the ball had entered and the fracture on the opposite side. Cheney asked the physician if his present testimony differed from testimony he had given during the coroner's inquest on June 4, 1874. Forsaith admitted that he had told the inquest jury that the victim had died instantly because of the wound. After the inquest he had consulted the latest medical literature and had changed his opinion. He now believed it possible that death was not instantaneous.

Jane Smith, the last witness on the first day of trial, described her relationship with Julia Hawkes and shared her knowledge of Julia's movements prior to her death. Smith testified that she had gone to East Braintree with her sister, Margaret Garibaldi, on May 27 and had identified Julia's body at the receiving tomb in Village Cemetery.

French introduced a russet-colored Saratoga trunk with "J. H. Costley" written across it and asked Smith if she recognized it. Smith replied that the trunk belonged to Julia. She also identified a comb found inside the trunk as Julia's property. The court granted French's request to enter the trunk and comb as evidence. The district attorney showed Smith the articles of clothing previously identified by the commonwealth's witnesses and asked her to identify them. Smith told French that the items were similar to the clothing Julia was wearing when Smith last saw her.

Given the late hour, the district attorney requested that Smith continue her testimony the next day. Defense counsel did not object, and court was adjourned.

~

Jane Smith completed her direct testimony on the trial's second day, Tuesday, December 29. Attorney Sanford cross-examined Smith extensively, focusing on Julia's clothing, the trunk, and the personal effects found in it, but the defense gained nothing helpful during this questioning.

Smith's sister, Margaret Garibaldi, testified next and told the court when she had last seen Julia and described the clothing Julia had been wearing at that time. French produced the clothing in evidence, and Garibaldi identified it as Julia's. The prosecution called four more witnesses, and all identified the clothing as the attire Julia Hawkes was wearing when they last saw her.

Johanna Randall, another of Jane Smith's sisters with whom Hawkes had occasionally boarded, testified about her knowledge of Julia's two trunks and the personal effects they contained. The DA showed her the trunk that had been previously identified by her sister, Jane. Randall confirmed that it was Julia's. She also identified the trunk's contents, including a comb she had given to Julia.

The next witness, Deborah Randall, corroborated her sister's testimony. She also recognized Julia's Saratoga trunk.

Mary Day, owner of the boarding house at 63 Camden Street, provided the court with important testimony regarding Costley and his appearance at her boardinghouse on May 14 to collect Julia Hawkes's property. Day told the court that Costley had the key to Julia's room. Costley's remarks that Julia "wouldn't want" personal items left in the room proved damaging to the defendant. Day identified Costley in the courtroom, and the court recessed until the afternoon.

When court resumed, Day returned to the witness stand to testify about a conversation she had with Costley at the Dedham courthouse. Day said she had gone to the courthouse to testify as a witness before the Norfolk County grand jury and saw Costley there. She greeted him, but Costley acted as if he didn't know her.

"Don't you remember Mrs. Day of Camden Street?" she asked Costley.

"I don't know Mrs. Day, and I don't know where Camden Street is," Costley answered.

The government called Sarah Cushing to testify. She was not in the courtroom. Doctors Woodbridge Howes and John French, both of Hanover, appeared on her behalf and told the court that Cushing was unable to appear due to "continued mental excitement and neuralgia pains in the spine;" that a trip from Hanover to Dedham might prove arduous for Cushing and endanger her life.

The DA was not satisfied with the doctors' explanation and advised the court that the government intended to request a capias warrant if Cushing continued to disregard the summons to appear. A judge may order a capias warrant to take into custody a person who refuses to appear in court.

The government summoned Minnie Arbuckle. She testified about her acquaintances with Julia Hawkes and the defendant. She told the court she had met Julia at the rooming house on Camden Street on May 2 and last saw her at 5:15 p.m. on May 13 in the South End of Boston. During a walk that evening, Julia had told her she was going to Weymouth Landing for two weeks and if Costley should come to Camden Street for her things, to let him have them. Arbuckle described the clothing Julia wore on May 13. It was consistent with the clothing found on Julia's body when it was discovered in East Braintree. She immediately recognized the apparel and Newport tie shoe shown to her by French as part of the ensemble Julia had worn on May 13.

Arbuckle said she had met Costley on several occasions during his visits to Julia. When the district attorney asked if Costley was in the courtroom, Arbuckle pointed toward the prisoner's dock and positively identified him.

James Riedell, owner of the stable where Costley had rented a horse and buggy on May 9 and May 13, testified about his knowledge of Costley's actions and remarks on both occasions. Riedell also identified Costley as the man he had spoken to at the stable and testified about the shoe and hammer that his employee, James Spillane, had discovered in Costley's rented buggy on May 14. The district attorney showed Riedell the shoe and hammer. After he identified them, the court admitted the evidence as commonwealth exhibits.

Spillane and other stablemen employed by Riedell corroborated their employer's testimony. All of the witnesses identified the Newport tie shoe and the hammer and identified Costley as the man they had seen at the stable.

The commonwealth called Simon Chandler of Quincy. Chandler testified that he knew Costley and had met him in Plymouth on Wednesday, May 13; that they had dined and afterwards taken a train together to Quincy. During a conversation on board, Costley told Chandler he had visited William Sturtevant at Plymouth Jail earlier in the day. A Plymouth County grand jury had indicted Sturtevant five days before for a triple murder in Halifax. Sturtevant had "made a bad piece of work" and "some foolish moves in trying to cover his tracks," Costley said. "I could cover up tracks better myself," he added. Just before they arrived in Quincy, Chandler asked Costley to stay with him. Costley declined. "I guess your engagement is with a woman," Chandler said, and Costley laughed.

Employees of Dow's Stable on Portland Street, Boston, testified that Costley appeared at the stable on May 14 and asked that someone pick up two trunks at the Old Colony Railroad depot, return them to the stable, and store them there until a future date. One of the employees, John Brown, testified that Costley had paid him for the trunk storage. All positively identified Costley as he sat in the prisoner's dock.

After he had identified Costley, the expressman, Cornelius Sullivan, was asked if the Saratoga trunk bearing Costley's name, previously marked as evidence, was one of the trunks he had transported with Costley from Dow's Stable to the Boston and Albany Railroad depot on May 16. Sullivan confirmed that it was.

The court excused Sullivan after a brief cross-examination by the defense and adjourned. A deputy sheriff handcuffed Costley, escorted him out of the courthouse and, with another deputy, walked him back to Dedham Jail.

~

Attorney General
Charles Russell Train

The third day of trial opened on December 30 with a motion by Attorney General Train to compel Sarah Cushing's attendance and testimony. Train asked the court to appoint a Boston physician to visit Cushing in Hanover and evaluate her condition. The court granted Train's request and dispatched Dr. Frederick Ainsworth to Hanover.

DA French called the first witness, John Burke, owner of Burke's Saloon, 176 Tremont Street, Boston, who testified that Costley had been in his establishment on May 13 and had left a black valise and umbrella there. Costley had returned to the bar three days later, May 16, in the company of the expressman, Cornelius Sullivan, and retrieved the valise but left the umbrella. Another employee at the saloon, John Kalbskopl, corroborated Burke's testimony. Both men positively identified Costley from the witness stand.

French next summoned three witnesses to testify about Costley's handwriting. Each compared signatures on the hotel registers with a known sample of Costley's handwriting and verified that the signatures were in Costley's hand. French showed handwriting expert George Sawyer the Saratoga trunk previously identified by several witnesses as belonging to Julia Hawkes. On the trunk was written "J. H. Costley." Sawyer testified that the signature on the trunk was written by the same hand that had signed the hotel registers.

James Williams, a photographer from South Scituate (later Norwell) who lived near Four Corners, testified that he and Costley had practiced their penmanship together at the Howard House on a number of occasions. The district attorney showed the witness several letters Costley had addressed to Franklin Howard, and Williams identified the signatures and handwriting as Costley's.

French turned his attention to the Newport tie shoe that James Spillane had found at Riedell's Stable on May 14. Lucius Evans, a

Wakefield, Massachusetts, shoe manufacturer, identified the Newport tie shoes in evidence as shoes made by his employee, Jason Knight. Evans confirmed that the shoes matched and that Knight had produced them in his factory.

On cross-examination, Evans told the court that his shop had produced about sixteen hundred pairs of the shoes between December 1873 and January 1874 and distributed them to markets in Boston, Taunton, and Charlestown in Massachusetts; Saco, Maine; and Cleveland, Ohio. He confirmed again that the shoes were identical based on his inspection of the unique pattern of each.

Jason Knight took the stand and testified that he started making Newport tie shoes for Evans in 1872. French presented the two shoes in evidence, and Knight positively identified both as shoes he had made, pointing out several characteristics that were unique to his methods. Knight also produced the form, called a last, that he had used to make the shoes.

Shoemakers Joseph Burdett and Edward Walton took the stand and, after evaluating the shoes, expressed their belief that Knight had made them. On cross-examination, Burdett and Walton admitted they had not seen Knight make the shoes in evidence.

Parker Cushing took the stand after Walton. The thirty-four-year-old Cushing, who was not related to Sarah Cushing, testified that while working at the Howard House in September 1874, he found a loaded .22-caliber Wesson & Harrington pistol hidden in a storage room above the stable office. The pistol was secreted behind a beam beside the chimney. Cushing found a baggage claim check, No. 2549, in the same spot about a week later. He gave the loaded pistol and the claim check to Franklin Howard, his

Wesson & Harrington .22 caliber revolver

95

employer. However, when French showed Cushing the evidence in court, he refused to say that they were the same items he had found.

On cross-examination, Cushing said he had never agreed with Mr. Howard not to say anything about finding the pistol and check and denied having said anything to anyone else about the discoveries. He could not explain why he had never mentioned the pistol and check to the police and didn't remember if Howard had told him what he was going to do with them.

When the court reconvened at 1:00 p.m., the commonwealth called fifty-six-year-old Franklin Howard to the stand. Howard identified himself as the proprietor of the Howard House and told the court he had leased his hotel to the defendant from November 1872 until May 1874. Howard moved to Danvers, Massachusetts, immediately after leasing the hotel to Costley.

Costley visited Howard in Danvers around April 1874 and told him he wanted to give up his lease and get out of the hotel business. Howard agreed to release Costley from the lease and consented to Costley's request to hold an auction of his personal property on the hotel premises. French showed Howard a poster that he identified as the one Costley had used to advertise the auction. Howard told French that he returned to the Howard House in May 1874 after Costley sold out.

The district attorney then showed the pistol and claim check found by Parker Cushing to the witness. Howard identified both and acknowledged that Cushing had given them to him in September 1874. Howard testified he had kept both items locked in his office desk but later placed them back in the storage room where Cushing had found them.

On cross-examination, Howard admitted he had withheld information about the gun and the check because he didn't want to get involved in the murder investigation. He also conceded he had told Cushing not to tell anyone about what he had found.

Howard testified that the day after he had returned the gun and check to the storage room, two friends, who he refused to identify, came to his office and told him they knew he had the items and advised him to turn them over to the police. Howard suspected Cushing had "leaked" that information to the men. When Howard demurred, the men threatened to call the police and expose him. Howard acquiesced, contacted Chief Constable Boynton, and delivered the loaded gun and the claim check to him on September 15. French offered the gun and claim check as evidence, and the court admitted them as commonwealth exhibits.

Baggage Master George Ingalls of the Boston, Hartford and Erie Railroad testified he had received a russet-colored Saratoga trunk bearing claim check No. 2549 on the morning of May 20 at the Boston and Albany depot. Written on the trunk was "J. H. Costley." The trunk had been sent from New York via the Norwich line. The trunk remained in the depot's baggage room for seventeen weeks until Chief Boynton appeared with the matching check and claimed it. French showed Ingalls the Saratoga trunk in evidence, and Ingalls identified it as the trunk he had received on May 20.

French called Chief Constable George Boynton to the witness stand. Boynton told the court about his involvement in the murder investigation and provided an account of his September 28 interview with Costley in Plymouth Jail.

French showed Boynton the pistol and claim check in evidence, and Boynton identified both as the items he had recovered from Franklin Howard at the Howard House on September 15. The chief constable told the court he had removed five cartridges from the pistol and had submitted several of the cartridges to a pharmacist for analysis.

The district attorney produced the Saratoga trunk bearing Costley's name and asked Boynton if he recognized it. Boynton identified it as the trunk he had claimed from George Ingalls at the Boston and Albany depot with claim check No. 2549 – the same check given to him by Franklin Howard.

The chief constable testified there were two shirts in the trunk and two handkerchiefs, both monogrammed "J.H.C." He also stated that a black valise was found in the trunk and that the interior of the valise was stained with what appeared to be blood. Boynton believed this was the black valise Costley had used to conceal the carriage robe, tailor's goose, and rope on the night of the murder. He had earlier theorized that Costley, after returning to Boston following the murder, stopped at Burke's Saloon and left the valise there, then brought the horse and buggy back to Riedell's Stable. Costley then returned to Burke's, picked up the valise, and placed it in the Saratoga trunk before shipping it from the Boston and Albany depot on May 16. Boynton told the court that Julia Hawkes's second trunk was never found.

Attorney Cheney subjected Boynton to an extensive cross-examination but elicited no new information or contradictions. Boynton did, however, deny he had made a statement to Costley at the jail about anchoring the victim's feet before submerging her in the river.

The government next called Dr. Edward Wood, an assistant professor of chemistry at Harvard Medical School who specialized in bloodstain identification. Wood testified he had received the stained valise from Chief Constable Boynton and had found several stains in an upper pocket of the valise and another stain in a lower pocket. Even though a fail-safe method for confirming whether blood was human had not yet been developed, Wood subjected the stains to microscopic examination and chemical analysis and testified that the stains were, in his opinion, consistent with human blood. Wood never testified about the bloody towel and carpet sample that Detective Pinkham had taken from the Howard House on May 27.

Associate Justice
Charles Devens

Attorney Cheney cross-examined the witness about the validity of the tests he had performed and how exact they could be in differentiating between human blood and that of "fish and fowl" in an attempt to discredit his testimony. Justice Devens excused Wood from the witness stand at the conclusion of his testimony. The court would leave it for the jury to decide if the physician's tests for the existence of human blood were valid.

Court then adjourned until the next day.

A *Boston Globe* reporter covering the trial shared his impressions of the defendant. "Costley is a well-proportioned, handsome man, dresses with scrupulous neatness in dark blue cloth, and while manifesting the closest interest in the evidence, pays no attention to the spectators, and, at the close of the day's proceedings, smilingly holds forth his wrists for the handcuffs and passes out of the courtroom in charge of the officers, apparently unconscious of the curiosity with which all eyes are bent upon him."

~

Analytical chemists, testifying about blood evidence during this period, sought to establish the validity of scientific testing. But the courts were skeptical and refused to accept the idea that science could conclusively determine, beyond a reasonable doubt, the difference between human blood and the blood of animals.

In 1868, Samuel Andrews was tried in Plymouth County for a murder in Kingston, Massachusetts. Chemists testified about the process used to determine evidence of human blood on a number of exhibits offered by the commonwealth. A chemical analysis called the guaiacum test involved placing a suspected stain into a mixture of glacial acetic acid and chloride of sodium. The test confirmed the presence of blood, but it did not enable the chemist to determine if the blood was human or animal.

In order for the chemist to determine whether the stain was human blood, he soaked the bloodstained item in glycerin and water for several hours and then scraped a sample of the stain onto a microscope slide. The chemist inspected the sample for particles of starch and fat globules and circular, biconcave, disc-like bodies that corresponded in their shape and size to human red blood corpuscles. Chemists compared those corpuscles with known blood corpuscle samples from humans, horses, cows, dogs, rabbits, and pigs by inspecting their shape and measuring their size. But the size and shape of the human corpuscle could be so varied that chemists could not conclusively state that a bloodstain was, in fact, human blood.

In 1895, Joseph H. Linsley, MD, professor of pathology and bacteriology at the University of Vermont, published an article in *Medical Record – A Weekly Journal of Medicine and Surgery* about the scientific examination of suspected human bloodstains. Linsley asserted that microscopic examinations used to measure the exact size of corpuscles in blood specimens could not conclusively determine whether the specimens were human blood. He found it regrettable that certain medical men, posing as experts, would offer testimony and declare they could positively identify a suspected bloodstain as originating from a human source.

Six more years would pass before chemists could confirm that a bloodstain was human. Dr. Paul Uhlenhuth, a German bacteriologist, in 1901 developed the precipitin test, a fail-safe chemical method for distinguishing human blood from animal blood by the presence of unique proteins. Naming and standardizing blood groups was established the same year. The precipitin test is still used today by forensic scientists to verify the presence of human blood.

~

Clear skies, frigid temperatures, and a biting wind prevailed on Thursday morning, December 31, 1874. Detective Pinkham was the government's first witness and told the court that he began his investigation at East Braintree on May 25 after being notified of the discovery of the victim's body. He provided details about his meeting with Costley at the Howard House on May 26, Costley's arrest the same day, and evidence he had collected during the course of his investigation. French never asked him, however, about the bloody towel and bloodstains found in the Howard House.

Pinkham's testimony was briefly interrupted to allow Dr. Frederick Ainsworth to report on his examination of Sarah Cushing. At sidebar, Ainsworth told the court that he and Dr. William Morland had visited Cushing in Hanover the day before and had found her not ill but suffering

100

from "nervous excitement." In Ainsworth's opinion, a trip from Hanover to Dedham would not jeopardize her health.

Defense Attorney Sanford protested Ainsworth's conclusion. The court, with an eye to compromise, instructed counsel to discuss a possible alternative to Cushing's attendance. The court suspended Pinkham's testimony and recessed for a half hour to allow counsel for both sides to confer on the issue.

When the court reconvened, the attorneys announced they had agreed to accept a written statement from Cushing in lieu of her testimony. Justice Wells asked Costley if he had any objection. When Costley stated he was not opposed, the judge ruled that the court would allow the statement as evidence and directed Pinkham to return to the stand.

Pinkham testified he had driven a horse and carriage from Riedell's Stable by way of the Neponset Bridge to Quincy and from Quincy to Weymouth Landing. When he reached the place where the victim's body was recovered in East Braintree, he retraced his route and returned to Riedell's. He estimated the trip took him four hours and twenty minutes and included a ten-minute stop.

He described the area between the stable and Neponset as thickly settled. From Neponset to the Monatiquot Bridge in East Braintree, the region became more rural and homes were spaced from a half mile to three-quarters of a mile apart. The road from Quincy to the bridge was heavily wooded.

Sanford objected to Pinkham's testimony about the carriage ride and the geography. The court sustained the defense attorney's objection regarding Pinkham's route and the duration of the ride but not to Pinkham's description of the route. The court recognized that various routes existed between Boston and Weymouth Landing and that Pinkham had followed only one of them. The court also acknowledged that any estimate about the time of travel was mere speculation. The court allowed Pinkham's testimony about the area's description, ruling it competent, and stated that the jury might consider that evidence in relation to other evidence in the case.

101

The court recessed until the afternoon when Sanford began cross-examining Pinkham.

"Did you swear to a complaint in court after your arrest of the defendant that the murder was committed in Hanover?" asked Sanford.

"Yes, I did," Pinkham answered.

"What prompted you to decide the murder was committed there?"

"I found a towel in the Howard House [on May 27] on which I thought were blood stains. I also found spots of what I believed to be blood on the dining room floor."

"Did you find any other stains you thought were blood?"

"I found a stain on the top rail of the gate [outside the hotel], but I had considerable doubt about its being blood. There was a tree there and I found similar stains all about and rubbed them off and satisfied myself they were not blood stains."

"Are you sure of that?" Sanford inquired.

"I don't know positive of my own knowledge that they were not bloodstains," Pinkham answered reluctantly.

Pinkham had taken the towel and bloodstained carpet from the hotel for testing but the items were never examined. Sanford hoped that the officer's unqualified opinion and his failure to submit the items to an expert would convince jurors that Pinkham was either careless, or purposely trying to hide exculpatory evidence.

Sanford was laying the groundwork for a directed verdict of not guilty based on his contention that there was "...not sufficient evidence of the commission of the homicide in Norfolk County and that on that ground the defendant must be acquitted." If the court denied the defense's appeal for a directed verdict and the jury's deliberations resulted in Costley's conviction, Sanford and Cheney planned to appeal to a higher court based on the same contention, that if the homicide occurred in a county other than Norfolk, the indictment against Costley was flawed and his conviction was, therefore, improper. If an appellate court should rule in favor of the defense's argument, then double jeopardy would apply and prohibit the government from trying Costley again.

After Sanford concluded his cross-examination, DA French called Albert Sawyer, a pharmacist with an apothecary shop at Washington and State Streets, Boston, who testified about the ballistics evidence. Sawyer explained that a cartridge consisted of a bullet, shell casing, powder, and primer. The hammer of a pistol, upon striking the cartridge, ignited the primer and powder and expelled the bullet from the shell casing. He told the court that he had weighed the bullet taken from Julia Hawkes's head in the presence of Chief Boynton and Francis Green, a firearms expert, and determined its weight as seventy-seven and a half grains. He then weighed two cartridges given him by Boynton and found them to measure eighty-one and eighty-two grains. Sawyer testified that the fatal bullet had probably been fired from a cartridge consistent with the two cartridges provided by Boynton.

Francis Green, a firearms dealer in Faneuil Hall Square, established himself as an expert witness. He confirmed that he was present when Albert Sawyer weighed the cartridges in evidence. French showed Green the .22-caliber Wesson & Harrington pistol in evidence. French asked Green if he had formed an opinion about the compatibility of the cartridges and the pistol. Green stated that all of the cartridges were consistent with ammunition manufactured for .22-caliber Wesson & Harrington pistols.

Judson Harris, manager at Thomas Barnes's hardware store in Boston, testified about the sale of a .22-caliber pistol on April 27, 1874. French displayed the pistol in evidence and asked Harris if he recognized it. Harris said it was similar to the one he had sold in April. French asked Harris if the man who had purchased that pistol was present in the courtroom. Harris said he couldn't be sure.

French showed Harris a second pistol, a Tycoon revolver the defendant had allegedly purchased as a gift for his fiancée, Sarah Cushing. Harris stated he did not recognize it. The defense had no questions for Harris, and the court excused him.

The prosecution and defense attorneys next approached the bench and informed Justices Wells and Devens that they had received Sarah Cushing's written statement of testimony. After inspecting the document, the court instructed Attorney General Train to read it aloud. Cushing swore to the following facts: She had known Costley ever since he had lived in Hanover, and on May 13, 1874, (the same day the government alleged Costley had murdered Hawkes) she accepted his proposal of marriage. Her personal worth was in excess of $12,000 (equivalent to $1.3 million in today's economy).

She acknowledged writing and sending the letter addressed to "Thomas I. Thomas" that Detective Philbrick found in Costley's trunk at the Howard House. She admitted that the letter was meant for Costley and that "Thomas" was a fictitious name she and Costley had devised to keep their correspondence confidential. She also acknowledged that she had received a Tycoon revolver from Costley as a gift. She surrendered the revolver to Detective Pinkham on or about May 30, 1874. The statement concluded with Cushing's admission that Costley had told her he was in New York from May 15 to May 19 and that she had received a letter from Costley purportedly written by him when he was there.

The court accepted Cushing's statement and entered it as evidence. The prosecution then called Constable Napoleon Furnald to the stand.

Furnald corroborated Detective Pinkham's previous testimony about the visit to the Howard House and the evidence found there, and he offered information he had solicited from witnesses during his investigation. He also testified about geographical conditions in the vicinity of Weymouth Landing. No new or conflicting evidence was obtained during cross-examination, and Furnald was excused. The court adjourned until the next day.

~

The fifth day of trial opened on a clear, cold Friday morning, January 1, 1875. The government called state detective Chase Philbrick who corroborated the testimony of Detective Pinkham and Chief Boynton. DA French approached Philbrick with a Tycoon revolver and asked if he recognized it. Philbrick identified it as the same revolver Sarah Cushing

104

had surrendered to him, and it was accepted as evidence. Philbrick underwent a lengthy cross-examination that elicited no new facts.

French recalled three witnesses, James Riedell, the stable owner, Cornelius Sullivan, the expressman, and Franklin Howard, owner of the Howard House, to clarify issues in their previous testimonies.

French had failed to ask Riedell during direct testimony if Costley had identified himself when he rented the horses on May 9 and May 13. Riedell confirmed that Costley had done so.

On cross-examination, Attorney Sanford asked Riedell if he had either shown or discussed with Costley the shoe that Spillane had found in the buggy. Riedell denied doing so.

Sullivan told the court about an encounter he had with Costley at the Plymouth jail the previous June. When detectives brought Sullivan to Costley's cell, Sullivan immediately recognized the prisoner.

"How do you do, Costley?" Sullivan asked.

"How do you do?" Costley responded, rising from his cot.

"That is a pretty scrape you have got me into with those trunks," the expressman said.

"What trunks?"

"Those I took from the stable on Portland Street to the depot," Sullivan replied.

"I don't know anything about any trunks," said Costley as he returned to his cot. He refused to speak any further with his visitor.

When Franklin Howard was called again, he denied he had owned the cartridges and tailor's goose found by police at the hotel. He said that he had kept a tailor shop near the hotel about twenty years before but had sold everything except his shears and a rule.

At the conclusion of Howard's testimony, Attorney General Train and District Attorney French rested the prosecution's case. The court declared a brief recess.

~

Attorney Horace Cheney delivered his opening statement for the defense when the trial resumed. The purpose of his statement was twofold: to convince the jury that the government had failed to prove his client's guilt; and to lay the groundwork for an appeal should Costley be found guilty. If he could prove that evidence was improperly admitted, that a person connected with the trial had committed a misconduct in court, or that a lower court did not have jurisdiction to hear the case, an appellate court might overturn his client's conviction.

Attorney Horace R. Cheney

Cheney attacked the government's attempts to connect the carriage robe, tailor's goose, and trunk to Costley. He also assailed the forensic testimony, stating that the government never proved the bullet recovered from the victim's head matched the cartridges found at the hotel and on Costley. He dismissed the notion that Costley had hidden the claim check and pistol in the storage room at the hotel and suggested that some other person had placed them there to falsely implicate the defendant.

Cheney commented on the government's failure to prove that the crime, as specified in the indictment, had occurred in Norfolk County, and he challenged the court's authority to take jurisdiction in the case.

Cheney noted other technical aspects of the case and shared his interpretation of circumstantial evidence and reasonable doubt with jurors. As to circumstantial evidence, Cheney said, "…no living witness had testified to seeing anything done, and [the jury] would have to distinguish between circumstantial and direct evidence. You are asked to infer certain proved facts, or certain facts claimed to be proved and from them you are asked to infer certain other facts which usually accompany and attend them…"

As to reasonable doubt, Cheney cited Massachusetts Supreme Judicial Court Chief Justice Shaw's definition, which first introduced in the 1850 Parkman-Webster murder trial in Boston. Shaw defined reasonable doubt as: "that state of the case, which, after the entire comparison and consideration of all the evidence, leaves the minds of jurors in that condition that they cannot say they feel an abiding conviction, to a moral certainty, of the truth of the charge. For it is not sufficient to establish a probability, though a strong one arising from the doctrine of chances, that the fact charged is more likely to be true than the contrary; but the evidence must establish the truth of the fact to a reasonable and moral certainty; a certainty that convinces and directs the understanding, and satisfies the reason and judgment, of those who are bound to act conscientiously upon it. This we take to be proof beyond reasonable doubt."

After finishing his opening statement, Cheney called his first witness, John Lovell, an expert in firearms. Lovell testified that the cartridges found by police at the hotel were .32-caliber, not .22-caliber as claimed by previous experts, and that they could be fired by twenty to twenty-six different pistols on the market at the time. The government had no questions for Lovell, and he was excused.

Eben Waterman was Cheney's next witness. Waterman testified that he had known the defendant for two years and had accompanied the defendant from the Howard House to the Hanover depot on May 9, 1874, in a wagon driven by expressman Horace Tower. He recalled taking a black valise from Costley and placing it in the wagon. Waterman said he didn't notice anything unusual about the bag's weight. When they reached the depot, Costley and Waterman took their belongings and boarded a 10:00 a.m. train for Boston.

During cross-examination by Attorney General Train, Waterman said he left Costley when they arrived at the Old Colony depot in Boston and didn't see him again for two days. He wasn't sure if Costley had taken the black valise with him or if he had placed it in the depot's baggage room.

Train then questioned Waterman about the inquest into Love Congdon's death. At first, Waterman said he didn't recall anything that had implicated Costley in Congdon's death, and he denied hearing rumors that Costley had poisoned her. When Train pressed him,

Waterman recanted and admitted that he "might have heard it suggested that Costley killed her," and "there was a good deal of talk about it in Hanover, one party asserting he poisoned her and the other party denying it."

Waterman told the court that he was a Plymouth County coroner as well as a justice of the peace in Hanover. He had assembled a coroner's jury to investigate Congdon's death, and when he presented the results of the inquest to a magistrate at the Plymouth Court, the magistrate took no action. This, to his mind, closed the case and eliminated the need for further inquiry.

The defense next called Horace Tower. Tower told the court that he was an expressman for Hiram Randall in Hanover. He corroborated Waterman's testimony and confirmed that he had taken Costley and Waterman to the depot on May 9, 1874. Tower said he had known Costley for about five years and considered him a "kind and humane man."

When cross-examined, Tower said he had not seen the contents of Costley's black valise on the day in question, nor could he estimate its weight. He didn't remember taking any other baggage to the depot for Costley on any other day, and he didn't recall anyone discussing Love Congdon's poisoning and Costley's possible involvement.

Defense witness Adeline Lindsay, who lived a short distance from the Howard House, testified that several officers had come to her house the day Costley was arrested and questioned her and Harriet McLaughlin, who boarded with Lindsay. The officers inquired about Costley and asked where they could find him. She directed them to the Howard House. Lindsay told the court that she had seen Costley before the officers arrived and asked him if he had heard about Julia Hawkes's death. She was holding a newspaper in her hand that detailed the incident. Lindsay said she watched Costley as he read the article, and she didn't observe any change in his expression.

The defense team introduced six more witnesses to testify to Costley's good character. Abner Stetson of South Scituate, Costley's first employer when he arrived in Hanover; Francis Arnold of Pembroke, a shoe manufacturer and grand master of the Phoenix Masonic Lodge; John Ellis; Michael Sylvester; George Bates; and Edward Sweeney. All six men, residents in the Four Corners area and members of the lodge, said they knew the defendant, a fellow Mason, to be a quiet, peaceable, and humane man.

DA French cross-examined each of the men in an effort to discredit their testimony about Costley's reputable character. He asked them what they knew about the Congdon death and if they had heard any talk about Costley's involvement in her poisoning. All of the men admitted to hearing rumors about Costley, but each considered the allegations as gossip and unfounded speculation. None of them believed Costley was in any way responsible for her death and all believed him incapable of foul play.

~

The court recessed for the morning, and defense counsel resumed its efforts during the afternoon to cast doubt on the time and place of the murder. Cheney recalled Dr. Forsaith to clarify the physician's previous testimony regarding his autopsy on Julia Hawkes.

Cheney handed Forsaith the anatomical skull in evidence and asked him to point out the location of the entry wound on the victim's head. Forsaith indicated that he had found a fracture on the right side of the head in the lower third of the parietal bone, near its juncture with the temporal and frontal bones.

French approached Forsaith for cross-examination. The district attorney ascertained the intent of Cheney's questions and wanted to prevent the defense from establishing that Hawkes's wound was not immediately fatal. French asked Forsaith if there were any differences between the skull presented in court and the victim's skull. Forsaith admitted that the skull exhibited in court was unlike the victim's. "Mrs. Hawkes's was much higher and a very different proportioned skull," he explained.

French then asked Forsaith if he knew where Julia Hawkes was buried. Forsaith said he didn't know and was then excused.

Cheney next called Dr. William Fifield of Dorchester, a Harvard Medical School graduate, who testified that he had reviewed Drs. Forsaith's and Tinkham's autopsy notes and had listened to their testimony. He asserted that Hawkes's wound was not necessarily fatal; that she could have survived such a wound, as the path of the bullet did not strike "...any important veins, arteries or sinuses, the destruction of which would lead to such effusion of blood upon the brain as to indicate speedy death therefrom..."

"What are the probabilities that life might be continued, resulting in restoration from the effects of the wound?" Cheney asked Fifield.

"Do I understand you to mean ultimate recovery?" asked Fifield.

"Yes, sir," Cheney said.

"I should say the probability of a recovery might be held," Fifield answered, "but I should make a reservation as to the amount of probability."

"Would, in your opinion, death within any given period of time be uncertain as the consequence of the wound?"

"Yes, sir," said Fifield.

Attorney General Train, on cross-examination, got Fifield to state that Hawkes's wound may or may not have been fatal. As to the time of death, Fifield said, "...the duration of life may be shortened or lengthened according to each particular case." He admitted that the victim's wound could have resulted in instantaneous death.

No evidence was offered during the trial to suggest that drowning, strangulation, suffocation, or any other cause contributed to, or was the actual cause of, Julia Hawkes's death. The issue was whether or not the victim died from the gunshot instantaneously or over a period of time.

Sanford and Cheney called two other physicians to address hypothetical questions about the manner of death. Dr. D. W. Cheever, a prominent physician and surgeon at Boston City Hospital, and Dr. George Gay, of Massachusetts General Hospital, agreed that a person could survive for a certain amount of time following a pistol shot to the brain. Cheever stated that would raise questions in the Hawkes case as to whether the pistol shot or drowning had caused her death.

Sanford called two additional witnesses to contest Pinkham's testimony about Costley's probable route from Riedell's Stable to East Braintree. The prosecution offered no rebuttal witnesses.

Sanford and Cheney decided, with Costley's consent, not to place him on the stand in his own defense and rested their case.

The court instructed the prosecution and defense to present their closing arguments the following day and then adjourned.

~

Light snow was falling when court reconvened at 8:00 a.m. on Saturday, January 2.

Attorney Baylies Sanford rose from the defense table and approached the jury to begin his closing argument at eight thirty. He spoke for five and a half hours.

Sanford first asked the jury if the prosecution had established Costley's guilt "beyond a reasonable doubt in the manner prescribed by law." If the jurors could not determine that the murder had been committed within Norfolk County, they had no right to convict Costley. If they were uncertain about the cause of Julia Hawkes's death, they must find Costley not guilty. Sanford tried to convince the jury that the prosecution had not proven that the pistol shot killed Hawkes instantly. She could have been shot elsewhere and survived until she was deposited in the river. He also argued that Hawkes's death could have been caused by drowning, strangulation, or some other means – not by the pistol shot alone.

Sanford next attacked the evidence presented by the prosecution. He argued that the carriage robe that was wrapped around Hawkes's head had never been identified as belonging to his client. He also questioned the ownership of the russet-colored trunk, stating it had never been positively identified as belonging to Hawkes. He challenged the testimony of handwriting experts who told the court that the writing on the trunk, "J. H. Costley," belonged to his client. Sanford dismissed the government's assertion that the pistol and baggage claim check found in the Howard House stable had been placed there by Costley and suggested that some other person, possibly the real murderer, had put the items there. He said the detectives who searched the hotel and stable when they first visited Hanover did not find the pistol and claim check. How could Costley have hidden them after his arrest and during his confinement in Dedham Jail?

Sanford discredited the testimony of the constables in the case, focusing particularly on the conversations they had with his client in Plymouth Jail. He suggested that constables are prone to overlook and distort facts and details that are unfavorable to their case which "…renders [them] absolutely unable – though it may be honestly unable – to report exactly what is said under the circumstances."

He believed it incredulous that the officers could recall everything that was said seven months after they had first interviewed Costley at the jail. The officers, "…are prejudiced witnesses, having an interest in the result of the case," the defense attorney charged.

Sanford then moved to motive. He told the jury his client's reputation had been untainted before May 26 except for "an idle, evanescent rumor that Costley's former housekeeper died suddenly." When he was arrested, Costley was engaged to marry "an accomplished lady in Hanover possessed in her own right of more property than ordinarily falls to any human being." Why would Costley jeopardize his future with this woman by murdering Julia Hawkes and risking imprisonment or death?

Sanford also tried to convince jurors that the woman who was said to live in the rooming house on Camden Street had never been proven to be Hawkes. He tried to discredit Minnie Arbuckle's testimony that Julia, on the afternoon of May 13, had told her she was leaving with Costley that evening for Weymouth Landing. He also questioned the testimony of the stablemen at Riedell's, alleging they didn't know for sure that Costley had returned the buggy that evening. If they didn't know for sure, how could the Newport tie shoe found in the buggy be connected to Costley?

With that, Sanford finished his summation.

Seated in the encaged dock, Costley remained composed as he had during the entire trial. On many occasions when court was in recess he laughed and smiled at spectators and conveyed a cavalier and self-assured demeanor. Costley was arrogant and manipulative. Even with his life at stake he remained confident that his charm and guile would convince both spectators and jurors of the absurdity of the charges against him. He was always smartly dressed and usually wore a navy blue suit. His physical appearance had changed little since his incarceration, although he had let his side whiskers grow longer.

~

Attorney General Train began the closing argument for the prosecution at about three o'clock. He summarized the prosecution's case, highlighting the testimony and physical evidence introduced during the trial that contradicted statements Costley had made to police. He delivered a powerful and convincing rebuttal to the defense's closing remarks. He employed simple logic and reasoning as he carefully reconstructed the planning and execution of the crime.

"It is true the evidence is circumstantial," Train told the jurors, "but it is more satisfactory than if four or five men from Quincy had testified that they were in a piece of woods on the night of the thirteenth of May and had seen, on that misty night, the woman shot down by a man resembling the prisoner, because they might have been mistaken if they didn't catch him in the act. There is no break in this chain of evidence, and it does not only constitute a chain made of iron links but a cable made of strands of hemp, from which no hypothesis, beyond a reasonable doubt, can be assumed that it is not consistent with the guilt of the prisoner."

The attorney general completed his statement at 6:15 p.m. He had spoken for three hours and twenty minutes. When he returned to the prosecution table, District Attorney French quietly congratulated him. The court ordered a recess until seven fifteen.

When the court reconvened and before the jury filed in, Baylies Sanford submitted twelve exceptions for the court's consideration.

113

Justice Wells allowed some of the exceptions, but dismissed the majority. The most important – and disappointing for the defense – concerned the issue of venue. Costley's attorneys filed an exception stating that the court must acquit the defendant if the government failed to prove that the crime had been committed in Norfolk County, "or within one hundred rods of the line…"

Justice Wells ruled "…it is necessary for the government to prove, as it is necessary for them to prove all the other facts in the case to your satisfaction, beyond any reasonable doubt, that the offense was committed in the county of Norfolk. It is not necessary to prove that the pistol was fired within the county of Norfolk. If the pistol was fired in Suffolk County, but she (Hawkes) died in Norfolk County, or within one hundred rods of the line, the offense may be prosecuted in the county of Norfolk."

Wells referenced Massachusetts General Laws, Chapter 171, Sections 17 and 18. "The statute is, 'If a mortal wound is given, or other violent injury inflicted, or poison administered, in one county, by means whereof death ensues in another county, the offense may be prosecuted and punished in either county.'"

After Wells ruled on the exceptions, the jury was brought into the courtroom and seated. The judge then addressed the defendant, advising him of his privilege to make a statement to the jury if he wished. Costley told the judge he had nothing to say. Wells then charged the jury, explaining the law as it pertained to the degrees of murder, jurisdiction, and circumstantial evidence. He concluded his charge at about nine o'clock and dismissed the jury to begin deliberations.

Many spectators remained in the courtroom to await the jury's verdict. Costley stayed in the prisoner's dock and chatted and laughed with some of the men in the room as if he were disinterested in the case's outcome. But some recognized his false confidence, watching as Costley occasionally stroked his beard or twirled his moustache. It was plainly evident, in the opinion of a *Boston Globe* reporter, that Costley was on the "ragged edge of anxiety and despair."

~

Two hours later, the court advised the prosecution and defense that the jury had reached a verdict. An eerie silence filled the courtroom when the justices took the bench at 11:12 p.m. and court officers escorted the jury into the chamber.

The foreman announced that the jury had found Costley guilty of murder in the first degree in the death of Julia Hawkes. Costley showed no emotion. Attorney Horace Cheney asked the court to poll the jury. The court told Cheney such action was not the usual custom and denied his request. Costley asked the court if he could make a statement to the jury, but that was also denied. The court adjourned at 11:20 p.m., and Costley was remanded to Dedham Jail to await sentencing.

A newspaper correspondent later asked Costley what he intended to say to the jury had he been given a chance. Costley said he simply wished to thank the jurors and say that he had no hard feelings against them.

~

On Saturday, March 13, 1875, Norfolk County deputy sheriff William Warren escorted Costley into the prisoner's dock at the Dedham court for sentencing. As Costley conferred with his attorney, Horace Cheney, the court clerk ordered Costley to stand and asked him if he had anything to say why sentence of death should not be pronounced. "I have nothing to say," Costley replied.

Justice Wells then pronounced the sentence: "James H. Costley, it now becomes the painful duty of the Court to award against you the judgment which the law affixes to the crime of which you stand convicted. Under the humane provisions of the laws, there is but one offense the commission of which subjects the guilty party to the forfeiture of life. In the brief and simple, but expressive and solemn language of the statute, it is enacted that whoever is guilty of murder in the first degree shall suffer death. Of this high and heinous offense – the taking of human life with deliberate, premeditated malice aforethought – you have been found guilty by a jury carefully selected by yourself, and after a patient and impartial trial, in which you were defended by

115

able counsel. To this verdict and to the sufficiency of the indictment, we have been able to find no valid objections by reason upon any error in law, nor upon a deliberate and careful survey of the case by the full bench. The verdict was the necessary and inevitable conclusion resulting from the evidence of your guilt. Nothing, then, remains for the Court but to pass the sentence of the law: which is, that you, James H. Costley, be removed from this place to the Prison of this County, there to be kept in close confinement until such time as the Executive Department shall, by their warrant, appoint, thence taken to the place of execution, and there to be hanged by the neck until you are dead. And may God, in His infinite wisdom, have mercy upon your soul."

Wells scheduled Costley's execution for June 25, 1875. Costley bowed his head but showed no emotion. The deputy sheriff led Costley back to the jail. Spectators noticed Costley smiling slightly as he passed them.

~

Costley spent much of his time in jail reading and writing. Prison officials considered him a model prisoner because he never caused a problem or was disciplined during his incarceration.

His brother, Peter, from California was the only family member to visit Costley at the jail. His parents and siblings had moved from Nova Scotia to California after the Civil War. His brother spent several hours with Costley and promised, as he departed, that he would not tell his parents of Costley's fate.

Costley's fiancée, Sarah Cushing, was devastated by the verdict and sentencing. She visited him frequently as did the prison chaplain, Rev. Zachariah Mudge, and the rector of Saint Andrew's Episcopal Church in Hanover, Rev. William Brooks. A Dedham florist, George Morse, in commiseration with his fate, sent Costley a bouquet of flowers. Costley thanked Morse with the following note:

Mr. Morse, Respected Sir: I much appreciate the favors you have presented, and my true friend (Cushing) wished me to say that every kindness shown to me is increased tenfold to her. A blooming flower in a cell, so grim and dismal, seems to keep the soul awake, 'sweet thoughts alive, and sordid ones dead,' or it helps to bear a sorrow that often seems unbearable. But I do not want to mar the comforts of others by my cup of bitterness, as every heart has trials to endure. I know you give cheerfully. I feel it much. Will simply say, 'Thanks!' Ever grateful, J. Henry Costley.

Costley made friends with his jailors and made every attempt to convince them he had not committed the crime. He developed a special relationship with jailor Isaac Porter, a good-natured man who sympathized with the prisoner and allowed him certain privileges. This friendship became such a bond between the two men that Costley believed he could trust Porter with his life.

~

As June 25, the scheduled date of his execution, neared, Costley and his fiancée became frantic. Cushing had funded Costley's legal representation during the trial and continued to pay his expenses during appeal. Chances for a reversal of his conviction seemed bleak, so the two contrived an escape plan. They hoped to enlist the aid of their mutual friend, Isaac Porter, by offering him a bribe of ten thousand dollars, an incredible sum that amounted to nearly all of Sarah Cushing's riches, a sum that she could raise only by selling her property or obtaining contributions from others who were sympathetic to Costley's cause.

Costley approached Porter with the proposition and offered the bribe. Porter agreed to cooperate, and Costley revealed two plans he had devised to escape.

Costley's fiancée would surreptitiously supply tools and acid during one of her visits. Workers had demolished a wall as part of a project to extend the jail's west wing and had left it inadequately secured. As soon as he had removed the bars from his cell window he would escape through the opening, through the compromised wall, and into a waiting carriage.

"If I can't saw through the bars," Costley continued, "I'll get the attention of the guard on duty, blind him with the acid as he nears the cell, relieve him of his keys, and escape through the jail's gate."

Sarah Cushing arrived at Dedham Jail on May 7. Warden Henry White had gone to Plymouth that day to witness the execution of William Sturtevant at Plymouth Jail.

Cushing met Porter who led her to Costley's cell. Prison rules prohibited visitors from having physical contact with prisoners, so Cushing had to remain a short distance from the cell. As she approached the cell, however, Cushing staged an episode of dizziness and nausea and collapsed to the floor within reach of Costley. She quickly passed a package containing files, saws, and acid through the bars to Costley. As previously agreed, Porter did not interfere. He did help Cushing "recover" and then accompanied her from the cell area to the prison exit.

But Porter had second thoughts later that day about his complicity. Costley had made a statement to him that was deeply troubling. "[I] would make nothing of killing two or three men," Costley said, "if they stood in the way of [my] liberty."

Porter urged Costley to surrender the tools and acid to minimize the risk of discovery by another guard. The unwitting Costley reluctantly yielded when Porter promised to return the tools whenever he needed them, but he would not relinquish the acid and warned Porter not to betray him.

Porter, racked with guilt and trepidation, went to Warden White and confessed his part in the escape plot. He surrendered the tools, told White about the acid in Costley's cell, and tendered his resignation.

White sent a guard to Costley's vacant cell to retrieve the acid while Costley was in the jail's workshop. Costley grew increasingly alarmed when Porter failed to visit his cell over the next several days. Sensing the inevitable, he looked under his cot for the acid, and when he discovered it was gone he realized his plan for freedom had failed.

Warden White notified Sheriff Thomas of Costley's escape attempt and asked for additional security. Thomas contacted Boston mayor Samuel Cobb who dispatched thirty officers from the West Roxbury station to take posts outside the jail's walls.

~

The full bench of the Supreme Judicial Court heard Costley's last appeal on June 21, 1875. Chief Justice Horace Gray and Associate Justices Wells, Morton, Devens, and Endicott presided over the hearing. Attorney Horace Cheney represented the defendant, and Attorney General Train and Associate Attorney General Waldo Colburn represented the government. After listening to the arguments of both sides, the court announced it would take the matter under advisement and adjourned.

The court overruled all exceptions and upheld the conviction of first-degree murder. The execution would be carried out as scheduled.

On Wednesday, June 23, two days before Costley's scheduled execution, Detective Hollis Pinkham told Norfolk County Sheriff John Thomas he had received information regarding a plot to free Costley by force. Thomas considered the information valid and made arrangements to hire additional security to prevent the escape.

That evening, a detail of Boston police officers led by Sergeant John Laskie reported to Sheriff Thomas and were assigned to posts outside the prison walls. Laskie and his officers remained at their posts the following day and evening. On Friday morning, the day of execution, Boston Police captain Alexander McDonald of the West Roxbury station arrived with Lieutenant Chase and thirty men to complement the officers already assigned to the jail.

~

The impending execution caused great interest and excitement in the little village of Dedham and beyond. Residents hadn't witnessed such a spectacle since George Hersey was hanged inside the jail in 1862 after a Norfolk County jury found him guilty of murdering Betsey Frances Tirrell in Weymouth. Thirty-three years before, a death sentence was carried out on Dedham Common when John Boies was hanged for the axe murder of his wife, Jane, in Milton.

So many persons wanted to witness Costley's gruesome hanging that

Sheriff Thomas ordered that a limited number of permits be issued for access to the gallows. Heavy cardboard tickets, bordered in black, were printed:

> Admit...........
> **TO THE JAIL, DEDHAM**,
> On *Friday, June 25, 1875*,
> At 9 o'clock A. M.
> No admittance after 9 ½ o'clock.
> JOHN W. THOMAS, Sheriff

~

The sheriff distributed tickets to trial witnesses and members of the press. Additional tickets were disseminated to the general public on a case-by-case basis for ten dollars.

Winslow Drew, a Plymouth carpenter, arrived at the jail on June 23 to begin constructing the gallows. Drew had designed and built the gallows used to execute triple murderer William Sturtevant in Plymouth six weeks before.

The scaffold, erected in the prison's rotunda and facing the entrance, consisted of two upright posts, eighteen feet high, connected by a cross beam. It was unlike the gallows used to execute Hersey in that it was without a "drop," or trap door, through which the prisoner plunged. Instead, a Manila hemp rope, half an inch thick, ran over a wheel in the center of the crossbeam. On one end was the noose that dangled above a low platform. On the other end was a one hundred sixty pound weight. The weight was secured with a mechanism that, when triggered, caused the weight to plummet and lift the condemned criminal six feet into the air.

~

It was stifling in Costley's cell when Attorney Horace Cheney visited his client on Thursday, June 24. The temperature outside had reached ninety-four degrees, the highest since July 1874. Costley sat dejected as Cheney advised him that all attempts at reversing his conviction had failed. The prison warden, fearing suicide or another attempt by Costley to escape, assigned officers Goodwin, Bailey, and Clifford to oversee Costley during a deathwatch.

Costley slept soundly Thursday night, getting up only once, when brilliant flashes of sheet lightning penetrated his cell window. He rose early Friday morning, bathed, dressed, and ate a hearty beefsteak breakfast prepared by the sheriff's personal cook. Reverend Brooks of Hanover visited him in his cell and prayed with him.

A *Boston Globe* reporter later wrote that Brooks had advised Costley to confess. Costley said, "I have nothing to confess. I did not commit the deed." "But," said the clergyman, "if you did not do it, you may be cognizant [of] who did it, and are equally guilty." Costley answered, "Yes, I suppose I am. I do not want to tell who it was. It would only criminate [*sic*] others and not help myself. I am prepared to die, and at eleven o'clock I shall be happier than any whom I leave behind."

Costley then wrote several letters, including one to his fiancée, Sarah Cushing. He composed a letter thanking Warden Henry White for his kind treatment while Costley was in his custody. It read:

Mr. White, Respected Sir: I think you know my feelings without my expressing them in writing. But the very kind words and acts while under your care bids me say here that the respect I bear to you and Mr. Goodwin was stronger than all precaution that might surround me. I know you will act faithfully to all you have under your charge. I will not multiply words, but my trust and respect is second to that of a brother. Truly gratefully, J. H. Costley.

Costley penned a letter to Detective Christopher Bailey of the state constable force.

Mr. C. Bailey, Respected Sir: You have asked me for information that is beyond my power to give in full, and betraying my word to give in part. I know you feel deeply for me, and would be pleased to do anything allowed by law that would benefit me. For all of which I feel extremely grateful. I will not multiply words, Mr. Bailey. But I feel as if you were an honorable friend. Good-bye. Very respectfully, J. H. Costley.

During their conversations, Bailey had asked Costley to confess or to at least tell what he knew of the murder. Costley had declined and suggested that someone else had been responsible, but he was not at liberty to tell who that person was.

Costley then wrote his final statement, professing his innocence to the end.

These are my last words. I have the kindest wishes for the just laws of this commonwealth, and the execution of the same. These laws would not allow my execution if my situation was made known. I assert no goodness, but in the fear, and almost presence of God, I say to one and all, I am innocent of murder. I now forgive my enemies, thank my friends, and submit myself to the mercy of God, and know my end shall be peace. I feel thankful to all the prison officers, and especially to Mr. White and Mr. Goodwin, in whose charge I have been for the last year. While strict to duty, they have shown every kindness allowed by law. I have no words to fully express my respects and good feeling to them. The many kind visits of Dr. Chase, the prison physician, are very dear to me. I am truly grateful to all the officers in whose charge I have been since my arrest. I am very thankful to all the followers of Christ for their sympathetic visits during these solitary hours, and am extremely grateful to Rev. W. N. Brooks of Hanover, and Rev. Z. A. Mudge of Dedham, the Chaplain of the prison. Friends not mentioned I thank again and again for every kindness. Gratefully, J. H. Costley - Dedham, June 25th 1875.

~

About three hundred fifty people had gathered outside the jail's entrance gate hours before Costley's scheduled execution. Heat and humidity did not deter the festive atmosphere as people chatted and laughed. Ladies fluttered gaily-colored fans beneath fashionable parasols, and men mopped their brows with handkerchiefs and fanned themselves with their hats.

At nine o'clock, two guards opened the jail gate and admitted the sworn witnesses to the execution, members of the press, and ticket holders. Inside, solemnity prevailed as deputies directed the assembly to the rotunda and to seats arranged in front of the gallows.

Shortly after 9:30 a.m., Costley entered the rotunda from the east wing of the prison with his arms strapped tightly to his body. He was accompanied by Rev. Brooks, Rev. Mudge, Dr. John Chase, the prison physician, Warden White, and Deputy Sheriffs Endicott, Wood, and Warren. The deputies were dressed in blue broadcloth coats with brass buttons and silk hats and were armed with pistols. Present and seated in the front row before the gallows was District Attorney Asa French, Worcester County Sheriff Augustus Sprague, Hampden County Sheriff Addison Bradley, Chief Constable George W. Boynton, and state detective Chase Philbrick.

Costley, dressed in a black suit, a black necktie, polished black shoes, and an immaculate white shirt, was, according to a *Boston Post* correspondent, "deathly pale but expressive of determined resignation. His firmness was not characterized by any bravado, but, on the contrary, indicated that he fully appreciated his position and was prepared for the ordeal."

Deputies wheeled the sixty-year-old Sheriff Thomas, who was suffering from rheumatism, in a chair to the left of the gallows. Four other deputies seated Costley in a chair directly beneath the gallows rope and noose. He scanned the assemblage before him, and when his eyes met Philbrick's, he nodded and smiled in recognition.

Thomas gave everyone present an opportunity to leave before the execution, but all remained. Reverend Brooks offered a prayer, "commending the soul of the condemned man to the mercy and goodness of God."

The sheriff solemnly read the warrant of execution signed by Governor William Gaston. When he finished, Thomas turned to Costley and asked if he had any last words. A *Boston Globe* correspondent heard Costley say, "I think what I intended to say I have committed to writing to my much honored and respected keeper, Mr. Henry White. I have no words that I can speak that can express anything of his kind attention and respect paid me at this place and now. This much I have to say and no more." The reporter watched as Costley, "so speaking, in a quiet but firm tone, bowed and stepped back under the noose, the chair having been removed."

Deputies fastened straps around Costley's knees and ankles. Warden White placed the noose over the condemned man's head and around his neck, securing the knot just behind his left ear. White then drew a black hood over Costley's face. At 9:43 a.m., Sheriff Thomas pronounced, "And now, James Henry Costley, in obedience to this warrant and by virtue of the authority vested in me, I now execute the command of the law, and may the Almighty God have mercy on your soul."

Thomas triggered the release lever, and "Costley's body bounded straight up about six feet and settled back with a sickening jerk," the *Globe* correspondent wrote. "There were some eight or ten convulsive contractions of the legs and shoulders, lasting for nearly a minute and a half, after which the inanimate corpse of the murderer hung without motion." One witness, William Ames, director of the Norfolk Mutual Fire Insurance Company, fainted, and deputies carried him out of the jail for fresh air.

Sheriff Thomas ordered everyone, except for those with official business, to leave the rotunda, and the body was lowered at 10:14 a.m. Dr. John Chase and several other physicians examined Costley's pulse and heart and pronounced him dead. There was no noticeable discoloration or distortion on the face, but the neck was bruised and the U-shaped hyoid bone in the larynx was crushed.

~

Costley was the last person hanged in Dedham Jail. Thirteen more men would swing from gallows in other county jails before sweeping legislative changes altered the course of capital punishment in the commonwealth. In 1898, Governor Roger Wolcott signed a bill that replaced the noose with the electric chair, prohibited capital punishment in the county of conviction, and directed that all executions take place at the state prison in Charlestown. The bill also eliminated public executions. Only certain officials – necessary physicians, the surgeon general of the governor's staff, the sheriff of the county where the crime was committed, and not more than three others – were authorized to attend the imposition of punishment.

~

Several hours before the execution, Sheriff Thomas had permitted Timothy Smith, an undertaker in Dedham, to deliver to the jail a rosewood coffin adorned with a cover of black broadcloth and silver mountings. It was purchased by Sarah Cushing. Thomas released the body at her request to undertaker Francis Arnold of Hanover.

Sarah had planned to bury Costley in the Cushing family plot at Hanover Center Cemetery where her father, Captain John Cushing, had been interred in 1871. But Sarah's mother was vehemently opposed to that. The widow would not allow a murderer to be laid to rest beside her husband, she chided, and if Sarah persisted, her mother would have her husband's remains exhumed and buried in another plot. Sarah relented and purchased a single grave beneath a large maple tree in the oldest section of the cemetery.

Few people attended Costley's burial, but many stopped by the gravesite during the days and years that followed and threw stones upon it in condemnation. As time went by and the memory of the tragedy faded, the persistent and deliberate effects of nature covered the stones with a blanket of grass and moss. The mound is plainly visible today, a pitiful marker of James Henry Costley's final resting place.

~

The commonwealth never prosecuted Sarah Cushing for her attempt to liberate Costley from jail. Neither the district attorney nor the attorney general saw a need to punish her. They viewed her as an innocent victim of Costley's wile and treachery.

Sarah married Godfried Turcotte, a cabinetmaker from South Abington, on December 27, 1879, four years after Costley's death. Sarah contracted pneumonia two years later and died in Boston on February 24, 1882. She was interred with her parents, John and Sarah Cushing, in the family plot at the Hanover cemetery less than thirty yards from Costley's grave. Some have claimed that in the evening Sarah's spirit –

the "lady in white" – visits the grave of her beloved betrothed.

~

During their preparations for the trial and in consideration of motive, prosecutors theorized that Costley had promised to marry Julia Hawkes, or, at the very least, had made some other type of promise or inducement to her. Train and French never proved this relationship during the trial, but they were convinced that Costley had become engaged to the wealthy Sarah Cushing sometime before May 13, the last day Julia Hawkes was seen alive. The prosecution firmly believed that Costley had eliminated Julia to expedite his plan to marry Sarah.

The court never ruled on Costley's involvement in the poisoning death of Love Congdon, as it was not a matter for consideration. Prosecutors alluded to Costley's connection to Congdon's death with rumors and innuendos, but they never introduced any material facts to confirm that Costley had taken Congdon's life. However, Train and French must have considered, and perhaps discussed, the possibility that Costley had made the same promises and inducements, and proposed marriage, to Congdon as he had to Hawkes. Had Costley disposed of Congdon in order to court Hawkes, just as he had eliminated Hawkes in order to court and marry Sarah Cushing?

The two prosecutors must have also wondered if Hawkes held a secret about Costley's connection to Congdon's death. Did she threaten to notify authorities about his involvement? Is it possible that Costley's real motive for killing Hawkes was to keep her quiet about his role in that woman's demise?

Why officials never ordered an autopsy on Congdon's body remains a mystery. The examination of her remains might have revealed whether she had, in fact, been murdered. Perhaps a thorough investigation might have led to Costley's arrest and prevented the brutal killing of Julia Hawkes

Costley truly believed he could get away with murder by carefully planning every step in his sinister scheme. Costley set his plans in motion by giving up his interest in the Howard House and telling Julia Hawkes that he was planning a new venture in Oregon with his brother and that he wanted her to accompany him. Julia was either unaware of his affair with Sarah Cushing or she did know about it and Costley convinced her that he intended to end his relationship with the other woman.

Before leaving the Howard House, Costley went to Camden Street to secure temporary housing for Julia. He told the landlady that the room was for a woman who did not want her friends to know where she was. Costley later gave Julia the room key, and she arrived there about May 1, 1874. Costley told Julia he'd handle the transfer of her travel trunks by shipping them to the railroad depot. He later told investigators he had given the claim checks for the trunks to Julia when he accidentally met her in Boston. But he never gave them to her. He planned to keep the checks and conceal the trunks.

When anyone at the Hanover House asked about Julia's whereabouts, Costley falsely answered that she had gone to Maine to visit friends. Once he had disposed of her, he could tell those who asked that he never heard from her again, that she had apparently decided not to return.

Costley rented a horse and buggy on May 9 in Boston and rode to Weymouth Landing and back to search for an isolated place for the murder and to estimate the length of time it would take him to ride to the Landing, murder Julia, submerge her body in the river, and return to Boston. Upon his return to the stable that evening, he left a black valise containing the rope, a hammer, the carriage robe, and the tailor's goose he would need to anchor Julia's body to the Monatiquot riverbed.

Costley executed his plan on the night of May 13. He rented a horse and buggy from the same stable, obtained the valise he had left there four days before, and picked up Julia at the Camden Street rooming house. He and Julia drove from the city through Quincy and Weymouth. Somewhere near Weymouth Landing, Costley stopped in a dark, isolated area he had selected during his trial run, removed the pistol he had concealed in his clothing, and shot Julia once in the head, killing her. Costley then removed any identifying papers and jewelry from her person, tied the rope attached to the gunnysack and tailor's goose around her neck, covered her head with the carriage robe, and tied the other rope around her neck to secure the robe. He then drove a short distance to the bridge spanning the Monatiquot River and tossed Julia's body into the water. Costley returned to the stable without the valise and left the horse and buggy with the stableman. Costley had secreted the valise at Burke's Saloon and retrieved it after depositing the buggy.

Costley next had to conceal any trace of Julia's existence. He went to the Camden Street rooming house with Julia's room key the morning after the murder. Costley told the landlady he was there to pick up Julia's things. Costley took some of Julia's personal items, but not all. When the landlady tried to hand Costley a nightdress, he told her to leave it, that Julia wouldn't need it anymore.

Costley went to the railroad depot to present the claim checks for Julia's trunks. He put the black valise he had used on the night of the murder into one of the trunks, marked with claim check No. 2549, wrote his name on the outside, and then took both trunks by train to New York. Costley later shipped the trunk tagged No. 2549 back to Boston. The other trunk was never found. Costley kept the claim check but never intended to retrieve the trunk until he knew it was safe to do so. He hid the claim check in Hanover along with the pistol he had used to kill Julia. The claim check and pistol were found during the murder investigation and were turned over to police. The chief constable took the claim check to the train station and retrieved the trunk with Costley's name written on it. Inside the trunk the constable found the black valise and a pocket handkerchief bearing the initials J.H.C. The valise was later found to contain bloodstains which Dr. Wood suggested during the trial were consistent with the characteristics of human blood.

Costley felt confident he had pulled off the "perfect crime." That was until constables came to the Howard House on May 25, asking questions about Julia Hawkes. Even before they got there, the investigators believed they had sufficient evidence to arrest Costley for Julia's murder, and as the investigation continued in preparation for trial, the evidence continued to mount. Costley was doomed.

He made two fatal errors. First, he failed to weigh down the lower part of Julia's body when he threw her into the Monatiquot River, leading to her discovery. Second, he unknowingly left one of Julia's Newport tie shoes in the buggy he had rented. The shoe verified Julia's presence in the buggy on the night of the murder.

Attorney General Train skillfully summed up the facts of the case during his closing arguments when he told the jury that Costley's motive "…was to get rid of Julia Hawkes to gratify lust, or love of property, or jealousy." Train believed Costley had spent considerable time planning Hawkes's murder and had been caught in a series of lies while trying to mask his intentions.

It is likely that the prosecution discounted Costley's later assertion that another person had been responsible for the murder and scoffed at his contention that he would not talk about the murder for fear that he would implicate others. Undoubtedly, there was never a hint of skepticism in their minds that Costley had been the lone killer in the Julia Hawkes affair. The evidence against him had been overwhelming and irrefutable. In this case, justice had been served.

Costley's conviction could never have been obtained without the skill and determination of the state constable force. Chief Boynton's men persisted in beating the bushes with good old-fashioned legwork until they found every possible witness and piece of physical evidence to tie Costley to the murder. The case was strictly circumstantial, because no one had actually witnessed Julia Hawkes's murder. But the testimonies and evidence presented during the trial were compelling and left the jury, all men "tried and true," to quickly decide, beyond a reasonable doubt, that James Henry Costley was guilty.

A Soap Box

Other sins only speak; murder shrieks out.
John Webster – The Duchess of Malfi, act 4,
sc.2.

Principal Characters

Victim:
Soo Hoo Yee Yoke, alias Quong Sing (about 1856-1904)

Accused:
Cyrus Lawrence Ryan (1883-1962)

Judges:
William Burnham Stevens (1843-1931), associate justice, superior court
A Stoneham, Massachusetts, native, Stevens graduated from Dartmouth College in 1865, studied law at Harvard, and was admitted to the Suffolk County bar in 1867. He was district attorney for the Northern District from 1880-1890 and was appointed to the superior court in 1898.

John Henry Hardy (1847-1917), associate justice, superior court
Hardy was born in Hollis, New Hampshire, and was a Civil War veteran. He graduated from Dartmouth College in 1870, studied law at Harvard, and passed the Suffolk bar in 1872. He was appointed associate justice of the Boston Municipal Court in 1885 and associate justice of the superior court in 1896.

Jury:
Andrew Gale (1850-1939), building mover, Brockton
Otis Barden (1849-1934), barber, Middleborough
Ezra Bumpus (1852-1930), farmer, Wareham
John Ferguson (1853-1935), undertaker, Scituate
George Gardner (1856-1907), farmer, Hingham
Calvin Hall (1841-1929), peddler, Brockton
Samuel Hammond (1857-1909), farmer, Mattapoisett
George Leavitt (1850-1921), shoemaker, Whitman
Henry LeLacheur (1845-1920), real estate dealer, West Bridgewater
Austin Pratt (1835-1919), shoemaker, Bridgewater
James Roberts (1848-1924), janitor, Middleborough
Francis Sheldon (1839-1921), milk dealer, Rockland
Bradford Wilder (1849-1933), unemployed, Hingham

131

Prosecution:
Asa Palmer French (1860-1935)
 French was born in Braintree, Massachusetts, graduated from Yale University and Boston University Law School, and was admitted to the Norfolk County bar in 1885. He was elected as district attorney for the Southeastern District in 1901. Before his election as a prosecutor, French was a defense advocate in two highly publicized capital cases.

 Thomas Bram, first mate on the bark *Herbert Fuller*, was charged with the July 1896 triple ax murders of the ship's captain, Charles Nash, his wife, Laura Nash, and the second mate, August Blomberg, while at sea. The U. S. Circuit Court in Boston appointed French to represent Bram. A jury found the defendant guilty, and he was sentenced to death. French appealed Bram's conviction on a technicality to the U.S. Supreme Court. The court overturned the conviction and ordered a new trial. Bram was again found guilty, but he was sentenced to life in prison.

 Ellen Seery was murdered on July 2, 1899, in Dedham. Her two sons, John and Joseph Seery, were indicted for her murder and stood trial in Dedham Superior Court beginning December 11, 1899. French and Benjamin Greenhood defended Joseph Seery. Joseph and his brother were acquitted after a ten-day trial.

Defense:
Frederick M. Bixby (1863-1909)
 Bixby graduated from Boston University Law School and was admitted to the Massachusetts bar in 1884. He was assistant district attorney for the Southeastern District in 1889, and he was appointed special justice of the Brockton Police Court a year later.

 Bixby also maintained a private practice and was a seasoned defender. He was junior counsel in the 1895 trial of Arthur Albee for the murder of Brockton barber Collins Leaman. A Plymouth County jury found Albee not guilty after a four-day trial.

 Bixby defended infamous nurse Jane Toppan in Barnstable Superior Court in 1902. Toppan was found not guilty by reason of insanity in the deaths of three people she had poisoned with morphine. Toppan later admitted to killing thirty-one people in the same manner.
John Callanan (1876-?)

Callanan was born in South Abington, Massachusetts (now Whitman). He graduated from Holy Cross College in Worcester, Massachusetts, in 1898, and received his law degree from Boston University in 1901. He had little experience in capital cases.

Medical Examiner:
Henry Watson Dudley (1831-1906), Plymouth County medical examiner
    Dudley graduated from Harvard Medical School in March 1864 and set up a practice in Abington, Massachusetts, where he remained for the rest of his life. Massachusetts Governor George Robinson appointed Dudley medical examiner for the Second Plymouth District in 1890.

Investigators:
William Henry Proctor (1861-1924), captain, Massachusetts District Police
    Proctor was born in Swampscott, a coastal town on the North Shore of Massachusetts. Known as "Harry" by family and friends, he had spent many of his formative years on the water with his father, a fisherman.
    Proctor joined the state force in 1888 and was soon promoted to detective. He was placed in charge of the state police vessel *Ocean Gem* several years later and then took charge of the new *Lexington* in 1898. Members of the force informally addressed him as captain, although he would not officially hold that rank until a year after the Ryan case, when he received his commission from Governor William Douglas. He was the first man to hold the rank of captain in the history of the state police.
    Proctor was on general assignment during the winter months, and he enforced the state's fishing and gaming laws and patrolled the state's coastal waters aboard the *Lexington* in the summer. During the previous three years, Proctor had played an important role in the investigation of five murders in the state before the Hanover murder.
Alfred Baylies Hodges (1840-1918), constable, Massachusetts District Police
    Born in Norton, Massachusetts, Hodges was a Civil War veteran and a lieutenant colonel in the 1st Massachusetts Infantry. He was wounded in his forehead during the battle and siege of Port Hudson, Louisiana,

in 1863. He was appointed to the district police in 1896 and assigned to Bristol County. Hodges was assistant city marshal and city marshal in Taunton prior to joining the force. Hodges solved the Joseph McMahon murder in Taunton in 1899, the Tillinghast Kirby murder in New Bedford in 1903, and assisted in the investigation of the 1900 murder of May L. Fosburgh in Pittsfield.

~~~

Hanover Four Corners, ca. 1900

Hanover's Four Corners had thrived during the quarter century following the murder of Julia Hawkes. By 1900, the little village was bustling with the commerce of hotels, dry goods and provisions stores, carriage makers, blacksmiths and wheelwrights, barbers and clockmakers, carpenters and shoemakers. Physicians and surgeons practiced in the village, among them Drs. William Grovestein, Clarence Howes, and Andrew MacMillan. William Curtis's drugstore provided for the area residents' medicinal requirements as well as bicycles for their transportation and recreational needs. Nearly all the houses in the neighborhood were heated with coal or woodstoves. John Loring, a plumber, sold stoves and ranges in his shop, as did Henry Magoun. M. E. Flavell and Company, "The Corner Store," specialized in dry and fancy goods as well as Allen's Kushion Komfort shoes for ladies.

The Hanover Branch Railroad, opened for service in 1868, was sold to the Old Colony Railroad in 1887, consolidated with the New Haven system in 1893, and merged with the New York, New Haven and Hartford Railroad in 1899. Passengers boarded at the Hanover depot and traveled to North Abington where they connected to trains bound for Boston, Plymouth, and beyond. Ten trains operated every day from 6:00 a.m. until 6:00 p.m.

~

135

Hanover Branch Railroad depot

Electricity had reached the village and was being used in most homes and businesses. The Southern Massachusetts Telephone and Telegraph Company installed telephone service at the Corners in 1903, using the railroad's telegraph poles for its wires. Joseph Tripp, owner of the Howard House, operated the telephone switchboard in his hotel. In 1900, Alonzo Josselyn converted a boarding house for Hanover Academy students opposite the Howard House into a hotel he named the Hotel Josselyn and competed with Tripp for guests.

Churches and schools completed the community's social fabric. Clergy conducted services at the Second Congregational Church on Oakland Avenue and at Saint Andrew's Episcopal Church, and teachers broadened the horizons of pupils at the Salmond School. By 1904, Hanover was a community of 2,152 people.

The North River Lodge of the Independent Order of Odd Fellows maintained a hall on Broadway as did the Freemasons at the Phoenix Lodge Masonic Building. The Freemasons occupied the second floor of the building and leased the first floor to retail businesses.

Phoenix Lodge Masonic Building

Quong Sing and his brother, Soo Hoo Yee Sing, opened a hand laundry in the Masonic building in 1902. Emily Freeman of Washington Street in Assinippi provided the only other laundry service in Hanover at the time. The brothers were industrious and quickly built a reputable business. In 1903, Soo Hoo Yee Sing took his share of the profits from the Hanover operation and moved to Beverly, Massachusetts, where he set up his own laundry shop.

Quong Sing's shop was typical of Chinese hand laundries in America during the nineteenth and early twentieth centuries. One out of four Chinese men in the United States were laundrymen by 1900, typically working ten to sixteen hours a day and earning between eight and twenty dollars a week.

Quong Sing lived and worked in his shop that consisted of four small rooms. He cooked and ate his meals in the room where he washed the laundry. He dried the laundry in another room and used the front room for ironing and wrapping finished laundry. He kept a small cot and his

137

personal belongings in a room off the front room.

A partition with a countertop divided the front and back of the shop, and a small gate in the partition allowed entry and exit to both areas. Quong Sing placed his finished laundry, packaged in brown paper, on shelves behind the counter, each package labeled with a ticket in Chinese to identify the customer. He charged ten cents for laundering shirts; two cents for handkerchiefs; and two cents for cuffs and collars, which were detachable dress shirt accessories of the era. He paid rent to William Bates, a Hanover merchant, in "fractional silver," coins worth less than one dollar. He kept a small sum for expenses and sent the remainder of his earnings to his wife in China.

Area residents respected and liked the Chinese man. They Americanized his name and affectionately called him "John." He was meticulous about his work and generous in extending credit to customers. According to the *Rockland Standard*, "Quong Sing was highly spoken of by all who knew him. He was very quiet and inoffensive, minded his business steadily, and never sought a quarrel with anybody. He was of a very good Chinese family and had a wife and four children in China, to whom he had hoped to return as soon as he had earned a competence."

~

The great California Gold Rush began in 1848. Fleeing economic constraints, political and religious persecution, hunger, drought, and disease, the Chinese immigrated to the United States to find their fortunes. As their numbers increased and gold became scarcer, the Chinese and other ethnic newcomers encountered resentment and hostility from native-born competitors who gradually forced them from the mines.

The animosity continued as industrialists, exploiting the Chinese immigrants' willingness to labor for low wages, employed them in the canning, timber, and garment industries and in railroad and canal construction.

Just as they had done when the Irish streamed into the country during the nineteenth century, American citizens perceived the overwhelming influx of Chinese immigrants as a threat to their own job prospects and as a negative influence on economic conditions. Cultural differences also exacerbated social tensions and discrimination. The Chinese man's queue, which prejudiced Americans mockingly called a pigtail, represented the vast differences between them. The Chinese man regarded his queue as a symbol of loyalty to his country and his plan to return home.

Bostonians during the early twentieth century negatively stereotyped the Chinese, mostly due to press accounts that depicted the Chinese as dishonest, crafty, money-grubbing, profoundly ignorant, and naturally violent.

Addressing the concerns of constituents, but risking diplomatic difficulties with China, President Chester A. Arthur signed the Exclusion Act into law on May 6, 1882. Although the law made immigration to the United States difficult, it did not make it impossible. Certain classes of Chinese people, such as merchants, diplomats, and scholars, were exempt from the law. The only way for other Chinese immigrants to enter America legally was to prove they were the sons or daughters of American-born citizens. Upon verification of the legal right to be in this country, each Chinese immigrant was issued a certificate of identification. Immigrants who did not obtain a certificate or failed to produce one upon demand of a public official were subject to immediate deportation.

Chinese immigrants living in America found ways to acquire false documentation to verify their status as American-born citizens. Once their citizenships were officially recognized, they claimed they had sons or daughters in China who wished to immigrate to the United States. The Chinese-American citizens then obtained false documents that proved the relationships between themselves and their "children." The Chinese-American citizens would then sell the "papers" to Chinese citizens seeking to immigrate. Once secured, the immigrants assumed the names that corresponded with the papers, carefully studied the documents of "proof," and prepared for questioning by immigration authorities. After the immigrants had convinced officials of their identity, they were allowed to enter the country.

Those who gained entry into the United States in this manner became known as "paper sons" or "paper daughters." It is likely that Hanover laundryman Quong Sing, whose true name was Soo Hoo Yee Yoke, was a "paper son" who had secured the papers of "Quong Sing" and entered the country under that alias.

Soo Hoo Yee Yoke, alias Quong Sing, immigrated to America sometime after 1882, when immigration laws changed, and before 1902, when his presence in Hanover was first documented. His surname, Soo Hoo, points to the Pearl River Delta region of Guangdong Province in southern China as his place of origin. Like so many of his countrymen, he fled the poverty and strife of his homeland to find peace and prosperity in America. He left his wife and four children behind and hoped to reunite with them someday.

~

Cyrus Lawrence Ryan was born to Michael and Elizabeth (Pierce) Ryan on April 12, 1883, in Charlottetown, Prince Edward Island, the sixth child in a family of nine. Cyrus attended school for six months as a youngster and wouldn't learn to read and write until he was an adult. His father had a low-paying position as a stevedore on the Charlottetown docks and expected his children to work and support the family.

When Cyrus was nine, his father sent him to strip tobacco in the Charlottetown factories of Hickey & Nicholson and T. B. Riley. Due to his small size, Cyrus had to stand on a box to reach a counter on which he manually removed tobacco leaves from individual stalks and rolled them into small bundles for final packing.

Cyrus worked in the tobacco factories until July 1903 when he hired on with the Plant Line Steamship Company as third cook on the *Olivette*, a steamer that transported passengers and freight between Charlottetown and Boston. He resigned three weeks later and disembarked in Boston. Short on cash and in need of clothing, lodging, and train fare, Cyrus borrowed seventeen dollars from the Washington Credit Company and agreed to repay the loan at a rate of one dollar a week plus interest. He bought an overcoat and other assorted clothing and proceeded to the South Station railroad terminal where he boarded a train bound for Hanover and the home of his half-brother, Frederick Pierce, on Water Street. Pierce took Cyrus in and helped him find work at the nearby E. H. Clapp Rubber Company a few weeks after he arrived. Cyrus received $1.50 a day in wages and paid his half-brother $4.25 a week for room and board. Cyrus's intended, seventeen-year-old Katie Murray, arrived from Charlottetown the next month, and Pierce provided her with room and board, charging Cyrus an additional $1.75 a week.

~

Residents enjoyed a respite from the harsh winter of 1904 when temperatures reached fifty degrees on Saturday, January 23. Many took advantage of the bright sunshine, running errands and shopping for necessities before the cold and snow again shut them in. Others took the opportunity to restock liquor supplies and visit the local taverns.

That afternoon, two intoxicated men entered Quong Sing's shop and demanded his money. When Quong refused to give it to them, one of them slapped the ninety-pound laundryman in the face. Quong ran to his bedroom, grabbed a gun from the shelf over his cot, and threatened to shoot them if they didn't leave. Startled, the two would-be robbers ran from the shop and were never seen again.

The *Rockland Standard* took note of Quong Sing's courageous stand in an article published six days later. "Quong Sing is very quiet, minds his own business, and will molest no one if they treat him decently, but he will not take many knocks from an assailant without showing that he is able to defend himself."

~

At about ten o'clock on Wednesday night, January 27, 1904, Mrs. Solomon Russell of Elm Street answered a knock at her house. A man she did not know devastated her with a message he said he had received from Boston that her daughter, Lucy, had been killed in a railroad

141

accident.

Russell, a seventy-five-year-old widow, lived alone. She had no way to contact Lucy and was afraid to travel alone into the city at night. Frantic, she made plans to take the eight-fifteen train to Boston the next morning. Russell departed for the Curtis Crossing station Thursday morning, and Cyrus Ryan joined her as she walked along Elm Street. At the station, Ryan chatted briefly with the stationmaster and left Russell in his care.

When Russell arrived in Boston, she learned that her daughter was alive and well. Confused, shaken, but relieved, she left the city on the 2:43 p.m. train and returned to Hanover. When she reached home, she discovered that someone had broken in and stolen cash, jewelry, and trinkets from her bedroom. She immediately suspected that the man who had visited her the evening before was the man responsible for the burglary. In an odd coincidence, someone had also burglarized the nearby home of Frederick Pierce.

Russell later told newspaper reporters that she was not sure if it was Ryan who had notified her of her daughter's death, but she was certain that he was the man who had walked with her to the station. Police never arrested anyone for the thefts.

~

It was four degrees when Quong Sing got up on the morning of January 28. He slipped a shan ku over his bedclothes, donned his jacket, melon cap, and slippers, wrapped himself in a wool blanket from his bed, and padded across the icy floor to the drying room where he stoked the fire in his stove and prepared for his day.

At about 11:10 a.m., Stanley Baker, a clerk at the nearby Phillips, Bates and Company, entered Quong Sing's shop to drop off some laundry. He interrupted a discussion between the laundryman and Cyrus Ryan, a young man who worked at Clapp's rubber mill down by Luddam's Ford. Baker nodded to Ryan, who stepped aside.

"Good morning, John," said Baker cheerfully, "I have a few items I'll need in the next few days."

While Quong Sing scribbled out a ticket for Baker and engaged him in friendly conversation, Ryan quietly slipped out the door.

At 11:30 a.m., Domingo Perry was cutting a customer's hair at his barbershop in the Howard House hotel on Broadway when Ryan came in for a shave. Ryan then told Perry he had changed his mind about the shave and left a few minutes later.

Ryan went back to Quong Sing's shop. While he was speaking with the laundryman in the front room, he saw William Appleton, a grocery clerk at Little's Market in Pembroke, ride by in his wagon as the 11:45 a.m. Clapp mill whistle blew. Appleton saw Ryan through the shop's front window and waved to him. Ryan waved back.

Ten minutes later, forty-five-year-old butcher William Paxton, owner of Wilkinson and Paxton, a provisions market in the Masonic building that adjoined Quong's laundry shop on the right, left his store with a pail to get some water from Quong Sing because Paxton's water pump had frozen overnight. As he entered, he saw a young man he recognized as Cyrus Ryan standing in the front room. He exchanged pleasantries with Ryan and called out to Quong Sing.

Quong Sing, who was in the back washroom eating a bowl of rice, came to the front room. Paxton asked Quong if he could pump some water. Quong consented, and Paxton filled his pail and returned to his market just before noon. He set the pail on a counter, locked up the market, and went to his nearby home for some lunch.

Henry Snell's barbershop adjoined Quong Sing's shop on the left. Snell and his friend, William Handy, left Snell's shop to get a bite to eat a few minutes before noon and saw Ryan talking with Quong in the front room of the laundry as Quong ironed a shirt.

At about 12:35 p.m., Ryan went to Howland's Livery at Four Corners and spoke with nineteen-year-old hostler Frank Chamberlain.

"I knew Ryan by sight," Chamberlain later stated. "He asked me for a team to go to Rockland. I said the boss would be back in a minute, that I did not want to let him one."

"I'm in kind of a hurry," Ryan replied. He left the stable a few minutes later and walked south along Broadway toward Elm Street and Curtis Crossing. Elm Street residents John Levings, Margaret Barry, Sarah Christy, and Catherine Ridgeway saw Ryan on the road from Four Corners to Curtis Crossing between 12:45 and 1:00 p.m. All said he was walking at a brisk pace.

Chester Hobart, a fifty-four-year-old shoe peddler, drove a cart in Hanover as part of his route. He was having lunch with Lucy Josselyn at her home on Water Street, talking about how some people in Hanover owed him money. He mentioned Cyrus Ryan's name. Ryan was passing the house on foot at that very moment. Hobart left Josselyn and followed Ryan next door to Fred Pierce's house.

Before Ryan went inside, Hobart called to him and asked Ryan for money he owed him. Ryan pulled a roll of bills and change from his pocket and handed Hobart five one-dollar bills and twenty-five cents in coin.

"I would like to pay all of my bills as easy as I can this one," Ryan declared.

Hobart later said that Ryan's hand trembled as he gave him the money. Other than that, he didn't notice anything unusual about Ryan's behavior or appearance but thought it odd that Ryan had the cash readily available. He gave Ryan a receipt, talked for a short time, and returned to his cart.

William Paxton returned to his market at 12:50 p.m. and went across the street to the post office a few minutes later. When he returned to his market, he noticed that the front door to Quong Sing's laundry shop was wide open. He looked inside the shop and saw signs of a struggle. His shouts of "Hello" were met with silence. Sensing that something was wrong, he went to Snell's barbershop and told Snell about the odd circumstances.

"There is certainly something wrong with John," Paxton told Snell, "and I mean to see what it is."

Paxton, Snell, and Alonzo Whiting, a customer in Snell's shop, went to the rear of the building to see if Quong Sing was there. When they couldn't find him, they returned to the front and entered the shop. Quong Sing's belongings were strewn about, and a hot iron was burning a hole in a shirt on Quong's ironing board.

The three men proceeded to the washroom in the back and saw that water from black, cast iron set tubs had spilled across the floor into the drying room. Inside the drying room they saw Quong Sing's still body, his face submerged in a portable tub, with a heavy soap box on his shoulders. The three men were shocked into momentary stillness before regaining their senses.

Paxton and Snell raced to the front door and shouted for help. Paxton went back inside, and Snell ran to Dr. William Grovestein's office on Broadway. Eben Waterman, chairman of the Hanover Board of Selectman, was running errands at Four Corners and saw the commotion at the Masonic building. He found Paxton and Whiting standing over Quong Sing's body in the laundry shop. Waterman saw Quong Sing's face submerged in water to his ears. Waterman helped Paxton remove the soap box, which he estimated to weigh about sixty pounds, from Quong's shoulders, rolled him over on the floor, and attempted to resuscitate him.

Snell returned with Drs. Grovestein and Andrew MacMillan. The two physicians made repeated attempts to revive Quong without success. They abandoned their efforts and pronounced him dead. Both doctors noticed marks on the windpipe and left side of Quong's neck as if the fingers of a hand had grasped it from behind.

Hanover police chief David Stoddard and Special Officer Thomas Tindale came to the laundry shop as did Selectman Edward Bowker. The three men, along with Selectman Waterman, Joseph Tripp, owner of the Howard House at Four Corners, and Benjamin White, a housepainter from Pembroke, searched the shop.

Waterman and Stoddard saw that someone had pried open a trunk inside Quong Sing's bedroom and had strewn its contents around the room. The bed was disturbed, but the intruder had apparently failed to search it thoroughly because Waterman found thirty-seven dollars in silver and bills tucked between the bedding. The men could not locate a revolver they knew Quong Sing owned.

Everyone at the scene quickly concluded that Cyrus Ryan, the last person seen with the laundryman before his death, was likely responsible for Quong's death.

Snell went to the telephone exchange at the Howard House to notify Massachusetts District Police Chief Rufus Wade about the murder and Ryan's possible involvement. Snell described Ryan as being about twenty years old, five feet eight inches tall, one hundred forty pounds, with hazel eyes and brown hair. Snell added that Ryan was wearing a black overcoat and a dark slouch hat when he was last seen. Wade sent a telegraph with Ryan's description to all of the railroad stations between Hanover and Boston.

~

William Bates, forty-three-year-old owner of Phillips, Bates and Company near Four Corners, went to Curtis Crossing to take the 2:15 p.m. train to Boston. Bates hoped to find Quong Sing's relatives in the city and notify them of his death. At the crossing, Bates, aware that police were looking for Ryan, was surprised and alarmed to see him on the platform in the company of two women. Ryan was carrying a small trunk and a satchel. Bates stepped inside the station and learned that Ryan had purchased a ticket for Boston. He asked the stationmaster to telegraph District Police Chief Wade with Ryan's intended destination and estimated time of arrival. As soon as he received the telegraph, Wade alerted Deputy Chief Joseph Shaw and sent Captain William Proctor and Detective Alfred Hodges to South Station.

When the local arrived at Curtis Crossing, Bates boarded with Ryan and his companions. Bates could see that Ryan was uneasy and watched him change his seat on the car four times between Hanover and North Abington.

When they reached North Abington, Bates, Ryan, and the two women disembarked and boarded the Boston-bound train. The conductor, who had obviously received the telegraph alert, knew Bates and asked him if he knew Ryan. Bates said he did and quietly pointed out Ryan as he took his seat on the car. The conductor informed Bates that he had received a telegraph at the depot from state police indicating that they were at Boston's South Station anticipating Ryan's arrival and had requested that someone on the train who knew Ryan point him out to them when Ryan disembarked.

Curtis Crossing Station

When the train arrived at the bustling South Station at 3:16 p.m., Proctor, bald and portly with a bushy moustache, and Hodges, a tall, graying, thin man with a handlebar moustache, were waiting. Bates quickly disembarked and found the two policemen, dressed in calf-length overcoats and derby hats, on the platform. As Ryan stepped down from the train with his two companions, later identified as his fiancée, Catherine (Katie) Murray, and his sister-in-law, Mary Pierce, Bates alerted Proctor, who immediately took Ryan by the collar.

"What...what's the matter?" the startled Ryan stammered.

"Well," said Proctor as he handcuffed Ryan, "I guess I'll take you along and find out who you are."

Ryan's shoulders slumped. Proctor searched Ryan while Hodges held the panic-stricken Murray and Pierce off to one side. Proctor found a revolver loaded with three cartridges and a baggage claim check in Ryan's coat and put both items in his pocket. A small crowd of curious passengers quickly gathered on the platform when they noticed the commotion. Proctor led Ryan to the baggage master's office inside the terminal to forestall any further attention. He searched the small trunk and satchel Ryan was carrying and found a small gold watch in the bottom of the

Captain William Henry "Harry" Proctor

trunk. Proctor turned to a porter standing nearby and handed him Ryan's baggage claim check. A few minutes later the porter returned with another trunk that Ryan identified as his own. Proctor inspected the trunk and found it contained men's and women's clothing. Proctor took possession of both trunks and the satchel and, with Hodges, escorted Ryan, Murray, and Pierce to the state police offices located in the basement of the statehouse on Beacon Hill. Proctor led Ryan into Deputy Chief Shaw's office. Murray and Pierce were detained in Proctor's office under Hodges's watchful eye.

Under questioning by Proctor and Deputy Chief Shaw, Ryan disclosed that he and his fiancée, Katie Murray, had made plans the day before to leave Hanover and stay at his sister's house in Brookline for several days. Ryan said he had taken a trunk that Murray had packed the night before to the stationmaster at Curtis Crossing station that morning. He then walked to Four Corners to pick up a shirt he had left to be laundered at Quong Sing's shop.

At the shop, however, he realized he had lost the ticket for the shirt. He said he tried to explain his predicament to the shop owner, Quong Sing, but the laundryman refused to accommodate him. He admitted he had heard of the man's death before leaving Hanover, but he adamantly denied that his disagreement with Quong had become violent.

Shaw and Proctor observed that Ryan's clothing was torn and that he had scratches on the left side of his face. When Proctor asked about them, Ryan said he had a good-natured scuffle with a coworker before he left Hanover.

"Where did you get the gun and the gold watch?" asked Proctor.

"I bought the revolver from a man in Rockland for a dollar," Ryan claimed.

"Who was this man?"

"I don't know."

"And the watch?" Proctor prompted.

"It was a gift from my sister," insisted Ryan.

When the interrogation ended, Proctor led Ryan to a damp subbasement, locked him in a cell, and returned to his office to interview Katie Murray. Murray confirmed she had made plans with Cyrus to leave Hanover. She had packed their clothing in a trunk the night before, and Cyrus had taken it to the stationmaster at the Curtis Crossing depot at Elm and Water Streets that morning. She told Proctor that she and Cyrus lived with Cyrus's brother, Fred Pierce, on Elm Street. She and Ryan left Fred Pierce's house in the afternoon with Fred's wife, Mary, to take the 2:15 p.m. train from Curtis Crossing to Boston. When Proctor asked where she was going with Ryan, Murray said they had planned to stay with her sister-in-law in Cambridge. Murray said she knew nothing of Cyrus's visits to the laundry shop in Four Corners and had detected nothing unusual about his behavior when he returned from the Curtis Crossing depot.

Murray asked Proctor if she could have a word with Cyrus. Proctor consented and led her down to the subbasement. Proctor thought he saw Ryan pass something to Murray as the couple conversed. When Proctor and Murray returned to his office, the policeman ordered her to surrender what Ryan had slipped to her. Murray retrieved eleven dollars and a cheap, silver Ingersoll watch from the bosom of her dress and handed the items to Proctor.

Proctor returned to Ryan's cell and asked him about the money and watch. Ryan said he had saved the money from his earnings and that he had bought the silver watch from a crewmember on the *Olivette* during his trip to Boston the year before.

Police never charged Murray with complicity in the deception. Proctor later learned that Quong Sing had purchased the watch at William Curtis's drugstore in Four Corners six months earlier.

Proctor briefly interviewed Mary Pierce and was satisfied that she knew nothing about the Hanover murder. Before he released them, Proctor told both women that the district attorney would likely require their testimony at Cyrus's trial.

In Hanover, Stanley Baker, William Paxton, William Handy, and Henry Snell boarded a train for Boston after district police called and asked them to identify Ryan. The four men met William Bates at South Station and went to the statehouse where they all identified Ryan as the man they had seen in the laundry shop earlier in the day. Paxton also identified the revolver seized from Ryan as the one owned by Quong Sing. Proctor showed the four men the gold watch he had found in Ryan's trunk and the Ingersoll watch he had seized from Murray, but none of the men could identify them.

The Plymouth County medical examiner, Dr. Henry Watson Dudley, arrived at the laundry shop at 3:30 p.m. and spoke with Eben Waterman and others. After inspecting Quong Sing's body, Dudley scheduled an autopsy for the next day.

~

On Friday morning, January 29, Proctor and Hodges escorted Ryan from the statehouse to South Station to travel to the Plymouth County Second District Court in Hingham for Ryan's arraignment. By sheer coincidence, Quong Sing's brother, Soo Hoo Yee Sing, and two companions were on the same train, headed for Hanover to claim Quong Sing's body and property.

Detective Alfred Baylies Hodges

At Hingham, Proctor and Hodges placed Ryan

in a holding cell and went to the court clerk's office to file a murder complaint against the prisoner. Court officers brought Ryan before Judge George Kelley an hour later. After Ryan entered a plea of not guilty, Kelley scheduled a February 6 hearing at the Plymouth County Second District Court in Abington and ordered Ryan held without bail. Sheriff's deputies took Ryan to Plymouth Jail. Captain Proctor and Detective Hodges left the courthouse and proceeded to Abington for Quong Sing's autopsy.

Two of Ryan's sisters, notified about his arrest the day before, mistakenly went to the Abington courthouse where a court officer informed them that Judge Kelley had already arraigned Cyrus in Hingham and sent him to Plymouth Jail. The two women went to Fred Pierce's house in Hanover. They left for Boston with Fred and Mary Pierce at one o'clock to retain a lawyer for Cyrus.

A *Boston Post* reporter went to the Pierce house after Cyrus's family had left and found Katie Murray there. Murray agreed to an interview and dramatically came to her fiancé's defense.

"Poor Cyrus is accused unfairly," she said. "I know that some great mistake has been committed and before the matter is settled, justice will be gained. My Cyrus is a good, upright man and I will stand by him to the last."

Murray told the *Post* correspondent that she was looking for work in Boston to help Cyrus pay his legal fees and had every intention of marrying him after his acquittal.

~

By the time Judge Kelley had arraigned Ryan at the Hingham court, Soo Hoo Yee Sing and his two companions had arrived in Hanover. William Bates and Eben Waterman met the three men as they alighted from the train and accompanied them to the Howard House in Four Corners to await the medical examiner and the district police.

Norwell undertaker Ernest Sparrell and his assistant removed Quong Sing's body from the laundry shop the same morning and delivered it to the medical examiner's office in Abington. Dr. Curtis, assisted by Dr.

Lewis Wheatley and his nephew, Dr. Frank Wheatley of North Abington, began the autopsy after Proctor and Hodges arrived from Hingham. Hanover Drs. Grovestein and MacMillan were also present.

An inspection of the body revealed slight wounds on the side of the head, neck, and chin, perhaps caused by fingernails. Scrutiny of the chest cavity showed a rupture of the right auricle of the heart, the wall of the organ being as thin as paper. The soap box placed on the body, the attempts at resuscitation, or attempts to breathe while asphyxiating might have caused the rupture. Dr. Dudley certified the cause of death as drowning and released the body to Sparrell and his assistant. Quong Sing was forty-eight when he died. Sparrell later delivered Quong's body to Lewis Jones & Sons, undertakers at 50 Lagrange Street, Boston, for final disposition.

Medical Examiner
Henry Watson
Dudley

Dudley returned to Hanover with Proctor and Hodges. The three men went to the Howard House where they met Quong Sing's brother, Yee Sing, and his two companions. Yee Sing spoke some English, but one of the companions was fluent and acted as Yee Sing's interpreter. Yee Sing had many questions about his brother's death and the disposition of his body and property. Dudley addressed Yee Sing's concerns and explained that authorities would turn over Quong Sing's property after the trial and after his estate had been settled in probate court.

Dudley authorized the return of the laundry in Quong Sing's shop to the proper owners. Selectman Waterman issued a notice asking patrons to contact him to claim finished and unfinished laundry.

Proctor, Hodges, and Waterman accompanied Yee Sing and his companions to the laundry. Yee Sing accounted for all of the laundry at the shop and deciphered the names attached to the laundry parcels that were ready for delivery.

Proctor found a shirt corresponding in size, fourteen and a half, to the one that Ryan had claimed was his. Yee Sing traced the shirt in an account book kept by his brother. The book revealed that Ryan had left the shirt for laundering months before.

Proctor and Hodges continued their investigation inside the shop. The officers found a box for a revolver in the bedroom trunk and one cartridge in the box. They also uncovered a roll of five-cent pieces in the trunk. They came across another box in the lower part of the trunk. The box, designed to store fifty .44-caliber cartridges, contained only forty-seven. The cartridges were stamped with the Union Metallic Cartridge Company (U.M.C.) brand name. The company manufactured small arms ammunition in Bridgeport, Connecticut.

The officers found a third box on the bed that contained a watch chain and $21.39 in cash. A dollar was found in Quong Sing's clothing, and nine more dollars were recovered from a locked cash drawer in the front room.

~

Newspaper correspondents spent Saturday, January 30, in Hanover interviewing Cyrus Ryan's friends and relatives. His supporters refused to believe that Ryan had committed the crime and told reporters they had evidence to prove his innocence. Ryan's family secured the services of Judge Fred Bixby of Brockton and Attorney John Callanan of Plymouth to defend him.

Ryan's supporters insisted that certain witnesses could provide an alibi for his whereabouts at the time of the murder by testifying about his movements and locations at certain times during the day.

"There is one thing that I wish the papers would correct, and that is the age of my stepbrother," Fred Pierce told a *Globe* reporter. "He will not be twenty-one until next April, and I wish that you would say in the *Globe* that none of his family believes him guilty of this deed, and we are doing everything possible to fix the time that he was seen walking between the Corners and his home here."

Ryan's family alleged that William Appleton had seen Ryan in the laundry with Quong Sing at 12:15 p.m., not 11:45 a.m. as he had claimed.

Mary Pierce maintained that Ryan had been in her house at twelve forty-five. His defenders believed it was not possible for Ryan to commit the murder, ransack the laundry shop, and walk to the Pierce home in a half hour. They reasoned that it would take a man at least twenty minutes to walk either of the only two routes – the main road or the railroad bed – between Four Corners and the Pierce house. Witnesses could confirm seeing Ryan on the road soon after 12:35 p.m. and that there was nothing unusual about his appearance. That left ten minutes unaccounted for.

Reporters asked several medical men if it were possible for someone to kill the victim and ransack his property in such a short time. They were evasive, but one man did state, "A man can do considerable in ten minutes."

Some town residents tried to link the robbery attempt of Quong Sing on January 23 with the murder. But police dismissed this theory and stated that no one fitting the description of the would-be robbers was seen in the vicinity of the laundry shop on the day of Quong Sing's murder.

Family and friends also refuted the claim that the revolver they had found in Ryan's possession belonged to Quong Sing because, they argued, there were thousands of pistols just like it.

As for the watch, Ryan insisted he had bought it from a crewmember on the *Olivette* during his trip to Boston in 1903. His half-brother, Fred Pierce, knew that Ryan owned a silver watch.

Other friends of Ryan's claimed another man committed the murder on January 28 and that Ryan was simply a victim of circumstances. Those friends alleged that this other suspect had been in Quong's laundry shop just before the murder. They said witnesses overheard the man and Quong Sing arguing over laundry the man had left at the shop. The witnesses insisted that the voice they had overheard was not Ryan's. They also claimed the man was considerably taller than Ryan and that he wore a cap and dark clothes.

Ryan's friends also thought that a statement made by Chester Hobart, the salesman who drove a boot and shoe cart in Hanover, clearly showed there was no possible way that Ryan could have been at Mrs. Josselyn's house at 12:40 p.m., where Hobart settled his financial affairs with Ryan, and then have the time to kill Quong Sing.

~

Katie Murray visited her fiancé at Plymouth Jail on January 31. Reporters were waiting for her when she left. She refused to provide details of her conversation with Ryan. She did tell reporters that she and Ryan were not on their way to be married when he was arrested. She also disclosed that the silver watch and revolver seized by the police belonged to Ryan and insisted he was innocent of the charge against him.

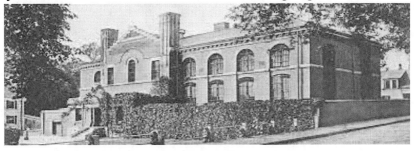

Plymouth County Jail

On that same day, Quong Sing's family buried him at Mount Hope Cemetery, Boston, in a small section reserved for Chinese. Soo Hoo Wing, a cousin of Quong's who owned a restaurant on Harrison Avenue, Boston, was in charge of the funeral and interment. A small cortege that included a hearse and two carriages carrying the deceased, his brother and cousin, and a few friends entered the cemetery at about 3:00 p.m. Mourners burned incense and "spirit money" at the graveside and offered ritual foods of pork, fowl, rice, and wine before the slain laundryman was laid to rest.

Eight years later, on September 21, 1912, Lewis Jones & Sons, at the request of the family and in accordance with Chinese custom, exhumed Quong Sing's body and shipped it to China for reburial.

~

A Plymouth County grand jury indicted Ryan for murder on

Thursday, February 4. Ryan was brought before Judge John Hardy at Plymouth Superior Court for arraignment. After accepting Ryan's not-guilty plea, Hardy scheduled Ryan's trial for June 6 and ordered the accused to continue being held without bail.

Two days later, Plymouth County deputy sheriffs transported Ryan to the Plymouth County Second District Court at Abington for his scheduled appearance before Judge Kelley. The state prosecutor informed Kelley that Ryan had been indicted for murder and had been arraigned in Plymouth Superior Court. Kelley dismissed the murder complaint in the Second District Court and ordered Ryan held in Plymouth Jail under the same conditions of bail pending his trial in Plymouth Superior Court.

~

Deputy sheriffs conveyed Ryan in the rain to Plymouth Superior Court on June 6 for the opening day of his trial. Dressed in a black suit and tie, Ryan showed little emotion as he was led to the front of the packed courtroom and placed in the open-topped iron enclosure that served as the prisoners dock. Attorneys Bixby and Callanan conversed

Plymouth County Courthouse

quietly with their client after the deputies removed his shackles.

Everyone in the courtroom rose as Associate Justices William Burnham Stevens and John Henry Hardy emerged from the judges' lobby, settled behind the bench, and called for the jury.

The judges were no strangers to capital cases. They had presided over Demetrio Bagni's 1902 trial. The same year, Stevens sat on the sensational Blondin murder trial, and Hardy presided at the trial of Michael Kilroy, who was charged with murdering his wife in East Boston. Kilroy was found guilty and sentenced to life in prison. Blondin murdered his wife, dismembered her body, and stuffed it in a trunk. Blondin received a life sentence. Stevens also presided at the 1901 murder trial of Robert Fosburgh, accused in the shooting death of his sister, May, in Pittsfield. Stevens ordered a directed verdict of not guilty.

~

The court crier, Deputy Sheriff George Wheeler, opened court by reading the declaration and proclaiming, "God save the commonwealth of Massachusetts." Rev. John Cuckson, pastor of the First Church at Town Square, Plymouth, offered a prayer, and trial proceedings began at 10:40 a.m.

District Attorney Asa Palmer French, whose father, the late Asa French, had prosecuted James Costley for the murder of Julia Hawkes in 1874, related to Justices Stevens and Hardy the steps leading up to Ryan's arrest and appearance before the court. He then moved for trial, and the court proceeded with selecting a jury.

The jury pool for the Ryan trial consisted of ninety people. The court drew sixty-nine names, and the attorneys for both sides examined those individuals. The

Asa Palmer French, Asa French, and Jonathan W. French (child), ca. 1892

commonwealth challenged twenty-four and the defense twelve. The court excused others because of prejudicial opinions, age, or infirmities.

The prosecution and defense selected the following twelve jurors and one alternate: Andrew Gale, Otis Barden, Ezra Bumpus, John Ferguson, George Gardner, Calvin Hall, Samuel Hammond, George Leavitt, Henry LeLacheur, Austin Pratt, James Roberts, Francis Sheldon, and Bradford Wilder. The median age was fifty-seven years; the eldest juror, sixty-eight, and the youngest, forty-six.

The court recessed after the jury was empaneled and reconvened at about 1:00 p.m. Judge Stevens, described as "nervous, quick, hustling, and bespectacled," ordered the sequestration of all witnesses. He consented, however, to exempt certain witnesses if counsel could show cause. The court also granted DA French's request to have jurors transported to the crime scene in Hanover.

Stevens detailed four deputy sheriffs to convey the jurors to Quong

Sing's laundry shop at Four Corners. Skies had cleared and the temperature was hovering around sixty degrees when the deputies assembled the jurors in front of the courthouse and escorted them to a special trolley that conveyed them the twenty miles to Hanover.

Jurors were met at the Masonic building by French, defense counsel, and Ryan, who was under guard. The DA summarized the

Judge William Burnham Stevens

events of the tragedy and led jurors through the various rooms in Quong Sing's shop. The assemblage departed after French's presentation and arrived back at the courthouse at 6:15 p.m. Judge Stevens polled the jury when court reconvened and then adjourned until the following morning.

~

The second day of the proceedings began at 9:00 a.m. on Tuesday, June 7. Light streamed in through the thirteen tall, arched windows on three sides of the courtroom. Deputy Wheeler opened several windows enough to allow the cool, ocean breeze off Plymouth Bay to flow into the room. Ryan, dressed in his black suit and tie, again smiled and appeared confident as deputies placed him inside the dock. "All rise," barked Deputy Sheriff Wheeler as the judges entered the room and took their places on the bench.

The district attorney solemnly approached the jury box and presented his opening remarks after court was called to order. French outlined what the commonwealth intended to prove, defined the degrees of murder, and gave the prosecution's version of Ryan's movements on the day of the murder.

The prosecutor didn't waste any time asserting the government's theory of Ryan's motive. The defendant, French said, earned a weekly wage of nine dollars at the rubber mill. He paid $4.25 a week to his half-brother, Frederick Pierce, for room and board, and an additional $1.75 per week for his fiancée, Katie Murray, who also boarded at Pierce's home. The rubber mill docked a portion of Ryan's weekly pay to repay the Washington Credit Company for the money he had borrowed to buy clothing when he first arrived in Boston ten months before. This, French told the jury, left very little money for Ryan's everyday expenses and savings. He also pointed out that Ryan settled a number of debts with creditors shortly before he left Hanover on the day of the murder.

French went on. He told the jury about the watch and the revolver that were missing from Quong Sing's shop and how investigators had found a box of ammunition there with three rounds missing. A revolver seized from Ryan upon his arrest was loaded with three new .44-caliber cartridges, similar to the ammunition missing from the box in Quong's shop.

French called John Sturtevant, a photographer, as his first witness. Sturtevant identified pictures he had taken of the Masonic building where Quong Sing's laundry shop was located. Harrison House, a thirty-seven-year-old civil engineer, described the Four Corners area and identified floor plans of the Masonic building. The court admitted the photographs and drawings as evidence.

The medical examiner, Dr. Henry Dudley, described what he saw when he arrived at the crime scene and provided the court with the details of Quong Sing's autopsy. Dudley stated that the air passages of the lungs were inflamed. The lungs were swollen and filled with soapy water. The tissue surrounding the heart was extremely thin, and the right auricle of the heart had ruptured. Dudley believed that the soap box placed on the body, the attempts at resuscitation, or Quong Sing's efforts to breathe while asphyxiating might have caused the rupture. In his medical opinion, Dudley said, the cause of death was drowning.

Dr. William Grovestein of Four Corners also testified about his observations in the laundry on the day in question and described his attempts to revive Quong Sing. He stated that he was present during Quong Sing's autopsy and concurred with Dudley's assessment that drowning was the cause of death.

Doctors Andrew MacMillan and Frank Wheatley added testimony consistent with the details provided by Dudley and Grovestein. MacMillan also said he had seen Quong Sing alive at 10:00 a.m. on January 28.

Defense attorneys had no questions for the medical witnesses. Fred Bixby did, however, state that the defense would present its own medical experts later in the trial.

The district attorney called Frederick Pierce who provided some background information about his half-brother's arrival in Hanover and his situation as a boarder in his home. Pierce testified that when Ryan appeared at his door in July 1903, it was the first time he had seen the defendant in fourteen years. Pierce told the court that Ryan had obtained work at the E. H. Clapp Rubber Company three weeks after he arrived.

Cyrus Lawrence
Ryan, 1912

Pierce said Ryan left his house in October to board with a cousin, Richard Smith, and that Ryan had returned in December. Katie Murray, Ryan's fiancée, arrived from Prince Edward Island the same month and, at Cyrus's request, Pierce allowed Murray to board at his home. Murray found work at R. C. Waterman's tack factory in Hanover soon after she arrived, Pierce added.

Pierce also testified that he never knew that Ryan owned a pistol. Ryan had a watch, the witness added, but Pierce said he had never looked at it closely. The prosecutor showed Pierce a gold watch, and Pierce said it had once been owned by his half-sister, Annie Ryan.

French next called Pierce's wife, Mary, who corroborated her husband's testimony. She testified she had heard about the murder about a half hour before she boarded a 2:15 p.m. train to Boston with Ryan and Katie Murray at Curtis Crossing. She said Ryan bought the train tickets for the three of them.

The prosecution's next witness, Henry Snell, recounted his role in the events of January 28.

"How well did you know Quong Sing?" French asked.

"I knew him. I saw him every day and often went into his laundry."

"Did you see him on January 28?"

"I did. I went to the laundry in the middle of the forenoon to get a pail of water."

"Was anyone in the shop at the time?"

"Yes. Ryan was in the front room near the ironing table."

"Did you see Ryan again?"

"I left my shop for dinner (lunch) and saw him in the laundry again. When I got back at five minutes of one, I didn't look in the laundry."

"What happened next?" French prompted.

"William Paxton came to my shop and said something to me, and I went with him to the laundry," Snell said. "The outer door was open. I didn't see anyone in the front shop, but there was an iron on a shirt half ironed. The bedroom door was open, and I saw a trunk there."

"What did you do next?" French asked.

"I went into the drying room and saw the Chinaman with his head in a tub of water and a box of soap on his shoulders. The tub was filled within two inches of the top, and the Chinaman's face was under water. Paxton and I went out and shouted."

Snell testified he had never seen Ryan in the laundry shop before, never knew Quong had owned a pistol, and did not know where the laundryman kept his money. He did acknowledge that Quong had owned an open-face watch.

On cross-examination, Defense Attorney Callanan tried to draw suspicion away from Ryan by asking Snell about another suspect seen near the laundry shop on the day of the murder. Snell repeated that he had never seen Ryan in the laundry shop before that day. He said he could easily see inside Quong's shop because the curtains were always up. He denied telling Joseph Tripp that he had seen a man with a cap outside the shop, but he admitted that he looked for a man fitting that description at Tripp's suggestion. He said he and Tripp had tried to find the man along the road to Rockland, but they never did.

Witnesses William Handy and William Paxton corroborated Snell's account of the events just before and after the murder. Paxton knew Quong owned a revolver and described it as a .44-caliber, five-shot

A Bull Dog revolver

American Bull Dog with a black handle. French showed him a revolver, and Paxton recognized it as similar to the one owned by Quong Sing. On cross-examination, Paxton stated he believed all .44-caliber revolvers to be the same. He also admitted he had not seen Quong's revolver in a box.

Snell, Handy, and Paxton all testified they had identified Ryan at the statehouse on the afternoon of his arrest. The court adjourned for the day following Paxton's testimony.

~

It was raining when French opened the trial's third day with witnesses who confirmed Ryan's movements during the day of the murder. Spectators gathered outside the courthouse with umbrellas, anxiously awaiting access. He called his first witness of the day, Stanley Baker, a clerk at Phillips, Bates and Company, who testified he had seen Ryan with Quong when he took his laundry to the shop at 11:10 a.m.

Domingo Perry recalled that Ryan had come to his barbershop for a shave that morning, but Ryan had changed his mind soon afterwards and left for Four Corners.

John Levings, Sarah Christy, Margaret Barry, and Catherine Ridgeway all testified they had seen Ryan hurrying along the road between Four Corners and Curtis Crossing. William Appleton testified he saw Ryan in the laundry shop at 11:45 a.m., not 12:15 p.m. as asserted by Ryan's family and friends.

Frank Chamberlain and David Tower, both employees at Howland's Livery, said Ryan had come to the stable to rent a team at about 12:35 p.m.

"Did you know Ryan before he came to the stable?" DA French asked Chamberlain.

"I knew him by sight."

"What happened when Ryan came into the stable on the day of the murder?"

"I was pitching off hay. He asked for a team to go to Rockland. I said the boss would be back in a minute; that I did not want to let him one. He said he wanted to go to Rockland in a hurry, so [he] left."

"When did you hear of the Chinaman's death?"

"I heard of it at 2:15 that afternoon."

"Did Ryan tell you his reason for going to Rockland?" Attorney Cheney asked after French concluded his direct examination.

"No, he did not."

"Did he say anything about his trunk?"

"No, he didn't mention his trunk."

David Tower next took the stand, and the district attorney asked him to tell the court what he had seen and heard when Ryan came to the stable.

"I was in Hanover with a load of hay for Mr. Howland," Tower recalled. "I got there about noon. I was in the haymow when I heard someone ask for a team to go to Rockland."

"What time was this?"

"It was between 12:45 and 1:00 p.m."

"How do you know that?"

"I fixed the time by the 12:45 whistle at the rubber works."

Cheney cross-examined Tower and asked if he had heard anyone say "I am in a hurry."

"No, I did not."

Charles Hunt testified he had seen Ryan at Pierce's home and had helped Ryan carry his trunk from the house to the Curtis Crossing station.

"On the day Quong Sing was killed I was taking Mr. Pierce's place at the crossing as flagman," Hunt said. "I saw Ryan coming from Curtis Street to [the] Water Street crossing along the railroad track. He went to the house where he lived."

"What time was this?" the district attorney asked.

"It was at 12:55 p.m."

"Did you see Ryan again?"

"Yes, I saw him about fifteen minutes later. He asked me to carry his trunk to the crossing, and I did so. A little later he went to the rubber mill yard and back to the house. I saw him leave the house with his sister-in-law and a young lady."

There was no cross-examination by the defense, and Hunt was excused.

Alonzo Whiting substantiated Paxton's and Snell's testimonies. He also testified he had seen Ryan at the depot on the day of the murder.

William Bates stated he had seen Ryan and two women board the 2:15 p.m. train at Curtis Crossing and that Ryan had appeared to be nervous. He saw Ryan get up and change his seat on the car four times between Hanover and North Abington.

John Smith, an employee at E. H. Clapp's, said he had never known Ryan to own a watch or gun. Herbert Cook, another employee, said he had seen Ryan with a gold watch. The prosecutor handed the witness the gold watch that police had seized from Ryan on the day of his arrest, and Cook identified it as similar to the one he had seen in Ryan's possession. He could not identify the silver watch and stated he had never seen Ryan with a revolver.

Annie Ryan, Cyrus's sister, identified the gold watch as once being hers. Annie stated she had given the watch to Cyrus and that he had it with him when he arrived in Hanover from Canada in 1903. This corroborated the previous testimony of her half-brother, Fred Pierce.

As for the revolver, Tom Sing of Pittsburgh, a nephew of Quong Sing's, identified the box and gun given in evidence as similar to the items he had given to his uncle in 1902. Sing said his uncle kept the gun on a shelf over his bed.

French called Quong Sing's brother, Yee Sing, and asked if he could identify the revolver. Yee confirmed it was the same one he had seen in his brother's shop.

Hanover selectman Eben Waterman testified about his observations of the laundry shop when the body was found.

"Did you know the defendant, Cyrus Ryan?" asked DA French.

"I never saw him before the murder," Waterman answered.

"How did you find out about the murder?"

"At 1:25 p.m. on that day I was going to the Masonic block to see about some fires. I was told of the murder and went directly to the laundry."

"Did you go inside?"

"Yes."

"Please tell the court what you saw."

"In the drying room I saw a soap box on Quong Sing's shoulders and his face, as far back as the ears, submerged in a tub containing about six and one half inches of water. His hands were also in the tub and were resting on the bottom. I removed the box of soap and tried to revive the man. The body was warm when I first took hold of it. He was placed on a boiler and rolled.

"I went into the washroom and saw a pair of slippers on the floor. The floor of the room seemed to be wet. There were two barrels of clear water in the washroom. I then went into the bedroom and saw a trunk partially open and the tray had been lifted up. The contents of the tray had been stirred up, but the other part had not been disturbed."

Waterman identified the revolver box and cartridges in evidence that he, Detective Hodges, and Captain Proctor had found in the bedroom. He also identified a cigar box containing cash that he had found under a pillow in the bedroom and said more money was discovered in Quong's clothing and in his cash drawer in the front room.

"Did you ever see a watch in the laundry?" Attorney Cheney asked on cross-examination.

"No."

"Did you handle the iron in the front room?"

"Yes, I noticed that it was warm, but could be held in one's hand without burning."

"Was there a fire in the backroom?"

"No, there was no fire in that room, and the door outside had been open more or less."

Waterman was excused, and the government called Detective Hodges who testified about his examination of the laundry shop and corroborated Waterman's testimony.

Loring Phillips, superintendent of the Clapp Rubber Company, testified that Ryan had quit work in the mill a week before the murder because of difficulty repaying his debt to the Washington Street Credit Company.

"Ryan came to work for me in August and worked until January 23, 1904, at 1:45 p.m.," Phillips said. "He was paid $1.50 a day. The last time he was paid was January 14."

"Please tell the court what happened on January 22," French prompted.

"On January 22 I told Ryan that I could not pay him any more money until I had a release from a credit house in Boston, to which he had assigned his wages."

"How did Ryan respond?"

"He said if that was so he would not work longer, as he had to have money to pay his board."

166

To establish a timeframe, French called Alexander Christy, an employee at Clapp's, who testified he had blown the factory whistle at 11:45 a.m. and again at 12:45 p.m. on January 28.

Chester Hobart testified that Ryan had paid him a debt of $5.25 at about 1:00 p.m. on January 28. Hobart stated Ryan's hand had trembled while handing over the money. Hobart was the final witness for the day.

~

Court reconvened at 9:00 a.m. on June 9, day four of the trial, and the district attorney continued to examine commonwealth witnesses. The first two, Martin Mullen and Daniel Kelley, who both worked at the Clapp Rubber Company, testified that Ryan had repaid money he had owed them on January 28.

Captain Proctor, dressed in a double-breasted frock coat, testified about the events leading up to Ryan's arrest, his capture, and his interrogation at the statehouse.

"I was first notified of the murder by Deputy Chief Shaw at three o'clock on January 28," Proctor began in his deep bass voice. "I then went to South Station and waited for the three-seventeen train. I saw Ryan coming up the platform."

"What happened next?" the district attorney asked.

"I searched him and found a revolver with three cartridges in it. I then took him to the statehouse."

"Did you question him there?"

"Yes, I asked him if he had heard of the murder of the Chinaman. He said 'Yes,' and 'is that what you have got me for?' I informed him that what he said would be used against him and asked him about the revolver."

"What did he say?"

"He said he bought it off a man in Rockland; that there were two cartridges in it. He did not know what caliber it was. He said he never bought any cartridges for it but had a box given him that had a few [cartridges] taken out. He told me he had shot at rats and had used all the cartridges."

167

"What happened after the interrogation?"

"I took Ryan downstairs, where there are two cells. Miss Murray and another young woman came to see him. I let them see him. He asked her (Murray) to get him some tobacco. I stopped Miss Murray as she was going out and took a watch and chain from her, also eleven one-dollar bills."

French showed the witness the watch and chain and the bills, and Proctor identified them.

"Did you speak with Ryan after this?"

"Yes. Ryan said he gave the watch and money to Miss Murray at the cell, that he bought the watch from a man on the steamer *Olivette*. Ryan was given the watch and could not open it. He said he got the watch in July."

"Did you recover Ryan's trunk at South Station?"

"Yes. His trunk was searched, and the other watch that has been offered into evidence was found in the bottom. It is a small gold one. He said he bought it in Halifax [Nova Scotia]."

Proctor identified the gold watch when French presented it to him.

"Did you go to the laundry shop in Hanover later?"

"Yes, I went the next day and searched the laundry. I found a box with forty-seven cartridges in it, the same kind as those in the revolver. I also saw other things that have been testified to."

French showed the witness the box and cartridges, and he verified they were the same he had found. He then showed Proctor the revolver.

"I have examined the revolver and have testified [at other trials] as an expert on firearms. I have the opinion that the revolver in evidence has not been fired over three times."

"Did Ryan ever tell you why he went to the laundry shop on the day of the murder?"

"Ryan said that the reason he had gone to the laundry was to get a shirt. I examined every shirt in the laundry. There was only one shirt of the size fourteen and one-half, the same size Ryan wore. This one looked as if it had been there a long time."

French had Proctor identify the shirt and concluded his direct examination.

Attorney Cheney cross-examined Proctor and asked him if Ryan had appeared apprehensive when he first interrogated him.

"Ryan was not nervous when I talked with him at the statehouse," Proctor said.

"Did Ryan only speak of one occasion in which he visited the laundry shop?"

"Ryan might have said he went to the laundry several times, and the Chinaman could not find his shirt."

Robert Smith of Dorchester and William Rose of Boston provided expert ballistics and firearms testimony about the pistol seized from Ryan. Both witnesses agreed the weapon had never been fired more than once or twice.

William Atkins of Bridgeport, Connecticut, an employee of Union Metallic Cartridge Company and an expert on ammunition, testified about the company's .44-caliber ammunition found in Quong's bedroom and the company's procedure of boxing the ammunition in quantities of fifty.

Harriet Stalling, a stenographer at Massachusetts District Police headquarters, was the prosecution's final witness. She read the notes she had taken when Captain Proctor and Deputy Shaw interrogated Ryan at the statehouse. DA French then rested his case.

~

Junior defense counsel John Callanan rose to make his opening remarks to the jury. Callanan startled everyone in the courtroom when he said his client intended to admit that he had killed Quong Sing – in self-defense. It is not clear when Ryan and his attorneys decided to make that change, but it's likely that Ryan, after hearing overwhelming eyewitness testimony placing him at the scene of the crime, decided he couldn't refute it. His only possible chance for an acquittal was to claim he was defending himself from an attack by Quong Sing.

"We will introduce evidence to show Ryan's good character and life

169

from a child up to the present time," Callahan said. "On the day of January 28, Ryan went into the laundry to get a shirt before he left town. The Chinaman could not find it, however, so Ryan went out. He returned at about noon and again asked for his shirt. The Chinaman looked again and could not find it. He then went out to the back room and immediately came out with a revolver in his hand, which he pointed at Ryan. Ryan grappled with him and both fell to the floor. Ryan took the revolver away and then noticed for the first time the Chinaman was dead. Ryan admits the whole affair, but contends the Chinaman died from heart failure, and that he attacked him in self-defense. We will show that Ryan was justified in what he did, and that he then left the laundry and later took the train for Boston."

Upon completion of Callanan's remarks, the court recessed until 1:00 p.m.

The afternoon session found the courtroom packed with witnesses, spectators, and journalists, all anxiously awaiting the testimony of Cyrus Ryan. Word about Ryan's claim of self-defense had apparently spread quickly.

Callanan called Ryan's fiancée, Katie Murray, to the witness stand. Murray testified that she had been keeping company with Ryan for two years and that they had intended to marry. She said they had made arrangements to leave Hanover on the Sunday (January 24) before the laundryman's death.

"I was to get work in Cambridge and Cyrus in Brookline," Murray explained. "Cyrus was not well, so we decided to postpone the trip until Thursday."

Murray went on to state that she and Cyrus got up early and had breakfast. She said that Cyrus took money from his trunk and left for Four Corners. "He told me to be ready for the 2:15 p.m. train, and we left Hanover at that time."

It seemed that Murray was willing to do or say anything to prevent Ryan's conviction. Her comment to a *Boston Post* reporter the day after Quong Sing's death that, "My Cyrus is a good, upright man and I will stand by him to the last," left little doubt about Murray's devotion and loyalty. She was obviously attempting to show that Ryan had planned to leave Hanover for some time; that he had not departed in haste. She wanted the jury to believe that Ryan had a future with her; that the reason he had money on the day of the death was because he had taken it from his trunk before leaving for Four Corners; and that he had planned in advance to leave on the 2:15 p.m. train. If Ryan had robbery and murder on his mind, wouldn't he have wanted to leave on the next available train?

During cross-examination, Murray testified she had first heard of Quong Sing's death when she was at the statehouse after Ryan's arrest. That's when she learned that Ryan was a suspect, but she did not know if Ryan had been in the laundry when the death occurred. She stated she had never heard that Ryan was "hard up for money."

DA French never challenged Murray's testimony about the plans she and Ryan had made nor about Cyrus's actions on the morning of the death. More than likely, French sensed that the jury saw through her statements and gave little weight to them.

Callanan called several character witnesses from Charlottetown following Murray's testimony. The Reverend J. F. Johnston, Donald Nicholson, Mayor Frederick Kelly, and Charlottetown police chief Charles Cameron, who had been incorrectly identified as Tamerson in the newspapers, testified to Ryan's good moral character. Johnston, a Catholic priest, told the court he knew Ryan well and that he had always been a "straightforward, inoffensive young man." Johnston also said Ryan had belonged to a total abstinence society.

At about 2:55 p.m., the defense called Cyrus Ryan. The defendant was released from the cage, sworn in, and escorted to the witness stand.

Sitting erect and perfectly composed, he answered all of Callanan's questions in a clear voice. He told of his upbringing and his trip to Boston on the steamer *Olivette* in 1903 and how he had gone to the home of his half-brother, Frederick Pierce, in Hanover. He recounted how he had bought some clothes and an overcoat on credit in Boston and had signed an agreement to pay a dollar a week until the balance was paid in full.

Ryan admitted he had been negligent in making regular payments to the credit company and that the firm informed the Clapp Rubber Company about his debt. The defendant said that on Friday, January 22, the Clapp superintendent, Loring Phillips, told Ryan that all of the money he owed the credit company would be deducted from his pay. Ryan told Phillips he couldn't work if he wasn't going to get paid and quit his job.

Ryan stated that he had begun saving money the first week he was in Hanover and had about thirty dollars in denominations of five-, two-, and one-dollar bills on January 28. He kept the money in a trunk in his room at Pierce's house, he said.

Ryan further testified that he had intended to leave Hanover with Katie Murray the following Saturday, January 23, but his sister had arrived that day and had persuaded him to stay a while longer. Ryan said he told his half-brother, Pierce, on Wednesday, January 27, that he would take the 9:15 a.m. train to Boston the next day. (Ryan had claimed immediately after his arrest and during his interrogation at the statehouse that he intended to leave Hanover to marry Katie Murray and move into his sister's house in Brookline.)

The defendant recounted how he went to the Hanover depot to pick up a baggage check for his trunk on Thursday morning, January 28. He was unable to do so and left the station. He went to the post office and then to the laundry to pick up a shirt he had left there ten days earlier. That statement markedly contradicted the previous testimonies by several witnesses that Quong Sing's account book showed an entry for Ryan's shirt months before the laundryman's death. Investigators did not find any other entry for Ryan.

Continuing his testimony, Ryan said Quong Sing asked him for a check for the shirt and Ryan informed the laundryman he had lost it. Ryan said Quong had promised to give Ryan his shirt as soon as he had time to look for it.

Ryan told the court he next went to the barbershop at about 10:00 a.m. but found no one there. He returned to the train station to locate the agent and was told that he could find him at Dr. Baker's dental office. Ryan said he found the agent at that office, and the agent said he could not check his trunk there; that Ryan had to check the trunk at the station.

Ryan stated he went back to the laundry. Quong Sing said he hadn't found time to look for his shirt. Ryan told the court he left the shop and went to the drugstore for his mail; then he went back to the depot to obtain his trunk check. At the depot, the agent told him he had to have the trunk with him in order to check it. Ryan said he then went to Perry's barbershop at about 11:30 a.m. for a shave but couldn't get one.

"At twelve o'clock, I went once more to the laundry," Ryan testified. "Quong Sing was in the back shop. Paxton came in and went into the back room and came out with a pail of water. The Chinaman was stirring something in a pot."

"Where did Paxton go?" Callanan asked.

"Paxton went out and left the door to the shop open," Ryan replied.

"What happened next?"

"The Chinaman came from his back room with his iron in his hand. I said, 'I want my shirt.' He took down a parcel and looked at it and said, 'You have no shirt here; get out.' He stepped into the back room, came out with a revolver, pointed it at me, and said, 'Me shoot you dead.'"

Ryan dramatically described what happened next.

"I jumped at him, and as I did so, he clicked the revolver. I got hold of it and took the Chinaman by the throat. We had a struggle into the back room and there the Chinaman put his arms out and fell back on the floor. His face looked queer, and I found he was dead. I did not know what to do. I pulled a tub of water over to where he lay and threw him into it, then put a box of soap on his shoulders. I put the revolver in my pocket, picked up the watch, and left the laundry. I went home and afterward went to Boston where I was arrested. I know I lied to the Boston police, but I was afraid to tell the truth, as I thought I would be put in jail."

DA French cross-examined Ryan about his movements and the events inside the laundry.

"When did you first take your shirt to Quong Sing's laundry?" French inquired.

"I took the shirt there about January 18 in the evening. I got a check for it and put it in my pocket."

"When did you return for the shirt?"

"I went to the Corners on Saturday and Thursday. On Saturday evening I thought he was going to bed, so I didn't go in."

"What happened on Thursday?"

"I went to Four Corners to get my shirt, check my trunk, and for a haircut and shave. I went to the station first, and to the laundry about nine o'clock. I explained to Sing about the loss of my check, and he remembered me. Sing said I could get the shirt 'bime by.'"

"What happened next?"

"When I went in at noon he opened a parcel on the lower shelf, looked into it, and tied it up. Then he said, 'You have no shirt.' I told him I had, and he told me to go out of the shop. I told him I wouldn't. He spoke loud and rather cross."

"Were you angry?"

"I was calm as I am now."

"How long was this after Paxton had been in the shop?"

"Paxton had been in and been gone about one-quarter of an hour."

"Please continue to tell the court what next happened inside the shop," French urged.

"After I declined to leave, he [Sing] went into the bedroom. When he came out there was a revolver in his right hand."

Judge Hardy interrupted French's cross-examination at this point and called for adjournment. The jury filed out, and after Ryan had a few words with his attorneys, he was handcuffed and taken back to jail.

~

French cross-examined Ryan for another hour and a half after the trial resumed for the fifth day at 9:00 a.m. Friday, June 10.

Ryan denied knowing that Quong Sing kept a trunk containing valuables in the laundry. He also denied knowing that the laundryman was a weak man and was unsure how tightly he had grasped Quong Sing around the throat.

"When I felt the Chinaman loosen his grasp on the revolver I let go of him and he fell back on the floor. I am sure he was dead," Ryan testified. "I put my hand over his heart and he did not breathe."

"What did you do next?" French asked.

"When I found that he was dead, I got excited. I went into the washroom and dragged the tub into the other room. The water splashed over."

"Why did you put Quong Sing in the tub?"

"I don't know why."

Ryan, overwrought by his situation, broke down on the witness stand and wept for several minutes before regaining his composure.

"There was a pail next to the tub when Quong Sing was found. Did you use the pail to put more water in the tub?" French continued.

"I didn't see a pail there and I did not put any water into the tub after the Chinaman was in it," Ryan insisted.

French informed the court that he had no further questions and took his seat. A deputy escorted Ryan back to the dock.

The defense next called several more witnesses on Ryan's behalf. Attorney Callanan recalled Ryan's sister, Annie, to clarify her brother's plans for leaving Hanover. She testified that she left Hanover on January 27 and that Ryan had made plans to leave on January 28 before she departed.

Domingo Perry, Ryan's barber, stated he had seen Ryan with a good-sized roll of bills on several occasions.

Benjamin Franklin White, another defense witness, testified that he was in the laundry on January 28 and helped remove Quong's body from the tub. He said he saw no water coming from the victim's mouth.

Attorneys Callanan and Bixby called four doctors to rebut the cause of death declared by Dr. Dudley. Dr. Henry Borden of Brockton, Dr. Wilfred Brown, Dr. Horace Arnold of Boston, and Dr. Timothy Leary of Boston, assistant professor of pathology at Tufts Medical School,

175

testified that Quong Sing had died from a rupture of the heart and not by drowning. The doctors asserted that when the heart ruptured, fluid, not the water from the washtub, had entered Quong Sing's lungs.

DA French recalled Ryan to the stand and asked him to describe the shirt he had left at Quong Sing's laundry.

"It was a size fourteen and one-half white shirt," Ryan testified.

French went to the evidence table and picked up the shirt introduced during Captain Proctor's testimony.

"Is this your shirt?"

"No, it is not," said Ryan.

French had no other questions and the court adjourned at 4:30 p.m. Justice Stevens announced that proceedings would continue at 9:00 a.m. the next day, June 11, a Saturday.

~

Trial proceedings on the final day began as scheduled. The defense did not call any further witnesses and informed the court it had rested its case. The prosecution and defense presented their closing arguments to the jury.

Judge Fred Bixby, senior counsel for Ryan, approached the jury and began.

"We have shown the character of Ryan from the cradle to the present time, and his character should stand for something. Would a man whose character has been all right suddenly turn a murderer? He saved his money and was seen with a roll before the day of the murder and the only way he spent his money was for his fare to Boston to visit his sister."

Bixby described Quong Sing's threatening demeanor and insisted that Ryan had acted in self-defense when he had clutched the Chinaman by the throat.

"If the Chinaman died in the struggle to get the revolver," Bixby continued, "the court will instruct you that the defendant is not guilty of the deed. Why he put the man in the tub he cannot tell. No one can tell why they do things when under excitement.

"Where is the trunk that the government says Ryan took the money from? Every other thing, the tub, box, and other things have been brought here as evidence. Why did not this defendant take the money in the cigar box, cash drawer, or that in the Chinaman's clothes if the intent was theft?

"Ryan left the laundry excited. When he got home he paid Mr. Hobart and others. He did not act like a murderer. He left on the two-fifteen train as he had arranged to do some time before. People do not kill and rob for the purpose of paying their legal debts."

Judge Fred M. Bixby

Bixby questioned the government's assertion that the shirt found in the laundry belonged to his client and had been left there by him a year before it was found. Why didn't the prosecution present the shirts in the trunk for comparison with the shirt in evidence?

"We asked the government for the shirts which they say were in Ryan's trunk. They have had two days to bring them here, but they are not here. Why have they not brought them if they have them?"

Bixby tried to rationalize his client's untruthfulness at the statehouse.

"When Ryan was questioned by the officers in Boston he lied about it. Others in the same predicament have done the same."

Bixby reviewed the medical testimony and stressed that the opinions of Drs. Borden and Leary refuted Dr. Dudley's claim that Quong's death was caused by drowning. If Quong Sing died as the result of a weakened heart, then his client was not responsible for his demise, said Bixby before taking his seat.

District Attorney French rose from his seat at the prosecution table and opened his argument.

"The question is: 'Did Ryan murder this man?' The men who first found the dead body could think of nothing but murder by drowning and began at once to try to find the person who did the deed.

"Ryan was seen there at twelve o'clock. What was he there for? Why did he wait until everyone in the building had gone home to dinner?

"Someone," French continued, "had been at the trunk at the laundry, looking for something. What was it? Why had Ryan been hanging around the laundry until all had gone from the building? His [Quong's] revolver and watch were gone; find them and you have the man. They were taken from Ryan; what does that mean? Does it not look as though he was a thief and a murderer?

"Where did Ryan get his money? All the facts together go to show he was hard up on the morning of January 28. He was going to Boston on Thursday at nine fifteen. Did he have it in mind to pay his little bills? It is inconsistent with his story. He had plenty of money at one o'clock.

"When he was arrested he had eleven dollars in one-dollar bills. Where a person is suspected of a crime and lies about it, it is strong circumstantial evidence against him.

"There was only one way to get out of the net – that was to lie. The evidence must be weighed, because he is defending himself – perhaps his life. He had to take the stand and tell the story he did."

French returned to his seat.

Judge Stevens turned his attention to Ryan. Ryan, Bixby, and Callanan stood up. "Cyrus L. Ryan, you now have a chance to say a word to the jury," Stevens said.

Ryan looked directly at the jury and in a clear and confident tone said, "Gentlemen, I am innocent not only of murdering him, but of robbing him."

Judge Hardy then charged the jury.

"It is admitted by the defendant that he was present at the death of the Chinaman. Other evidence offered by the commonwealth is also admitted by the defense. You must consider the evidence of the defendant. The mere fact that he was indicted by the grand jury must not prejudice you in this case.

"If you find that the Chinaman met his death by other means than by the manner set forth in the indictment, he [Ryan] cannot be

Judge John Henry Hardy

convicted. You are to be controlled by your own opinion, assisted by the arguments by both counsel as to the verdict."

Hardy explained the applicable law and legal theories and dismissed the jury at 3:00 p.m. Court officers led the twelve men to the jury room where they deliberated for three and a half hours.

The court notified DA French and defense counsel at 6:30 p.m. that the jury had reached a verdict. French, Bixby, and Callanan arrived at the courthouse within fifteen minutes and took their places inside the bar. A hush fell over the crowded courtroom as deputies escorted Ryan to the dock at 6:52 p.m. According to one observer, Ryan was "seemingly the least concerned of any in the courtroom."

Judges Stevens and Hardy briskly emerged from their chambers, took the bench, and signaled for the jury. When the jury was seated, the court clerk turned to Ryan and told him to face the jury. "When called, he [Ryan] stood without a tremor, held up his head, and gazed steadily at the jury," according to one reporter.

The clerk asked foreman Andrew Gale if the jury had reached a verdict.

"We have," said Gale.

"What say you, Mr. Foreman and gentlemen? Is Cyrus L. Ryan, the defendant at the bar, guilty or not guilty?"

"Guilty," Gale answered. A collective gasp came from the gallery. Ryan showed no emotion.

"What say you as to the degree of murder?" asked the clerk.

"In the second degree," Gale said in a low but clear and distinct voice.

Ryan's friends and family were in the courtroom when they heard Gale's pronouncement. Ryan's mother and Katie Murray wept.

Ryan turned to a deputy standing on his right and whispered, "I wish it'd been the chair," but later retracted his statement.

Judge Stevens asked the defendant if he had anything to say to the court. Ryan once again proclaimed his innocence and denied he had robbed and killed Quong Sing.

Stevens thanked the jurors for their service and dismissed them. He then informed Ryan that he would pronounce sentence on June 15. Ryan shook hands with his defense team and thanked them before deputies shackled him and led him to the prison wagon for the trip back to Plymouth Jail.

~

Ryan appeared for sentencing before Justice Stevens at Plymouth County Superior Court on Wednesday, June 15, 1904. Ryan's mother and sister, Fred Pierce and his wife, and Katie Murray were in the courtroom when Judge Stevens sentenced Ryan to life without parole in the state prison at Charlestown, the maximum penalty for second-degree murder. He would serve his first three days in solitary confinement. Pierce did his best to console the four sobbing women after the sentence was pronounced. Ryan, seemingly unaffected, acknowledged his devastated family with a smile as deputies led him from the courtroom for his transfer to Charlestown.

Prison guards received Ryan later that day and assigned him convict No. 13408. During his entry interview, Ryan insisted he had been unfairly punished. He maintained he should have been convicted of manslaughter, not second-degree murder.

After the interview and the necessary documents had been processed, two guards had Ryan change into a prison uniform and led him to a cell in the prison's west wing that was reserved for solitary confinement. He was in a hard place. One of the prisoners was the Boston "boy fiend" Jesse Pomeroy, who was serving a life sentence of solitary confinement following his 1876 conviction for murdering several children.

The Massachusetts State Prison at Charlestown had grown in size and population since Seth Perry's incarceration in 1845. The warden had converted the prison's guardroom into a cell block and installed one hundred additional cells by 1867. The west wing constructed in 1886 added sixty more. By the early 1900s, the prison contained eight hundred fifty cells. The warden's staff included a deputy warden, a clerk, a chaplain, a physician, three engineers, an electrician, four turnkeys or jailers, who supervised fifty-three watchmen and five assistant watchmen.

There were 812 prisoners at the prison when Ryan was admitted. He became the ninth prisoner serving a life sentence.

The practice of isolating individual prisoners had changed little during the half century since Perry's release. Cells were furnished with a simple bed, a table, a chair, a wash pail, and a slop bucket. Narrow slits high in the granite walls provided a minimum of light and ventilation in the seven-by-nine-foot cells. An inner, solid iron door, kept each prisoner secure, and a wooden outer door kept prisoners out of the sight of others. Like Perry, Ryan was given bread and water. Prison officials released him from solitary after three days and assigned him to work in the prison shoe shop.

During his first few years at the prison, Ryan was accused of being troublesome and quarrelsome and of cursing an officer an average of once a year. He was placed in solitary confinement for three and a half days in January 1907 for refusing to obey a guard; for four days in May 1908 for assaulting a convict; for five days in May 1909 for refusing to obey; and for three days in January 1912 for fighting in the shoe shop.

He was transferred to Bridgewater State Hospital on October 24, 1912, because of his violent, disruptive behavior. The facility had previously been called the State Asylum for Insane Criminals and the Bridgewater State Farm. Situated on twelve hundred acres of land, the facility was rebuilt in 1883 after a fire. The new complex included a prison, three dormitories, a hospital building, a kitchen, and a superintendent's house, all constructed with brick, stone, and concrete.

Ryan was not considered insane. He was believed to be psychopathic. He was of average intelligence, but he was impulsive, neurotic, and unable to adjust to the prison environment. Hospital officials at Bridgewater discharged him after psychometric testing and treatment and sent him back to Charlestown on September 8, 1913.

Ryan's behavior improved after 1913, but he was nonetheless placed in solitary confinement three times for insolence, for writing filthy notes to prisoners, and for talking in line and resisting an officer. The warden also punished him seven times within three years for "gambling, issuing worthless transfers and writing letters to other inmates inducing them to claim insanity in order to go to Bridgewater." The warden described Ryan as "unreliable temperamentally, dishonest, untrustworthy, and profits very little from punishment."

~

On October 26, 1916, the Massachusetts Board of Parole's Advisory Board of Pardons held a hearing at the state prison in Charlestown on Ryan's application for a pardon. Ryan was represented by Attorney Peter Maher, who argued that Ryan had been denied effective assistance by counsel during his trial. The lawyer alleged that Ryan's attorneys had advised him to plead guilty to the lesser crime of manslaughter several days after the trial had begun. The two lawyers were apparently convinced, Maher continued, that evidence presented by the prosecution would ensure a murder conviction and possible execution.

Ryan refused to accept their advice, insisting he was not guilty of any crime. He firmly believed the Chinese laundryman had assaulted him

Cyrus Lawrence
Ryan, 1919

and that he had only used force to defend himself. Maher said Ryan told him that because he insisted on continuing with the trial, his lawyers believed the only way he could avoid conviction was to testify as they instructed. Ryan alleged that his defense team concocted a story for him to convey on the witness stand. Ryan followed their advice and was convicted of murder. According to Maher, if Ryan had been allowed to tell his own story and not the tale fabricated by his attorneys, he would not have been convicted. Maher told the hearing officers that Ryan's attorneys, Judge Fred Bixby and John Callanan, were unavailable for questioning because Bixby had died and Callanan's whereabouts were unknown.

Maher gave Ryan's account of what actually happened on the day of

Quong Sing's death. He related the same version Ryan had given when he first entered prison, but Maher added a critical fact Ryan had testified to at trial but had failed to mention to prison officials – that while he was trying to wrest the gun from Quong Sing's grasp, he heard the trigger "snap." There was no discharge. The gun had either misfired or the hammer had struck an empty cylinder. Maher hoped to convince the board that Quong Sing had tried to kill Ryan and that Ryan was only trying to defend himself.

Maher told the board that Quong Sing did not die from drowning but from heart disease. Maher apparently hadn't checked his facts, or perhaps he purposely misled the board, because the medical examiner, Dr. Henry Dudley, had clearly testified at the trial that the presence of soapy water in Quong Sing's lungs confirmed he had drowned.

The hearing officer asked why Ryan had taken Quong Sing's watch. Ryan replied that he saw the watch on the floor after the scuffle and thought it was his, because it was an Ingersoll. Ryan said he got the watch at a picnic on Prince Edward Island. When he boarded the train for Boston, he realized he had two watches, his own and Quong Sing's. He also had Quong's revolver in his pocket. He threw them away, Ryan explained, because he knew that police would implicate him in Quong's death if they found the watch and revolver in his possession. Unfortunately, he threw away the wrong watch – his own – and was found with Quong Sing's watch after his arrest.

Ryan was unaware that the hearing officer had a case file that included a report from Captain Proctor outlining the details of Ryan's arrest in 1904 and the recovery of Quong's gun from Ryan's coat pocket and Quong's silver watch from Ryan's sweetheart, Katie Murray.

Ryan's elderly mother vouched for his reputation while testifying on her son's behalf. She told the board that her son was a good boy, that he had worked since he was nine or ten years old, and that he always gave her his pay.

The hearing was adjourned, and Ryan was returned to his cell to await the governor's decision.

Ryan sent a letter to the state's Bureau of Prisons director, Cyrus Adams, on December 20, 1917, requesting the status of his petition. Adams forwarded Ryan's letter to Frank Brooks, chairman of the Board of Parole. Brooks wrote to the Charlestown warden, Nathan Allen, on January 4, 1918, requesting that Allen inform Ryan that the board had not yet received notice from the governor's office.

Ryan grew impatient and eight months later wrote directly to Governor Samuel McCall. McCall's office forwarded Ryan's letter to Brooks. Brooks wrote to Warden Allen on September 4, 1918, asking him to inform Ryan that his case was about to be reported to the governor with a recommendation. Shortly thereafter, Brooks advised Ryan through Allen that the governor had rejected his petition for pardon.

~

Ryan was illiterate when he entered the prison but he took advantage of the institution's educational opportunities and, according to prison records, became "…capable of writing a fairly good letter and is interested in good reading…" Ryan wrote a Mother's Day letter to his mother on May 12, 1918. The letter reflected his highly emotional, agitated state. He wanted out of prison, and would do anything to gain his release.

It is good to be able to write to you today, but you will not expect a cheerful letter as you know I have nothing to say that would bring cheer to you at this time. You have nothing to make you happy on this Mother's Day but do not let the gloomy outlook discourage you. I will prove my right to be out of here if I am given a chance to prove it and I will get out this summer if the warden here approves of it. All those who had him on their side went out and some of them were here only about half of my time and their crimes were bad – so bad that they were forced to plead guilty to save themselves from the chair. A man pleads guilty because he knows it's useless to fight.

I know this letter will interest you more than any other I could write because you need a home more than kind words written on paper and as I am the only one left to you able to make a home for you the thing to do is to get me out and if you have stumbling blocks thrown in your way you can get the best of them by getting up that petition. Do not let anything stand in your way or you will be fooled into believing that I will have to stay here another year.

It is up to you all outside to call the bluff and I will expect you to brush everything aside and fight for my life and soul. I have no religion now and I will not have any until I get out of here.

Last week I wrote to the parole board asking that my case be properly investigated and that if I am given the right to ask questions I will prove my record in here to be as good as the best. I do not know what they will do, but if I am not accorded fair treatment you will have to go ahead with the petition. Within a short time I will write to the governor and explain things more fully and it will be up to him to take action one way or the other. All I ask is a chance to prove my right to the outside and if the governor grants me this chance I will want to see him go to Washington in Mr. Weeks's place (John Wingate Weeks, the U.S. senator from Massachusetts)*, but if he refuses to take a hand in this matter I will not want to see him hold a public office of any kind.*

If anything serious should happen to me do not except [sic] *a gold brick as a compensation, but forget nothing and make everything public. I am warning you that I am going to make known the truth and I will not be afraid to tell anyone he is a liar or worse when I know I am right. I will let it be known that Bessie* (his sister) *is forced to pay your board out of her small earnings and that Frank* (his brother, Ambrose) *is almost too blind to earn his own living. This will be open to investigation and the brute who would oppose my release from here should be sent to hell.*

Let us hope that I will be granted a commutation of sentence and when Mother's Day comes around again you will have something worth living for.

Your affectionate son,

C. L. Ryan

~

Ryan's efforts to obtain a pardon or release on parole failed. Ryan was sent back to Bridgewater on October 21, 1919, after he again became disruptive. He returned to the state prison on December 17, 1920. Charlestown's warden punished him with twenty-four days of solitary confinement between July 1927 and July 1931 for four different offenses including assaulting an inmate and assaulting an officer with a chair.

The prison was the scene of great excitement during this stretch of Ryan's misconduct. Nicola Sacco and Bartolomeo Vanzetti had been convicted of murder in Norfolk Superior Court on July 14, 1921, and were sentenced to die in Charlestown's electric chair. After six years of appeals and international protests and demonstrations, the two men were executed at the prison on August 23, 1927.

Ryan wrote to his sister, Annie (Ryan) Brennan, in 1931. He told her he didn't want any visitors and asked her to tell the rest of the family not to send him any money unless he asked for it.

He conveyed a sense of paranoia and persecution as he continued: *Ed* (his brother Michael Edward Ryan) *should be careful not to let the gang frame him as they did me and if they find out he is trying to help me they sure will get him. Be careful about what you eat because if they don't get you one way they will another; when you see people vomiting and not able to walk you know someone is putting something over. They do these things to get you to talk and then they frame you up and send you to prison or a crazy house.*

Ryan wrote that he "...doesn't sleep and can't walk sometimes and the heart stops." He then changed his mind about visitors and told his sister "...Perhaps I will have you visit me anyway." He concluded by writing, "Tell Ed and the rest at home to be careful and I will tell you all about it later. Love to all from Cyrus."

In 1932, prison officials created a social case history on Ryan that included comments about his personality and institutional behavior. Ryan, who was about forty-eight, was regarded as "quite lively in physical mannerisms as well as speech. He appears pleasant and agreeable in conversation and although somewhat nervous, does not appear to be very much upset. He is completely convinced of his innocence and has suffered tremendously since his incarceration, but he bears no grudge against society in general, or anyone in particular."

Prison officials transferred Ryan back to Bridgewater on April 24, 1935. He stayed at the institution for about a month and was returned to the prison on May 31. Ryan was transferred to Bridgewater for the last time fifteen months later.

Although he had made great strides to improve himself, Ryan was not a model prisoner at the state prison. He was reprimanded twenty-four times for rules infractions, including fighting, insolence, disobedience, dishonesty, and poor work, and was placed in solitary confinement eleven times for more serious violations.

Cyrus Lawrence
Ryan, 1935

~

Clinical psychologists Scott O. Lilienfeld and Hal Arkowitz, in a December 2007 *Scientific American Mind* article, described a psychopath as someone who is incapable of feeling guilt, remorse, or empathy and is self-centered, dishonest, and undependable. Psychopaths display superficial charm and employ deceit and manipulation to attain their ends, the psychologists wrote. They will not accept responsibility for their actions and blame others instead.

As a youngster, Ryan had been arrested for throwing stones at a dog. He insisted during a 1932 interview with prison officials that he was later acquitted of the charge. Cruelty to animals, however, is a known sign of psychopathic behavior and a trait common to rapists and murderers.

During his incarceration at Bridgewater State Hospital, psychiatrists evaluated Ryan and determined that his behavior was consistent with the mannerisms of psychosis and psychopathic personality disorder. His conduct in prison – his deception, dishonesty, and unreliability – supported this diagnosis. Ryan never expressed any remorse or guilt over the murder of Quong Sing in his letters to his mother and sister. He

Cyrus Lawrence
Ryan, 1949

denied responsibility for the killing. Instead, he blamed the laundryman and insisted that he was only defending himself from Quong's attack. He placed the blame for his conviction on his attorneys and believed they had denied him proper counsel.

Ryan's home life and upbringing may have amplified his disorder. He grew up in poverty. His alcoholic father likely spent the meager wages he earned as a stevedore on his addiction. That left little for the family. His mother and father removed Cyrus and his siblings from school at an early age and sent them to work fourteen hours a day, seven days a week, in the factories and mills of Charlottetown, Prince Edward Island.

It is not known if Cyrus suffered any specific abuse in the Ryan household or at the workplace; or if any other circumstances may have influenced his adult behavior. But the long hours he spent at work and away from home likely prevented him from receiving the parental supervision and nurturing he desperately needed during his formative years.

Ryan died on December 4, 1962, at the age of seventy-nine, a broken, forgotten, and penniless man. He had spent fifty-eight years, nearly three-quarters of his life, in confinement.

Dr. Samuel Allen, a clinical psychiatrist at Bridgewater, certified his cause of death as atherosclerotic heart disease due to generalized arteriosclerosis. In Allen's opinion, "psychosis with psychopathic personality contributed to Ryan's death, but was not an underlying cause."

Cyrus Lawrence
Ryan, 1954

Ryan donated his body to Harvard Medical School for scientific study. Harvard agreed to pay for the removal and transportation of the corpse as well as associated expenses for the final disposition of his remains.

Funeral director Albert Sullivan of Rockland, Massachusetts, removed Ryan's body from Bridgewater and delivered it to the medical school.

After completing its study, Harvard arranged for Ryan's body to be transported to Pine Hill Cemetery in Tewksbury, Massachusetts, for burial at a private facility maintained by Boston-area medical schools.

Ryan's sweetheart, Katie Murray, returned to her hometown of Clyde River, Prince Edward Island, married a local man in 1906, and had eight children. Katie died in 1970 in Cornwall, Prince Edward Island.

Frederick Pierce and his wife, Mary, adopted a child and remained in Hanover until about 1930, then moved to Rockland, Massachusetts. Mary died in 1933, Frederick in 1949. Both were buried in Rockland.

Cyrus's mother, Elizabeth, died in Boston on Christmas Day 1935, and was buried with one of her sons and a daughter in New Calvary Cemetery. All of her children except one son, John, eventually settled in the Boston area where several married and had children.

Notes

Foreword

xiv   "…either expressed or implied": Sir William Blackstone, Knight, *Commentaries on the Laws of England in Four Books, Book Four: of Public Wrongs* (Philadelphia: Rees Welsh & Co., 1902) 1591.

xiv   "…sufficiently violent provocation": Ibid., 1599.

xiv   "…commission of some unlawful act": Ibid., 1587.

xiv   right to a trial by jury: Alan Rogers, *Murder and the Death Penalty in Massachusetts* (Amherst and Boston: University of Massachusetts Press, 2008), 41.

xiv   during a trial and an appeal: Ibid., 77.

xv   did allow challenges for cause: Ibid., 118.

xv   opponents had been purged: Ibid., 297-299.

xv   was punishable by life imprisonment: Ibid., 112-113.

xv   no presumptions about his or her guilt: Ibid., 116.

xvi   real or supposed predisposition: Ibid., 118.

xvi   from three to two: *Report of the Attorney General for the year ending January 15, 1902* (Boston: Wright & Potter Printing Company, 1902), xviii.

xvi   Supreme Judicial Court to the Superior Court: Rogers, *Murder and the Death Penalty in Massachusetts,* 121.

xvi   to two or more and in 1910 to one: Ibid., 430-431.

xvi   first day of January as a legal holiday: Massachusetts Secretary of the Commonwealth, *General Acts Passed By the General Court of Massachusetts in the Year 1916, Together With the Constitution, List of the Officers of the Civil Government, Tables Showing Changes in the General Statutes, Etc., Etc.* (Boston: Wright & Potter Printing Company, 1916), 83-84.

xvi   on Monday, January 1, 1917: "New Year's Day Now a Legal Holiday; First Observance Monday, January 1, 1917; Measure Before Legislature For Many Years," *Boston Daily Globe*, December 21, 1916.

xvi   deputies who served under their jurisdiction: "Retires Today; Sheriff Endicott Leaves That Office; Has Served Norfolk County More Than 36 Years," *Boston Daily Globe*, January 4, 1899.

xvi   public order and decency throughout the state: Mitchel P. Roth, *Crime and Punishment; a History of the Criminal Justice System,"* 2nd ed. (Belmont, CA: Wadsworth Publishing, 2011), 150.

xvii   reinstated the office of chief constable: Ibid., 150.

xvii   in suppressing riots: H. Kenneth Bechtel, *State Police in the United States, A Socio-Historical Analysis* (Westport, CT: Greenwood Press, 1995), 36-37.

xvii   after Wade's death in 1904: William F. Powers, *The One Hundred Year Vigil, the Story of the Massachusetts State Police* (Foxboro, MA: The Foxboro Company, 1965).

xvii   in the Northwestern District: Charles Allen, Uriel H. Crocker, James M. Barker, *The Public Statutes of the Commonwealth of Massachusetts* (Boston: Rand, Avery and Company, 1882), 189.

xvii   state agency with a specific request: "State Police Force of Massachusetts; Men Who Have Had Charge of Many Notable Criminal Cases and Enforcement of Many Laws," *Boston Daily Globe*, November 24, 1902.

xvii   competitive civil service examination: Massachusetts Civil Service Commissioners, *First Annual Report of the Civil Service Commissioners of Massachusetts* (Boston: Wright & Potter Printing Company, 1885), 8-10.

xviii   veterans with the same score. Massachusetts Civil Service Commissioners, *Thirteenth Annual Report of the Civil Service Commissioners of Massachusetts* (Boston: Wright & Potter Printing Company, 1897), 146-148.

Rum

2   married in Pembroke...1786: John Stetson Barry, *A Historical Sketch of the Town of Hanover, Massachusetts: with family genealogies* (Boston: S. G. Drake, 1853), 357.

2   were born in 1793: Ibid., 357.

2   still stands at 1170 Broadway): Hanover Historical Preservation Plan, Hanover, MA, September 2007 by Town of Hanover Historical Commission and Hanover Planning Department; Appendix A, page 2.

2   Seth married Melinda: Jedediah Dwelley, et al., *A Copy of the Records of Births, Marriages and Deaths and of Intentions of Marriage of the Town of Hanover, Mass., 1727-1857, As Recorded by the Several Town Clerks for the Said Town of Hanover* (Rockland: Press of the Rockland Standard, 1898), 145.

2   in a drowning accident: Arthur Foster, ed., *Vital Records of Hanson, Massachusetts, to the Year 1850* (Boston: New England Historic and Genealogical Society, 1911), 92. Seth Cox died on August 4, 1826.

2   Julia Ann in 1836: Barry, *A Historical Sketch of the Town of Hanover*, 357.

2   and Lydia Tilden Bates: Ibid., 253.

2   law degree from Harvard in 1831: William Thomas Davis, *History of the Judiciary of Massachusetts* (Boston: Boston Book Company, 1900), 181.

3   "…strove to rear its head": Frederic Hathaway Chase, *Lemuel Shaw, Chief Justice of the Supreme Judicial Court, 1830 – 1860* (Boston and New York: Houghton Mifflin Co., 1918), 216-217.

3   "…wholly irrelevant and collateral": Ibid.

3   "…could not exist in Massachusetts": Ibid., 164.

3   was brought into the state unintentionally: Paul Finkleman, *An Imperfect Union: Slavery, Federalism, and Comity* (Union, NJ: The Lawbook Exchange, Ltd., 2000), 103-125.

3   "…an unerring judicial mind": Davis, *History of the Judiciary of Massachusetts*, 189.

3   appointed him to the Supreme Judicial Court: *Memorial Biographies of the New England Historic Genealogical Society, Volume VI, 1864-1871* (Boston: Published by the Society, 1905), 179.

3   "…in the application of general principles": Ibid., 180.

4   to the Supreme Judicial Court in 1842: Conrad Reno, LL.B., *Memoirs of the Judiciary and Bar of New England for the Nineteenth Century with a History of the Judicial System of New England*, Volume III (Boston: The Century Memorial Publishing Company, 1901), 502-503.

4   Massachusetts bar in 1830: D. Hamilton Hurd, *History of Bristol County Massachusetts with Biographical Sketches of Many of its Pioneers and Prominent Men,* Illustrated, (Philadelphia: J.W. Lewis & Co., 1883), 12.

4   "…guilt of the accused, is fearful": Conrad Reno, LL.B., *Memoirs of the Judiciary and Bar of New England for the Nineteenth Century with a History of the Judicial System of New England*, Volume II (Boston: The Century Memorial Publishing Company, 1901), 164.

4   served for one year: Hurd, *History of Bristol County*, 13-15.

4   resumed private legal practice: Ibid.

5   for his wit and anecdotes: "Editor's Drawer," *Harper's New Monthly Magazine* (New York: Harper and Brothers, 1870), Volume XL, December 1869-May 1870, 631.

5   "…was almost an impossibility": Leonard Bolles Ellis, *History of New Bedford and its Vicinity, 1602-1892* (Syracuse, NY: D. Mason and Company, 1892), 646.

5   "...of all others I know of": Hurd, *History of Bristol County, Massachusetts*, 8-9.

5   "...a faithful counselor and trustworthy lawyer": Jedediah Dwelley and John F. Simmons, *History of the Town of Hanover, Massachusetts: with Family Genealogies* (Hanover: Town of Hanover, MA, 1910), 99-100.

6   graduated from Harvard College in 1839: D. Hamilton Hurd, *History of Plymouth County Massachusetts with Biographical Sketches of many of its Pioneers and Prominent Men,* (Philadelphia: J.W. Lewis and Company, 1884), 825.

6   "...always very bustling and businesslike": Dwelley and Simmons, *History of the Town of Hanover*, 108.

7   nearly sixteen hundred souls: 1850 United States Federal Census, Hanover, Plymouth County, Massachusetts, September 5, 1850.

7   scattered across its pastoral countryside: Massachusetts Historical Commission Reconnaissance Survey Town Report: Hanover: 1981, 6-8.

7   constituted as a separate township: Dwelley and Simmons, *History of the Town of Hanover*, 9.

7   source of income for many of Hanover's residents: 1850 United States Federal Census, Hanover, Plymouth County, Massachusetts, September 5, 1850.

8   iron and steel ship construction: Dwelley and Simmons, *History of the Town of Hanover*, 174.

8   its first church in North Hanover the following year: Ibid. 54-76.

8   "higher mathematics," navigation and surveying: Barry, *A Historical Sketch of the Town of Hanover*, 93-94.

8   issuance of new licenses for the same purpose: Barry, *A Historical Sketch of the Town of Hanover,* 174.

8   maximum fine of one hundred dollars: *Revised Statutes of the Commonwealth of Massachusetts*, passed November 4, 1835, Printed and Published by Virtue of a Resolve of November 3, 1835; under the direction of Theron Metcalf and Horace Mann – Chapter 47 of the Regulation of Licensed Houses, (Boston: Dutton & Wentworth, State Printers, Nos. 10 & 12 Exchange Street, 1836), Sections 1-3, 375-376.

9   "...which ally us to the angels": Barry, *A Historical Sketch of the Town of Hanover*, 169.

9   "...which threatened to overwhelm": Ibid., 168.

10   ...balance of his losses by selling rum": "The Murder of the Stapletons at Hanover," *Boston Post*, June 19, 1845.

10 resumed his illegal activities: *Plymouth Court Records, 1686-1859,* Boston, MA, Volume 15, page 233, #47 and #48: New England Historical and Genealogical Society, Boston: 2002.

11 "civilized domestic cattle": Thomas H. O'Connor, *The Boston Irish: A Political History* (Canada: Little, Brown and Co., 1995), 64.

11 "...nature of papal authority": Ibid., 43-44.

11 "...Pope in Rome was the real enemy": William V. Shannon, *The American Irish: A Political and Social Portrait* (Amherst: The University of Massachusetts Press, 1966), 41.

11 "...twelve dollars a month for wages": Edward Wakin, *Enter the Irish-American* (New York: Thomas Y. Crowell Co., 1976), 50.

11 expanding transportation system: Lon Cantor, *What Makes America Great? Land of Freedom, Honor, Justice, and Opportunity* (Lincoln, NE: iUniverse, Inc., 2003), 164.

11 "...work of the nineteenth century": Barbara A. Driscoll, *The Tracks North: The Railroad Bracero Program of World War II* (Austin: University of Texas Press, Center for Mexican American Studies, 1999), 13-14.

12 "...under every railroad tie": Wakin, *Enter the Irish-American,* 50.

12 "...horror of liberal-minded Concordians": William Barksdale Maynard, *Walden Pond: a history* (New York: Oxford University Press Inc., 2004), 52.

12 through Abington, Hanson, and Kingston: Charles Eben Fisher, *The Story of the Old Colony Railroad* (Taunton: By the author, 1919), 134.

12 On a chilly Monday, March 17: S. N. Dickinson, *Boston Almanac for the year 1846* (Boston: Thomas Groom and Company, 1846), 10. The 1846 *Boston Almanac* recorded variable weather conditions with temperatures of 28 degrees at 7:00 a.m. and 40 degrees at 2:00 p.m. on March 17, 1845. Microfiche held at Boston Public Library, Fiche 1, *Boston Almanac 1846,* Brookbauer Press, LaCross, WI.

13 attached shed, and a single fireplace: "The Murder of the Stapletons at Hanover," *Boston Post,* June 20, 1845.

13 A fifty-two-year-old man of medium height...: Charlestown State Prison, Commitment Registers, 1805-1930, HS 9.01, Sec. 289X, Roll 2, Commitment register of October 1840-December 1856, Massachusetts State Archives, Boston, MA.

13 "...his yard stained with blood...": "Shocking Outrages," *Quincy Aurora,* March 20, 1845.

13 with "sandy whiskers": "The Murder of the Stapletons at Hanover," *Boston Post,* June 21, 1845.

13   less than a mile from Perry's shanty: Anne Bonney Henderson and Fanny Hitchcock Phillips, *Map of Hanover, Mass., as it was in the 1850s,* Hanover Historical Society, Hanover, MA.

13   "...a good deal excited...": "Dreadful Affray at Hanover; Two Men Killed, and Another Dangerously Wounded," *Old Colony Memorial* [Plymouth, MA] March 22, 1845.

14   "...Bates argued against it," Lynch later said: "The Murder of the Stapletons at Hanover," *Boston Post,* June 19, 1845.

14   "...handle any man, Irish or Yankee": "The Murder of the Stapletons at Hanover," June 20, 1845.

14   "...among the brush in the corner," Lynch recollected: "The Murder of the Stapletons at Hanover," June 19, 1845.

15   "...when the shot passed my ear": Ibid.

15   and shattered his jaw: "Shocking Outrages," March 20, 1845.

16   threatened to demolish it: "Deadly Affray at Hanover," March 22, 1845.

16   ...as fast as they came in reach: "Murder of Three Men at Hanover!" *Massachusetts Temperance Standard,* March 17, 1845.

16   to the custody of Old Colony Railroad administrators: "Rum and Murder," *Quincy Patriot,* March 22, 1845; also, Plymouth County Probate Court, Plymouth, MA, Probate Case 19200 and 19201, Petition for Administration, Appointment, Bond Letter, May 6, 1845, Volume 11, 327 and 328.

17   celebrated by Rev. Bernard Carraher: *Historical Records and Studies, Volume II, Part I* (New York: the United States Catholic Historical Society, 1900), 247.

17   in the churchyard: "Rum and Murder," *Quincy Patriot,* March 22, 1845.

17   not responsible and released him: Deadly Affray at Hanover," March 22, 1845.

17   taken to Plymouth Jail: Ibid.

17   without bail to await trial: Ibid.

18   "...selling strong drinks, to change their business": "The Murder of Three Men," *Boston Courier,* March 22, 1845.

18   "...the facts just as they occurred": "For the O. C. Memorial; Mr. Editor," *Old Colony Memorial,* March 29, 1845.

19   inherit their assets...commonwealth: Plymouth County Probate Court, Plymouth, MA, Probate Case 19200 and 19201, Petition for Administration, Appointment, Bond Letter, May 6, 1845, Volume 11, 327 and 328.

19   within one year: Ibid.

19   depleted the assets: Plymouth County Probate Court, Plymouth, MA, Volume 89, page 66, Administration Account, February 15, 1847.

19   before the Supreme Judicial Court: "Indictment for Murder" *Barre Patriot*, May 9, 1845.

20   remain held without bail: Ibid.

20   in the back of the courtroom: "The Murder of the Stapletons at Hanover," June 19, 1845.

20   when the court generally adjourned: James Thacher, *History of the Town of Plymouth* (Boston: Marsh, Capon & Lyon, 1832), 309.

21   "…patients once considered incurable": William Richard Cutter, A. M., *New England Families – Genealogical and Memorial: A Record of the Achievements of Her People in the Making of Commonwealths and the Founding of a Nation* - Volume II (New York: Lewis Historical Publishing Company, 1914), 1055.

21   "…passions which war against the soul": "The Murder of the Stapletons at Hanover, June 19, 1845.

21   "…one such indictment at a time": Ibid.

21   Jury empanelment began…: Ibid.

22   "…the deceased making a disturbance at his place": Ibid.

26   "…but I might get hit": "The Murder of the Stapletons at Hanover" June 19, 1845.

26   "I did not," Lynch answered: Ibid.

27   "…in a row that day at Perry's": Ibid.

28   ball for the jury's inspection: "The Murder of the Stapletons at Hanover," *Boston Post*, June 20, 1845.

29   "…the Stapletons were mad," Bates replied: "Trial of Seth Perry," *Quincy Advertiser and Patriot*, June 23, 1845.

30   served as a home for Perry and his wife until she died: "The Murder of the Stapletons at Hanover," June 20, 1845.

31   he could, "handle any man, Irish or Yankee": Ibid.

32   "…the first gun was fired": Ibid.

33   "…and brown pants," answered Connor: Ibid.

34   "…after he left the shop": Ibid.

35   "…given them their breakfast that morning": Ibid.

35   "…in with him on the road": Ibid.

37   to say before the trial: Ibid.

40   "…drumming on a tin pail," White said: "The Murder of the Stapletons at Hanover," *Boston Post*, June 21, 1845.

40   in the habit of drinking later on: Ibid.

41   "…in any manner molested Perry": Ibid.

42   "…in such an extreme emergency": Ibid.

42   "…who might offend him": Ibid.

43   "…convict him with their murder": Ibid.

43   as presented during trial: Lemuel Shaw Papers, 1648-1923, Microfilm Call Number P-206, Part III-B, Minutes of the Supreme Judicial Court, 1830-1860, Reel 23B, File 4, Frame 921-1377, Massachusetts Historical Society, Boston, MA.

43   "…what he was doing was wrong": Alan Rogers, *Murder and the Death Penalty in Massachusetts* (Amherst and Boston: University of Massachusetts Press, 2008), 209.

44   because of his mental state: Ibid., 209.

44   could not lead to the truth: Ibid., 209.

44   not guilty by reason of insanity: Ibid., 209-210.

45   "…and reduces it to manslaughter": "The Murder of the Stapletons at Hanover," June 21, 1845.

45   "…of manslaughter," Thompson declared: "Trial of Seth Perry," *Boston Daily Advertiser*, June 23, 1845.

46   pled guilty to manslaughter: Plymouth County, Supreme Judicial Court – *Commonwealth v Seth Perry* (1845), Record Box 2196338, January 1, 1813 – December 31, 1853, Massachusetts State Archives, Boston, MA.

46   the charge was dismissed: "Trial for Murder," *Quincy Patriot*, June 28, 1845.

46   "no direct proof of the fact": "Trial of Perry," *Boston Courier*, June 21, 1845.

46   "…in cases of this kind": Ibid.

47   convicted of the lesser crime of manslaughter: Rogers, *Murder and the Death Penalty in Massachusetts*, 94.

47   but the bill never passed: Ibid., 80-81.

47   precept of "Thou shalt not kill.": Ibid., 81-82.

47   proponent for eliminating the death penalty: Louis P. Masur, *Capital Punishment and the Transformation of American Culture, 1776-1865* (New York: Oxford University Press, 1989), 124.

47   arguments proposed by Rantoul: Ibid., 83.

48   "…could, and should, be reformed": Rogers, *Murder and the Death Penalty in Massachusetts*, 83.

48   petitions for commuting punishments: Ibid., 83.

48   "…justice is defined and administered": Ibid., x-xi.

49   for the death of James Stapleton: "Trial of Perry," June 21, 1845.

49   ($47 million today): L. Officer and S. Williamson, *Purchasing Power of Money in the United States from 1774 to 2008.* Measuring Worth, 2009.

197

49   each seventeen feet by eleven feet: O.F. Lewis, PhD., *The Development of American Prisons and Prison Customs, 1776-1845* (Albany: Prison Association of New York, 1922), 69.

49   ninety-eight thousand square foot prison yard: Lewis, *The Development of American Prisons and Prison Customs,* 69.

49   perched atop the walls: Maturin Murray Ballou, ed., *Gleason's Pictorial Drawing Room Companion,* Vol. IV, *American Periodical Series, 1850-1900* (Boston: F. Gleason, 1853), 95.

49   impossible to undermine: Lewis, *The Development of American Prisons and Prison Customs*, 69.

49   with doors of wrought iron: Ibid., 160.

49   wing was added in 1850: Gideon Haynes, *Pictures From Prison Life: An Historical Sketch of the Massachusetts State Prison* (Boston: Lee and Shepard, 1869), 65.

49   four coal stoves in each building: Ibid., 49.

50   sufficient light during daytime: Ibid., 48.

50   when gas lighting was installed: Ballou, ed., *Gleason's Pictorial Drawing Room Companion*, 197.

50   serving time for manslaughter: Prison Discipline Society, *Reports of the Prison Discipline Society – 1846-1847* (Boston: Press of T. R. Marvin, 1855), 22.

50   shaved off his "whiskers: *Laws of the Commonwealth for the Government of the Massachusetts State Prison, with the Rules and Regulations of the Board of Inspectors, and Details of the Police and Discipline, Adopted by the Warden on the Completion of the New Prison, October 1829* (Charlestown: Press of the Bunker Hill Aurora, 1830), 58.

50   two blankets, and a cap: Ibid., 11.

50   made of coarse cloth: Lewis, *The Development of American Prisons and Prison Customs*, 71.

50   large scar on his left knee:, Charlestown State Prison, Commitment Registers, 1805-1930, HS 9.01, Sec. 289X, Roll 2, Commitment register of October 1840-December 1856, Massachusetts State Archives, Boston, MA.

50   and a "slop bucket": Harold Schechter, *Fiend: The Shocking True Story of America's Youngest Serial Killer* (New York: Pocket Books/Simon & Schuster, 2000), 261.

50   failed to follow prison rules: Ibid., 263.

51   a knife, fork, and spoon: Haynes, *Pictures From Prison Life: An Historical Sketch of the Massachusetts State Prison*, 265.

51   "...resembles a great manual-labor school": Francis Calley Gray, *Prison Discipline in America* (Boston: Charles T. Little and James Brown, 1847), 47.

51   reported violations to the warden: Ibid.

51   set aside for rest and reflection: Ibid., 39-40.

51   Indian bread and rye coffee: L. A. Abbott, *Seven Wives and Seven Prisoners, or Experiences in the Life of a Matrimonial Monomaniac – A True Story* (New York: published for the author,1870), 26-27.

51   pea or bean porridge: Lewis, *The Development of American Prisons and Prison Customs*, 70.

52   received fifty lashes intermittently: Gray, *Prison Discipline in America*, 48.

52   cut every three months: Haynes, *Pictures From Prison Life*, 267.

52   in the northwest section of the prison yard: Ibid., 267-268.

52   "...regulated by the physician": Gray, *Prison Discipline in America*, 48.

52   "...vegetables for their own use": Ibid., 51.

52   to the prison's small library: Ibid., 53.

52   Society in Aid of Discharged Convicts: Prison Discipline Society, *Reports of the Prison Discipline Society*, 38.

53   of his description and demeanor: John Ross Dix, "A Visit to the State Prison – A Prison Poet" in *Local Loiterings, and Visits in the Vicinity of Boston, by a Looker On* (Boston: Redding and Company, 8 State Street, 1846), 89-92.

53   attacking him or the prison guards: Ibid., 89.

53   "...almost massacred another": Ibid., 90-91.

53   "...the very incarnation of evil": Ibid., 91.

53   "...with a cry of vengeance": Ibid., 91.

54   "...that hardened-looking old man": Ibid., 92.

54   for one dollar: Plymouth County Registry of Deeds, Plymouth, MA: Land Records, Volume 294, page 206, 1859, Cephas Perry to Seth Perry.

54   was known locally as Sand Hill: Hanover Town Clerk, Hanover, MA; Valuation List, 1863, page 23.

54   lived in seclusion: "Suburban Short Notes," *Boston Post*, December 12, 1874.

54   dead in his home: Ibid.

54   cause of death as "old age": Vital Records and Statistics, Deaths, Hanover, 1874, Volume 266, page 302, Item 29, Massachusetts State Archives, Boston, MA.

54   sister and brother-in-law, Wealthy and Albert Stetson: 1850 United States Federal Census; Hanover, Plymouth County, Massachusetts, September 5, 1850.

54   Turner, of Hanson, Massachusetts in the spring of 1853: Vital Records of Hanover 1727-1857 (*A Copy of the Records of Births, Marriages and Deaths and of Intentions of Marriage of the Town of Hanover, Mass. 1727-1857; as Recorded by the several town clerks for the said town of Hanover. Prepared under the direction of ... a committee appointed by said town for that purpose.* (Rockland, MA: Press of the *Rockland Standard*, 1898), 182-183. The couple married on May 15, 1853.

54   of Hanover, that fall: Ibid., 184-185. The couple married on November 24, 1853.

54   Julia died in 1870 in Hanover: Massachusetts Vital Records and Statistics, Deaths, Hanover, 1870, volume 230, page 311, Massachusetts State Archives, Boston, MA. (She died of "convultion [*sic*] fits" on December 20).

54   died in Danvers, Massachusetts, in 1902: Massachusetts Vital Records and Statistics, Deaths, Danvers, 1902, volume 528, page 457, Massachusetts State Archives, Boston, MA. (She died of heart disease on December 2).

54   enlisted in the Fourth Regiment, Massachusetts Volunteer Infantry: *Massachusetts Soldiers, Sailors, and Marines in the Civil War*, Volume 1 (Norwood, MA: Norwood Press, 1931), 216. (He enlisted for three months of service on April 16, 1861).

54   in the Seventh Regiment: *Massachusetts Soldiers, Sailors, and Marines in the Civil War*, Volume 1, 513. (He enlisted on August 24, 1861 for three years duty in Company K).

54   deserted at Yorktown, Virginia: *Annual Report of the Adjutant-General of the Commonwealth of Massachusetts for the year ending December 31,1864* (Boston: Wright & Potter, State Printers, 1865), 248.

54   died of unknown causes at Hampton, Virginia: *Massachusetts Soldiers, Sailors, and Marines in the Civil War*, Volume 1, 513.

55   auctioned off and his debts were paid: Plymouth County Probate Records, Plymouth, MA: Docket 15727, volume 129, page 353; volume 146, page 13; volume 137, page 361; and volume 130, page 140.

55   mother died in 1852: Massachusetts Vital Records and Statistics, Births, Hanover, 1852, volume 67, page 249, Massachusetts State Archives, Boston, MA.

55   four children to supplement his income: 1860 United States Federal Census; Hanover, Plymouth County, Massachusetts, July 25, 1860, 12.

55   at Arlington National Cemetery: *Massachusetts Soldiers, Sailors and Marines in the Civil War*, Volume II, 338.

55   Minnie Leland Larkum, on June 21, 1863: Massachusetts Vital Records and Statistics, Births, Hanover, 1863, volume 160, page 280, Massachusetts State Archives, Boston, MA.

55   Congregational Church in Hanover fourteen months later: Massachusetts Vital Records and Statistics, Marriages, Hanover, 1864, volume 172, page 258, Massachusetts State Archives, Boston, MA.

55   in infancy before 1870: Massachusetts Vital Records and Statistics, Deaths, Hanover, 1867, volume 203, page 294, Massachusetts State Archives, Boston, MA. Charles died on November 26, 1867, of consumption; Massachusetts Vital Records and Statistics, Deaths, Hanover, 1870, volume 230, page 311: Rosa died on April 7, 1870, of brain fever.

55   Cora Perkins in 1897: Massachusetts Vital Records and Statistics, Marriages, Hanover, 1897, volume 470, page 580, Massachusetts State Archives, Boston, MA. The couple married in Boston on April 28, 1897.

55   in Weymouth in 1944: Massachusetts Vital Records and Statistics, Deaths, Weymouth, 1944, volume 91, page 454, Massachusetts State Archives, Boston, MA.

55   he died of "old age": Massachusetts Vital Records and Statistics, Deaths, Hanover, 1886, volume 374, page 328, Massachusetts State Archives, Boston, MA

56   Enos's wife and two children: Plymouth County Probate Records, Plymouth, MA: Docket #2605, volume 167, page 597.

56   on February 16, 1899, reportedly of hepatitis: Massachusetts Vital Records and Statistics, Deaths, Hanover, 1899, volume 494, page 177, Massachusetts State Archives, Boston, MA

A Tailor's Goose

58   Bullock...of the Massachusetts Supreme Judicial Court in 1866: William Thomas Davis, *History of the Judiciary of Massachusetts* (Boston: Boston Book Company, 1900), 194.

58   was sentenced to life in prison: *Annual Report of the Attorney General* [of Massachusetts] *for the year ending December 31, 1873* (Boston: Wright & Potter, State Printers, 1874), 6.

58   under President Rutherford B. Hayes: Davis, *History of the Judiciary*, 195-196.

59   by Governor John Long: Ibid.

59   became Attorney General of Massachusetts in 1872: Davis, *History of the Judiciary*, 289.

59   Alley was acquitted: Franklin Fiske Heard, *Report of the Trial of Leavitt Alley: Indictment for the Murder of Abijah Ellis* (Boston: Little, Brown & Co., 1875).

59   solitary confinement for life: John Lothrop, reporter, *Massachusetts Reports, 117, Cases Argued and Determined in the Supreme Judicial Court of Massachusetts* (Boston: Houghton, Mifflin and Company, 1875), 143-150.

59   district attorney for Norfolk and Plymouth Counties: Duane Hamilton Hurd, *History of Norfolk County, Massachusetts with Biographical Sketches of Many of Its Pioneers and Prominent Men* (Philadelphia: J. W. Lewis and Company, 1884), 25.

59   French prosecuted John Moran: "The Stoughton Murder; Second Day of Trial; Additional Testimony; the Case Given to the Jury," *Boston Post*, May 25, 1871; "The Stoughton Murder Case; A Verdict of Murder in the Second Degree," *Boston Post*, May 26, 1871; "Moran, the Murderer, Sentenced," *Boston Post*, July 6, 1871.

59   a sentence of death by hanging: "Execution of William E. Sturtevant, the Halifax Murderer; The Preliminaries! Last Hours of the Prisoner; No Confession; He Continues Defiant! Exercise in the Prison! The March to the Gallows! His Firmness on the Fatal Platform! The Last Act! *Old Colony Memorial* [Plymouth, MA] (Extra), May 7, 1875.

60   assistant district attorney in Suffolk County for a short time: Jeremiah Wadleigh Dearborn, ed., *A History of the First Century of the Town of Parsonsfield, Maine* (Portland, ME, Brown, Thurston and Company, 1888), 292.

60   indefatigable to a fault": Stanton, J. (1877). The Late Horace R. Cheney, Esq. *The Bates Student*, 87-90.

60   returned to Massachusetts in 1869: William Thomas Davis, *Bench and Bar of the Commonwealth of Massachusetts*, Volume II (Boston, MA, Boston History Company, 1895), 373.

61   Massachusetts First Cavalry Regiment: Massachusetts Adjutant General's Office, *Massachusetts Soldiers, Sailors and Marines in the Civil War*, Volume VI, (Norwood, MA: by the Adjutant General's Office, 1933), 167.

61   quartermaster of the Second Cavalry Regiment: Ibid., 278.

61   as a lieutenant colonel in 1863: Ibid. Volume II, 187.

61   appointed to the state constabulary: H.A. Wadsworth, compiler, *History of Lawrence, Massachusetts, with Portraits and Biographical Sketches* (Lawrence, MA: Lawrence Eagle Steam Job Printing Officer, 1880), 161-162.

61   to the state constabulary in 1872: *Biographical Review, Volume XXV, Containing Life Sketches of Leading Citizens of Norfolk County* (Boston: Biographical Review Publishing Co., 1898) 48.

61   and Vermont University: Gilbert Nash, compiler, *Historical Sketch of the Town of Weymouth, Massachusetts, from 1622 to 1884* (Weymouth: Weymouth Historical Society, 1885), 208.

61   Harvard University Medical School in 1871: Ibid., 210.

62   clear, bright, Sunday morning: *Climatological Record of the Weather Bureau, 1819-1892*, Microfilm Publication T907A, Roll 228, Fort Independence Station, Boston, MA, National Archives, Northeast Region, Waltham, MA.

62   locally called Whitmarsh's: Charles Devens Notebook, call number mss. N-1114, box number 8, folder F61-V58, Norfolk County Special Term for Trial of J. H. Costley, December 1874, Massachusetts Historical Society, Boston, MA.

62   "...jim-jams!" retorted Pelleran: "Murder Near Braintree; The Dead Body of a Woman With a Weight About Her Neck Found in the River; The Woman Shot Before Being Put Into the River; No Clew [*sic*] To Her Name," *Boston Daily Advertiser*, May 26, 1874. (jim-jams – colloquial: a state of nervousness or agitation; *delirium tremens*).

62   slowly rowed back to shore: Ibid.

63   red lining on the reverse: "Braintree; Mysterious Tragedy; The Body of a Murdered Woman Found in River," *Boston Journal*, May 26, 1874, morning edition.

63   extremities to the surface: David Owen, *Hidden Evidence, 40 True Crimes and How Forensic Science Helped Solve Them* (London: Copyright 2000, Quintet Publishing Limited, 2000), 100-105.

63   At the engine house: "The Gallows! Execution of Costley for the Murder of Julia Hawkes; History of the Crime; An Attempt to Escape Frustrated!; Details of the Execution; Picture of the Murderer and His Victim; Scenes and Incidents at the Execution," *Norfolk County Gazette*, June 26, 1875.

63   and a broad forehead: "Murder Near Braintree," May 26, 1874.

64   a ten-pointed star: Ibid.

64   seen the woman before: "Braintree; Mysterious Tragedy," May 26, 1874.

65   for further evidence: Ibid.

65 before she entered the river: "Criminal; Opening of the Costley Murder Trial," *Boston Daily Globe*, December 29, 1874.

66 pictures of the woman's features: "Braintree; Mysterious Tragedy," May 26, 1874.

66 Cemetery in Weymouth Landing: Ibid. She is buried in lot 81EE per Village Cemetery Superintendent Arthur Rogers.

66 replaced the coffin lid: "An Awful Murder," *Quincy Patriot*, May 30, 1874.

67 the manager of a hotel in Hanover: "The Monatiquot River Mystery; Body Fully Identified; Robbery the Motive of the Crime; Rumored Arrest of the Murderer," *Boston Journal*, May 27, 1874, morning edition.

67 in or near Saint John, New Brunswick: "The Murder of Julia Hawkes; Trial of J. H. Costley at Dedham; Second Day," *Boston Journal*, December 30, 1874; also, Massachusetts Vital Records, Deaths, Braintree, 1874, volume 266, page 228, Massachusetts State Archives, Boston, MA.

67 domestic servant in his home: *Massachusetts State Census, 1855, Brookline (Julia Hocks)*

67 worked there as a cook: "The Murder of Julia Hawkes; Trial of J. H. Costley at Dedham; Second Day," *Boston Journal*, December 30, 1874.

68 Savin Hill section of Dorchester, Massachusetts: Ibid.

68 as a cook at the Howard House: Ibid.

68 was unemployed: Ibid.

68 on Bedford Street in Boston in 1872: Union Institution for Savings Bank Records, Account #16757, manuscript collection of John J. Burns Library, Boston College, Chestnut Hill, MA.

68 closed her account on April 3, 1874: Ibid.

68 dissuaded Julia from pursuing that idea: "The Monatiquot River Mystery," May 27, 1874.

69 at the Hanover depot: Charles Eben Fisher, *The Story of the Old Colony Railroad* (Taunton: By the author, 1919), 52.

69 directed the men to the Howard House hotel: "The Hawkes Murder; Additional Evidence for the Government; Third Day's Proceedings in the Supreme Court at Dedham; How the Prisoner Appears; Further Evidence Connecting Him with the Tragedy; Testimony of Chief Constable Boynton, Etc.," *Boston Daily Globe*, December 31, 1874.

69 renamed it the Howard House: Dwelley and Simmons, *History of the Town of Hanover, Massachusetts* (Hanover: Town of Hanover, MA, 1910); 265.

69   an annual rate of $475: "The Murder of Julia Hawkes; Trial of J. H. Costley at Dedham; Third Day," *Boston Journal*, December 31, 1874.

69   moustache and goatee: "The Weymouth Tragedy; The Guilt of Costley Apparently Proven; The Money of the Murdered Woman in His Possession, Etc.; *Boston Daily Globe*, May 29, 1874.

70   shipped her trunks to Boston: "The Hawkes Tragedy; Fourth Day of the Trial of James H. Costley," *Boston Daily Globe,* January 1, 1875.

70   with the initials J. H. C.: "The Weymouth Tragedy; Additional Disclosures," May 29, 1874.

71   end was freshly cut: "Suburban Notes; The Hanover Murder," *Boston Daily Globe*, May 30, 1874, page 8.

71   "...got away on the four o'clock train": "The Murder of Julia Hawkes; Trial of J. H. Costley at Dedham," *Boston Journal*, January 1, 1875.

71   marked Union Institution for Savings: "The Murder of Julia Hawkes; Startling Disclosures; The Victim's Money Found in the Possession of Costley; A Bloody Room in the Hanover House," *Boston Journal*, May 29, 1874, morning edition.

71   brought them home from the service after the war: "The Murder of Julia Hawkes," January 1, 1875.

71   no improper use...of them: "The Hawkes Tragedy," January 1, 1875.

72   to Plymouth Jail without bail: "An Awful Murder," *Quincy Patriot*, May 30, 1874.

72   the goose they had found: "The Murder of Julia Hawkes," January 1, 1875.

73   imbedded in Hawkes's brain: "The Hanover Murder," *Boston Daily Globe*, June 1, 1874.

74   "...the stripes are different": "The Hawkes Tragedy," January 1, 1875.

74   and returned to Hanover: "The Murder of Julia Hawkes," January 1, 1875.

74   "...nothing further to say," Costley retorted: Ibid.

75   as a teamster: "Took Tickets at Circus; But is Now a New Hampshire Lawmaker; The Manager of Whitmore and Clark's Minstrels; Tells the Interesting Story of His Life – Hank White," *Boston Daily Globe*, November 2, 1891. (Ezra P. Hardy, wagon master for the Thayer and Noyes Circus, hired Costley in a small town near Halifax, Nova Scotia, to drive a team).

75   and a watchman for the ticket wagon: "The Hanging of James H. Costley for the Murder of Julia Hawkes," *The Sun*, [New York, NY], June 26, 1875.

75   assumed the hotel's management: "The Murder of Julia Hawkes; Third Day," December 31, 1874.

76   "...otherwise acted very strangely": "The End! Execution of Costley," *Dedham Transcript*, June 26, 1875.

76   caused by lead poisoning: Massachusetts Vital Records, Deaths, Hanover, 1873, volume 257, page 363, Massachusetts State Archives, Boston, MA.

77   liquor from the nozzle: "The Murder of Julia Hawkes; Additional Evidence Against Costley; Discovery of Her Missing Shoe; New Cartridges Found in the Chimney of the Hanover House," *Boston Journal*, June 1, 1874.

77   McCurdy never saw her again: "The Murder of Julia Hawkes: Second Day," December 30, 1874.

78   Stedman produced Julia's...passbook: "The Murder of Julia Hawkes; Startling Disclosures," May 29, 1874.

78   her usual and buoyant happy self: "The Weymouth Tragedy; Additional Disclosures," May 29, 1874.

78   open his own hotel: "The Murder of Julia Hawkes; Additional Particulars," *Boston Journal*, May 30, 1874.

79   until Costley completed his plans: "Criminal; Opening of the Costley Murder Trial," December 29, 1874.

79   to them, at least temporarily: "The Weymouth Tragedy; Additional Disclosures," May 29, 1874.

79   hadn't seen her since then: "The Murder of Julia Hawkes; Second Day," December 30, 1874.

80   "...insist on it, put it in": Ibid.

80   that evening for several months: Ibid.

80   last time Arbuckle saw Julia: Ibid.

81   "J. H. Costello and wife, Duxbury, Mass": Ibid.

81   take the team to Weymouth Landing: "The Murder of Julia Hawkes; Additional Evidence Against Costley," June 1, 1874.

81   one seemed unusually heavy: "The Hanover Murder," *Boston Daily Globe*, June 1, 1874.

81   square box buggy for Costley: "The Murder of Julia Hawkes; Second Day," December 30, 1874.

81   "I wish it was," Costley replied: Charles Devens Notebook.

82   could not positively identify him: "The Murder of Julia Hawkes," January 1, 1875.

82   11:00 a.m. Saturday, June 13: "Untitled," *Lowell Daily Citizen and News*, June 8, 1874, Column F.

83   "...murder of the said Julia Hawkes": "The Hawkes Murder," *Quincy Patriot*, June 6, 1874.

84   "...his face showed mental discomposure": "Costley," *Weymouth Weekly Gazette and Reporter*, June 19, 1874.

84   north, east, and west sides: Frank Smith, *A History of Dedham, Massachusetts* (Dedham: The Transcript Press, Inc., 1936), 540-541.

84   ladies' seminary rather than a prison": "Dedham's Jail; Amy Robsart Visits the Institution," *Boston Post*, April 21, 1893.

84   under the roof supplied water: Smith, *A History of Dedham*, 541.

84   caused a mortal wound: "Costley," June 19, 1874. Also, "Saturday," *Quincy Patriot*, June 20, 1874.

85   Judicial Court for trial: "Costley Indicted," *Boston Daily Globe*, Friday, September 11, 1874.

85   using the first name "John": "The Murder of Julia Hawkes; Trial of J. H. Costley at Dedham," *Boston Journal*, December 29, 1874.

86   after he entered the depot: "The Murder of Julia Hawkes; Second Day," December 30, 1874.

87   ever held in Norfolk County: "Dedham; The Hawkes Murder," *Boston Daily Globe*, December 2, 1874.

87   light rain was falling: "Meteorological: The Weather in Boston Yesterday," *Boston Daily Globe*, December 29, 1874; also, *Surface Weather Observations* (Boston: Signal Service, U.S. Army, Division of Telegrams and Reports for the Benefit of Commerce, 1874), 174, 203; Boston Public Library call number QC984.M4 S97x. (It was 44 degrees at 7:00 a.m. and 48 degrees by 2:00 p.m. with light rain).

88   fancy wrought-iron latticework: Bruce Watson, *Sacco and Vanzetti: The Men, the Murders, and the Judgment of Mankind* (New York: Viking Penguin, 2007), 103.

88   eight feet from the jury box: Watson, *Sacco and Vanzetti*, 145.

88   The original building in 1863: Dedham Historical Society, *The Dedham Historical Register, Volume IV* (Dedham: Dedham Historical Society, 1893), 8-14.

88   terra cotta walls: Watson, *Sacco and Vanzetti*, 104.

88   from Norwood as jury foreman: "The Murder of Julia Hawkes," December 29, 1874.

88   "...informal and sufficiently void": Ibid.

89   Justice Wells overruled Cheney's motion: Ibid.

90   the wound caused the woman's death: Ibid.

90   at the receiving tomb in Village Cemetery: Ibid.

90   Smith last saw her: Ibid.

91   When they last saw her: "The Murder of Julia Hawkes; Second Day," December 30, 1874.

91   proved damaging to the defendant: Ibid.

91   "...I don't know where Camden Street is": Ibid.

92   "...neuralgia pains in the spine": Ibid.

92   positively identified him: Ibid.

93   the man they had seen at the stable: Ibid.

93   and Costley laughed: Charles Devens Notebook.

93   confirmed that it was: "The Murder of Julia Hawkes; Second Day," December 30, 1874.

98   an attempt to discredit his testimony: "The Murder of Julia Hawkes; Third Day," December 31, 1874.

99   "...eyes are bent upon him": "The Hawkes Murder; Additional Evidence for the Government," December 31, 1874.

99   blood was human or animal: Charles G. Davis, *Report of the Trial of Samuel M. Andrews, Indicted for the Murder of Cornelius Holmes, Before the Supreme Judicial Court of Massachusetts, December 11, 1868, Including the Rulings of the Court Upon Many Questions of Law, and a Full Statement of Authorities Upon the Subject of Transitory Insanity* (New York: Hurd and Houghton, 1869) 66-67.

100   originating from a human source: George F. Shrady, Editor, *Medical Record – A Weekly Journal of Medicine and Surgery* (New York: William Wood and Co., 1895), 685.

100   developed the precipitin test: Colin Evans, *Criminal Investigations: Crime Scene Investigation* (New York: Infobase Publishing, 2009), 11.

100   established the same year: Ibid.

100   Clear skies, frigid temperatures, and a biting wind: "The New Year," *Boston Post*, January 1, 1875.

100   Detective Pinkham was the government's first witness: "The Murder of Julia Hawkes," January 1, 1875.

104   $1.3 million in today's economy: L. Officer and S. Williamson, *Purchasing Power of Money in the United States from 1774 to 2008.* Measuring Worth, 2009.

104   adjourned until the next day: "The Murder of Julia Hawkes," January 1, 1875.

104   The fifth day of trial opened: "The Murder of Julia Hawkes; Trial of J. H. Costley at Dedham; Fifth Day," *Boston Journal*, January 2, 1875.

105   Riedell denied doing so: Ibid.

105   any further with his visitor: "The Julia Hawkes Tragedy," *Weymouth Weekly Gazette and Reporter*, June 12, 1874.

105   When Franklin Howard was called again: "The Murder of Julia Hawkes, Fifth Day," January 2, 1875.

107   "...proof beyond reasonable doubt": "The Murder of Julia Hawkes, Fifth Day," January 2, 1875.

110   could have resulted in instantaneous death: Ibid.

111   the following day and then adjourned: Ibid.

111   Light snow was falling: *Surface Weather Observations* (Boston: Signal Service, U.S. Army, Division of Telegrams and Reports for the Benefit of Commerce, 1875), 4; Boston Public Library call number QC984.M4 S97x.

111   reconvened at 8:00 a.m. on Saturday, January 2: "The Murder of Julia Hawkes; Costley Found Guilty of Murder; Arguments of Counsel and Charge of the Court," *Boston Journal*, January 4, 1875.

112   "...ordinarily falls to any human being": "The Murder of Julia Hawkes; Costley Found Guilty of Murder," January 4, 1875.

112   finished his summation: Ibid.

113   side whiskers grow longer: "The Murder of Julia Hawkes," December 29, 1874.

113   Attorney General Train began the closing argument: "The Murder of Julia Hawkes; Costley Found Guilty of Murder," January 4, 1875.

113   the court ordered a recess until seven fifteen: Ibid.

114   "...prosecuted in the county of Norfolk": Ibid.

114   "...punished in either county'": Ibid. Also, *Cases Argued and Determined in the Supreme Judicial Court of Massachusetts; Commonwealth vs. James H. Costley; Norfolk; February 1-16, 1875*, volume 118, page 19, (Boston: Houghton, Mifflin and Co., 1876).

114   "ragged edge of anxiety and despair": "Costley's Doom; He is Found Guilty of Murder in the First Degree," *Boston Daily Globe,* January 4, 1875.

115   no hard feelings against them: "The Murder of Julia Hawkes; Costley Found Guilty of Murder," January 4, 1875.

115   "I have nothing to say": "The End!" June 26, 1875.

116   smiling slightly as he passed them: Ibid.

116   tell his parents of Costley's fate: Ibid.

117   *...Ever grateful, J. Henry Costley*: Ibid.

117   sympathetic to Costley's cause: "Murdered Julia Hawkes Was Possibly Not Henry Costley's Only Victim. An Old Hanover Tragedy and a Dedham Hanging Vividly Recalled, Doubts About the Man's Guilt and the Doubts About His Burial," *Boston Daily Globe*, August 13, 1887.

118   "...escape through the jail's gate": "The Story of the Plot; The Details as Gained by *Globe* Reporters; An Interview With Sheriff Thomas; He Admits the Facts; The Nicely Laid Plan by Which Costley Was to Gain His Freedom," *Boston Daily Globe*, June 23, 1875.

118   from the cell area to the prison exit: "Attempted Liberation of James H. Costley," *Old Colony Memorial* [Plymouth, MA], June 24, 1875.

118 "...stood in the way of [my] liberty": "The Hanging of James H. Costley for the Murder of Julia Hawkes," June 26, 1875.

118 tendered his resignation: "The Story of the Plot," June 23, 1875.

118 his plan for freedom had failed: "Attempted Liberation of James H. Costley," June 24, 1875.

118 outside the jail's walls: "The Hanging of James H. Costley for the Murder of Julia Hawkes, June 26, 1875.

119 court overruled all exceptions: "Costley; The Condemned Murderer, Who Hangs, Friday; Exceptions in His Case Heard by the Full Bench, Yesterday; No Probability of a Stay of Proceedings; History of the Man and His Crime," *Boston Daily Globe*, June 22, 1875.

119 already assigned to the jail: "The End!" June 26, 1875.

119 murdering Betsey Frances Tirrell in Weymouth: Louis Atwood Cook, *The History of Norfolk County, Massachusetts, 1622-1918*, Volume 1 (New York-Chicago: The S. J. Clarke Publishing Company, 1918), 49.

119 his wife, Jane, in Milton. "Execution," *New-Bedford Mercury*, July 10, 1829; see also, Daniel Allen Hearn, *Legal Executions in New England; A Comprehensive Reference, 1623-1960* (Jefferson, NC: McFarland and Company, 1999), 213.

120 case-by-case basis: Ibid.

120 for ten dollars: "The Hanging of James H. Costley for the Murder of Julia Hawkes, June 26, 1875.

120 six feet into the air: Ibid.

120 the highest since July 1874: *Surface Weather Observations* (Boston: Signal Service, U.S. Army, Division of Telegrams and Reports for the Benefit of Commerce, 1875), 93; Boston Public Library call number QC984.M4 S97x.

121 lightning penetrated his cell window: Ibid.

121 "...happier than any whom I leave behind": "The Execution of Costley; His Last Hours; He Denies the Commission of Murder; The Final Act of the Tragedy; Death Calmly Met," *Boston Daily Globe*, June 26, 1875.

121 *...Truly gratefully, J. H. Costley*: "The End!" June 26, 1875.

121 *...Very respectfully, J. H. Costley*: "The Execution of Costley," June 26, 1875.

122 *...Gratefully, J. H. Costley – Dedham, June 25th 1875*: "The End!" June 26, 1875.

122 About three hundred fifty people: "The Execution of Costley," June 26, 1875.

122 fanned themselves with their hats: "Class Day," *Boston Post*, June 26, 1875; also, Army Signal Corps, *Annual Report of the Chief Signal-*

Officer, 1875 (Washington, D.C.: Government Printing Office, 1875), 153. The chief signal-officer reported a high temperature of eighty-eight degrees on June 25, 1875.

123   state detective Chase Philbrick: "The Gallows," *Boston Post*, June 26, 1875.

123   "...was prepared for the ordeal": Ibid.

123   he nodded and smiled in recognition: Ibid.

123   "...mercy and goodness of God": "The Execution of Costley," June 26, 1875.

124   "...the chair having been removed": Ibid.

124   "...have mercy on your soul": "The Gallows," *Boston Post*, June 26, 1875.

124   "...the murderer hung without motion": "The Execution of Costley," June 26, 1875.

124   out of the jail for fresh air: Ibid.

124   was lowered at 10:14 a.m.: "The Gallows," *Boston Post*, June 26, 1875.

124   pronounced him dead: Ibid.

124   hyoid bone in the larynx was crushed: Ibid.

124   hanged in Dedham Jail: Records of the Norfolk County Sheriff's Office; also, Watt Espy and J. O. Smykla, *Executions in the United States, 1608-1987: The Espy File*. [Machine-readable data file]. (Ann Arbor, MI: Inter-University Consortium for Political and Social Research, 1987).

124   at the state prison in Charlestown: Alan Rogers, *Murder and the Death Penalty in Massachusetts* (Amherst and Boston: University of Massachusetts Press, 2008), 110.

125   to attend the imposition of punishment: Frank Moore Colby and Harry Thurston Peck, eds., *The International Year Book, 1898* (New York: Dodd, Mead and Company, 1899), 504.

125   Francis Arnold of Hanover: "The End!" June 26, 1875.

125   buried in another plot: "The Execution of Costley," June 26, 1875.

125   oldest section of the cemetery: Hanover Center Cemetery, Hanover, MA, Cemetery Records.

125   Costley's final resting place: Lowell Ames Norris, "Evidence from a Low-Studded Attic" *Yankee Magazine*, September 1966 edition; Curt Norris, "The Case of the Scarlet Slipper" *True Police Cases,* June 1975 edition.

125   a cabinetmaker from South Abington: Massachusetts Vital Records, Marriages, Boston, 1879, volume 308, page 303, Massachusetts State Archives, Boston, MA.

125   died in Boston on February 24, 1882: Massachusetts Vital Records, Deaths, Boston, 1882, volume 339, page 48, Massachusetts State Archives, Boston, MA.

125   yards away from Costley's grave: Hanover Center Cemetery, Hanover, MA, Cemetery Records.

126   the grave of her beloved betrothed: "Ghosts and Gossip Tour," November 21, 2012, Hanover Historical Society, Rachel Lovett and Judy Grecco.

A Soap Box

131   to the superior court in 1898: William Thomas Davis, *History of the Judiciary of Massachusetts* (Boston: Boston Book Company, 1900) 266-267.

131   associate justice of the superior court in 1896: William Richard Cutter, ed., *Historic Homes and Places and Genealogical and Personal Memoirs Relating to the Families of Middlesex County, Massachusetts,* Volume IV (New York: Lewis Historical Publishing Company, 1908), 1563.

132   for the Southeastern District in 1901: Samuel Atkins Eliot, A.M., D.D., *Biographical History of Massachusetts: Biographies and Autobiographies of the Leading Men in the State*, Volume II (Boston: Massachusetts Biography Society, 1909).

132   was sentenced to life in prison: Ibid.

132   Joseph and his brother were acquitted: "Seerys Innocent; Jury's Verdict 'Not Guilty' on Charge of Matricide," *Boston Daily Globe*, December 21, 1899; also, "Jury Complete; Trial of John and Joseph Seery Begun in Earnest," *Boston Daily Globe*, December 13, 1899.

132   of the Brockton Police Court a year later: *Men of Progress: One Thousand Biographical Sketches and Portraits of Leaders in Business and Professional Life in the Commonwealth of Massachusetts*, Edwin M. Bacon, ed. (Boston: New England Magazine, 1896), 368.

132   after a four-day trial: "For His Life; Arthur A. Albee to be Tried at Plymouth" *Boston Daily Globe*, September 30, 1895; also, "Not Guilty; Verdict of the Jury in Albee Murder Trial," *Boston Daily Globe*, October 43, 1895.

132   people in the same manner: "Toppan Trial; Alleged Prisoner in Court Today," *Boston Daily Globe*, June 23, 1902; also, "Jane Toppan Insane, Found Not Guilty," *Boston Daily Globe*, June 24, 1902.

133 Boston University in 1901: Historical Register of Boston University; Fourth Decennial Issue, 1869-1901 (Boston: Boston University, 1901), 121.

133 Second Plymouth District in 1890: Henry Harrison Metcalf and John Norris Clintock, eds., *The Granite Monthly: A New Hampshire Magazine devoted to History, Biography, Literature and State Progress*, Volume XLI (Concord: Granite Monthly Publishing Company, 1909), 261-263.

133 by family and friends: "State Police Force of Massachusetts," *Boston Daily Globe*, November 24, 1902.

133 with his father, a fisherman: 1860 United States Federal Census, Swampscott, Essex County, Massachusetts, July 28, 1860, 17.

133 history of the state police: "Full-Fledged Captain," *Boston Daily Globe*, May 9, 1905.

133 around the state before the Hanover murder: "Hand of the Defence [*sic*] Shown in Blondin Case," *Boston Post*, December 13, 1902.

133 First Massachusetts Infantry: "Death in Taunton of Col. Alfred B. Hodges," *Boston Daily Globe*, May 7, 1918.

133 the battle and siege of Port Hudson, Louisiana, in 1863: *Grand Army of the Republic: Department of Massachusetts; Personal War Sketches of the Members of William H. Bartlett Post No. 3 of Taunton* (Philadelphia: L. H. Everts, 1890), 18. (Original at Old Colony Historical Society, Taunton, MA)

134 in Taunton prior to joining the force: Alanson Borden, *Our County and Its People; A Descriptive and Biographical Record of Bristol County Massachusetts*, (Boston: The Boston History Company, 1899), 115.

135 Kushion Komfort shoes for ladies: Massachusetts City Directories: *Rockland, 1902, Hanover Directory*, 140.

135 New York, New Haven and Hartford Railroad in 1899: Charles Eben Fisher, *The Story of the Old Colony Railroad* (Taunton: By the author, 1919) 53, 134.

136 competed with Tripp for guests: Jedediah Dwelley and John F. Simmons, *History of the Town of Hanover, Massachusetts with Family Genealogies* (Hanover: Town of Hanover, 1910), 265.

136 was a community of 2,152 people: Massachusetts City Directories: *Rockland, 1902, Hanover Directory*, 140.

136 leased the first floor to retail businesses: Barbara U. Barker and Leslie J. Molyneaux, *Images of America: Hanover* (Charleston, SC: Arcadia Publishing, 1904), 25-66.

137 laundry service in Hanover at the time: Massachusetts City Directories – *Rockland 1902, Hanover Directory, Laundry*, 178.

137   set up his own laundry shop: *The Salem and Beverly Directory 1904* (Salem, MA: Henry M. Meek Publishing Co., 1904), 663, listing of Quong Sing, Laundry, 79 Cabot Street, Beverly, MA.

137   typically working ten....day: Judy Yung, Gordon H. Chang and Him Mark Lai, eds., *Chinese American Voices, From the Gold Rush to the Present* (Berkeley, CA: Regents of the University of California, 2006), 183.

137   between eight and twenty dollars a week: Shehong Chen, *Reconstructing the Chinese American Experience in Lowell, Massachusetts, 1870s-1970s, Making a Living as Laundry Men, 1876-1920* (Boston: Institute for Asian American Studies, University of Massachusetts, 2003).

138   shirt accessories of the era: Renqiu Yu, *To Save China, To Save Ourselves: The Chinese Hand Laundry Alliance of New York* (Philadelphia: Temple University Press, 1992), 11.

138   called him "John": "Chinaman Foully Slain; Quong Sing Murdered in Hanover Yesterday Noon; Body Found in Tub of Water; Alleged Assailant in Custody," *Rockland Standard and Plymouth County Advertiser*, January 29, 1904.

138   as soon as he had earned a competence: "Hanover," *Rockland Standard and Plymouth County Advertiser*, February 5, 1904.

139   his plan to return home: Frankie Hutton and Barbara Strauss Reed, eds., *Outsiders in 19th Century Press History: Multicultural Perspectives* (Bowling Green, OH: Bowling Green State University Popular Press, 1995), 72.

139   profoundly ignorant, and naturally violent: Alan Rogers, *Murder and the Death Penalty in Massachusetts* (Amherst and Boston: University of Massachusetts Press, 2008), 140.

140   entered the country under that alias: Tom Chin, e-mail message to author, August 15, 2008. Chinese Historical Society New England, Boston, MA.

140   Southern China as his place of origin: Tom Chin, e-mail message to author, "Re: Help with Name," August 15, 2008.

140   hoped to reunite with them someday: "Hanover," February 5, 1904.

140   on April 12, 1883: Prince Edward Island Baptismal Index, Saint Dunstan's Basilica Baptismal Records, book 4, page 211.

140   in a family of nine: HS9.01/Series 305, Charlestown State Prison, Inmate Case Files, #13408 – Social Summary, Massachusetts State Archives, Boston, MA.

140   work and support the family: Ibid.

140   Hickey & Nicholson and T. B. Riley: "Ryan's Dramatic Murder Defense; Admits Killing Quong Sing, Claiming That Chinaman Attacked Him," *Boston Daily Globe*, June 10, 1904; see also, HS9.01/Series 305, Charlestown State Prison, Inmate Case Files.

140   small bundles for final packing: HS9.01/Series 305, Charlestown State Prison, Inmate Case Files, #13408; Social Case History, page 3, Massachusetts State Archives, Boston, MA. Also, Mullgart, Louis Christian, *All About Tobacco* (Las Vegas, NV: Epic Publishing, 2014).

140   between Charlottetown and Boston: "A Dead Chinaman; A Strange Crime," *Boston Herald*, January 29, 1904.

140   disembarked in Boston: Charlestown State Prison, Inmate Case Files.

141   from the Washington Credit Company: Ibid.

141   one dollar a week plus interest: "Ryan's Dramatic Murder Defense," June 10, 1904.

141   at the home of…Pierce, on Water Street: Ibid.

141   seventeen-year-old Katie Murray: Fifth Census of Canada, 1911, Prince Edward Island, District 141, Queens County, page 8.

141   an additional $1.75 a week: "Seen Running; Ryan's Movements on Day of Murder; Some Testify He Appeared Ill at Ease; His Money Affairs Gone Into at the Trial," *Boston Daily Globe*, June 9, 1904; "Murder of Quong Sing the Charge," *Boston Herald*, June 8, 1904.

141   fifty degrees on Saturday, January 23: J.W. Smith, U. S. Department of Agriculture, Climate and Crop Service of the Weather Bureau: Central Office: Washington, DC. New England Section: Boston, MA, Volume XVI, Number 1, page 8: Boston Public Library, Government Documents, Climatological Data – New England, Microfiche 16.

141   the ninety-pound laundryman in the face: Charlestown State Prison, Inmate Case Files.

141   "…he is able to defend himself": "Hanover," *Rockland Standard and Plymouth County Advertiser*, January 29, 1904.

142   the eight-fifteen train to Boston: "Quong Sing Killed at Laundry in Hanover," *Boston Daily Globe*, January 29, 1904.

142   left Russell in his care: "His Property; Revolver and Watch of Cyrus L. Ryan; That Claim is Made for Him by His Sweetheart, Katie Murray; She Says They Were not on Way to be Married," *Boston Daily Globe*, February 1, 1904.

142   the man responsible for the burglary: "Quong Sing Killed at Laundry in Hanover," January 29, 1904.

142   the nearby home of Frederick Pierce: "Chinaman Foully Slain," January 29, 1904.

142   It was four degrees: J.W. Smith, U. S. Department of Agriculture, Climate and Crop Service of the Weather Bureau: Central Office: Washington, DC. New England Section: Boston, MA, Volume XVI, Number 1, page 8: Boston Public Library, Government Documents, Climatological Data – New England, Microfiche 16.

143   slipped out the door: "C. L. Ryan's Trial; Accused of Murder of Quong Sing; Defendant Admits the Chinaman Died in His Hands," *Old Colony Memorial* [Plymouth, MA], June 11, 1904.

143   came in for a shave: Ibid.

143   left a few minutes later: "Ryan's Dramatic Murder Defense," June 10, 1904.

143   Ryan waved back: "C. L. Ryan's Trial," June 11, 1904.

143   called out to Quong Sing: Ibid.

143   nearby home for some lunch: "Robbery the Motive; C. L. Ryan Followed to Boston and Arrested," *Boston Post*, January 29, 1904.

143   Quong ironed a shirt: "C. L. Ryan's Trial," June 11, 1904.

143   "...I did not want to let him one": "Seen Running," June 9, 1904.

144   toward Elm Street and Curtis Crossing: Ibid.

144   walking at a brisk pace: "C. L. Ryan's Trial," June 11, 1904.

144   returned to his cart: "Seen Running," June 9, 1904.

144   "...I mean to see what it is": "Quan [*sic*] Sing Killed in Laundry in Hanover," *Boston Daily Globe*, January 29, 1904.

145   hole in a shirt on Quong's ironing board: Ibid.

145   into the drying room: Ibid.

145   box on his shoulders: "C. L. Ryan's Trial," June 11, 1904.

145   attempted to resuscitate him: "Seen Running," June 9, 1904.

145   hand had grasped it from behind: "C. L. Ryan's Trial," June 11, 1904.

146   they knew Quong Sing owned: "A Dead Chinaman; A Strange Crime," January 29, 1904.

146   Wade sent a telegraph: "C. L. Ryan's Trial," June 11, 1904.

146   a small trunk and a satchel: "A Dead Chinaman; A Strange Crime," January 29, 1904.

146   four times between Hanover and North Abington.: "Seen Running," June 9, 1904.

147   took Ryan by the collar: "Robbery the Motive," January 29, 1904.

147   "...find out who you are": "Caught at South Station; Ryan Arrested by Capt. Proctor of State Police as He Stepped from Train," *Boston Daily Globe*, January 29, 1904.

148   basement of the statehouse on Beacon Hill: "Ryan Confesses He Killed Quong," *Boston Herald*, June 10, 1904.

149   with a coworker before he left Hanover: "Probe Murder of Chinaman," *Boston Post*, January 31, 1904.

149   "It was a gift from my sister," insisted Ryan: "A Dead Chinaman; A Strange Crime," January 29, 1904.

149   with her sister-in-law in Cambridge: Ibid.

149   handed the items to Proctor: "Claims Ryan Not Murderer," *Boston Herald*, January 30, 1904.

150   to Boston the year before: Ibid.

150   could identify them: "A Dead Chinaman; A Strange Crime," January 29, 1904.

150   to claim Quong Sing's body and property: "Ryan Is Held Without Bail," *Boston Daily Globe*, January 30, 1904.

151   ordered Ryan held without bail: Ibid.

151   marrying him after his acquittal: "Probing Murder of Drowned Chinaman; Ryan's Sweetheart Says Cyrus Accused Unjustly," *Boston Post*, January 30, 1904.

152   cause of death as drowning: "C. L. Ryan's Trial," June 11, 1904.

152   released the body to Sparrell: Massachusetts Vital Records, Deaths, Hanover, 1904, volume 47, page 83, Massachusetts Archives, Boston, MA.

152   forty-eight when he died: Ibid.

152   for final disposition: Mount Hope Cemetery records, Boston, MA: Soo Hoo Yee Yoke, burial, 1904, Section E, Grave 56. Exhumation, 1912.

152   estate had been settled in probate court: Ibid.

152   claim finished and unfinished laundry: "Hanover," *Rockland Standard*, February 12, 1904.

153   left the shirt...months before: "C. L. Ryan's Trial," June 11, 1904.

153   dollar was found in Quong's clothing: "Seen Running," June 9, 1904.

153   nine more dollars: "A Dead Chinaman; A Strange Crime," January 29, 1904.

153   "...between the Corners and his home here": "His Property," February 1, 1904.

154   "A man can do considerable in ten minutes": "To Clear Ryan," *Boston Daily Globe*, January 31, 1904.

154   knew that Ryan owned a silver watch: Ibid.

155   have the time to kill Quong Sing: "His Property," February 1, 1904.

155   innocent of the charge against him: Ibid.

155   pork, fowl, rice, and wine: "Funeral of Murdered Chinaman Free From All Disturbance," *Boston Daily Globe*, October 12, 1903.

155   laundryman was laid to rest: "Slain Chinaman Rests in Grave," *Boston Herald*, February 1, 1904.

155   shipped it to China for reburial: Mount Hope Cemetery records, Boston, MA: Soo Hoo Yee Yoke, burial, 1904, Section E, Grave 56; Exhumation, 1912.

156   being held without bail: "For Murder," *Boston Daily Globe*, February 5, 1904.

156   for trial in Plymouth Superior Court: "C. L. Ryan's Trial," June 11, 1904.

156   enclosure that served as the prisoners dock: "Held for Trial; Arraignment at Plymouth of Henry Gunn for the Murder of his Father at Bridgewater, Mass.," *Boston Post*, February 20, 1880; also, "To Report Murder Trial; Sheriff Porter Makes Arrangements for Newspaper Men At Trial of Mrs. Eaton," *Old Colony Memorial*, Plymouth, MA, October 10, 1913.

157   Bagni's 1902 trial: "Jury Disagrees; Were Out 24 Hours in Bagni Murder Trial," *Boston Daily Globe*, July 4, 1902.

157   Blondin murder trial: "Blondin Scores First Point, Jury Goes to Lowell Today," *Boston Post*, December 2, 1902.

157   sentenced to life in prison: "To Prison for Life; Sentence Imposed Upon Michael J. Kilroy," *Boston Daily Globe*, October 11, 1902.

157   Blondin received a life sentence: "Blondin Dies in Prison; Served 17 Years for Murder of His Wife," *Boston Post*, December 17, 1919.

157   directed verdict of not guilty: "Fosburgh's Acquittal Ordered by Court; Event of Morning of Aug. 20 Now More Than Ever a Mystery; Scene of Enthusiasm in the Court Room as the Judge Took Unusual Action," *Boston Daily Globe*, July 27, 1901.

157   "God save the commonwealth of Massachusetts: "On Trial for His Life," *Rockland Standard*, June 10, 1904

157   First Church at Town Square: Massachusetts City Directories, *Plymouth, 1905*, page 199.

157   trial proceedings began at 10:40 a.m.: Ibid.

158   and Bradford Wilder: "Ryan Faces Murder Charge," *Boston Herald*, June 7, 1904.

158   the youngest, forty-six: Massachusetts Bureau of Vital Records and Statistics, Boston, MA; all ages determined by consulting birth records for each juror.

158   "...nervous, quick, hustling, and bespectacled": "Blondin Scores First Point, Jury Goes to Lowell Today," *Boston Post*, December 2, 1902.

158   hovering around sixty degrees: "Weather," *Boston Daily Globe*, June 6 and June 7, 1904.

158   court was adjourned until the following morning: "C. L. Ryan's Trial," June 11, 1904.

158   The second day of proceedings: "In Laundry," *Boston Daily Globe*, June 8, 1904.

159   smiled and appeared confident: "Murder of Quong Sing the Charge," June 8, 1904.

159   movements on the day of the murder: "C. L. Ryan's Trial," June 11, 1904.

159   a number of debts with creditors: "Murder of Quong Sing the Charge," June 8, 1904.

160   air passages of the lungs inflamed: "In Laundry," *Boston Daily Globe*, June 8, 1904.

160   three weeks after he arrived: Ibid.

162   adjourned for the day following Paxton's testimony: "C. L. Ryan's Trial," June 11, 1904.

162   It was raining when French opened the trial's third day: "Seen Running," June 9, 1904; also, "Weather," *Boston Daily Globe*, June 8, 1904.

163   to the shop at 11:00 a.m.: C. L. Ryan's Trial," June 11, 1904.

163   by Ryan's family and friends: Ibid.

163   2:15 that afternoon": "Between 11 and 12 o'clock; Witnesses Saw Ryan in Sing's Laundry; Government Further Presents Case at Plymouth; Court Room Crowded at Today's Opening," *Boston Daily Globe*, June 8, 1904.

163   "...didn't mention his trunk": Ibid.

164   "No, I did not": Ibid.

164   "...and a young lady": Ibid.

165   had never seen Ryan with a revolver: Ibid.

165   her half-brother, Fred Pierce: "Seen Running," June 9, 1904.

165   on a shelf over his bed: "C. L. Ryan's Trial," June 11, 1904.

165   in his brother's shop: "Seen Running," June 9, 1904.

166   "...had not been disturbed": "Between 11 and 12 o'clock," June 8, 1904.

166   "...open more or less": Ibid.

166   corroborated Waterman's testimony: "C. L. Ryan's Trial," June 11, 1904.

167   "...money to pay his board": "Seen Running," June 9, 1904.

167   while handing over the money: Ibid.

167   Hobart was the final witness for the day: Ibid.

167   Court reconvened at 9:00 a.m.: "Admit the Killing; Counsel for Ryan Claim Self Defense; Attorneys Spring Surprise at Plymouth; Commonwealth Rests Its Case," *Boston Daily Globe*, June 9, 1904.

167   in his deep bass voice: "Hand of the Defence [*sic*] Shown in the Blondin Case," *Boston Post*, December 13, 1902.

169   could not find his shirt": "Admit the Killing," June 9, 1904.

169   fired more than once or twice: Ibid.

169   in quantities of fifty: Ibid.

169   DA French then rested his case: Ibid.

170   "We will introduce evidence…took the train for Boston": "On Trial for His Life," June 10, 1904.

170   recessed until 1:00 p.m.: "Ryan's Dramatic Murder Defense," June 10, 1904.

170   "…we left Hanover at that time": "Ryan Confesses He Killed Quong," June 10, 1904.

171   "…stand by him to the last": "Sweetheart Says Cyrus Accused Unjustly," June 10, 1904.

171   "hard up for money": "Ryan's Dramatic Murder Defense," June 10, 1904.

171   belonged to a …society: "Ryan Confesses He Killed Quong," June 10, 1904.

171   defense called Cyrus Ryan: "Ryan's Dramatic Murder Defense," June 10, 1904.

173   "…I would be put in jail": Ibid.

174   "…there was a revolver in his right hand": "C. L. Ryan's Trial," June 11, 1904.

175   the Chinaman was in it," Ryan insisted: "Ryan Weeps Like a Child; Rigidly Examined by Dist. Atty. French; Further Describes the Fatal Struggle with Quong Sing; Don't Know Why He Put Body in Tub," *Boston Daily Globe*, June 10, 1904.

176   not by drowning: "Say Quong Sing Was Not Drowned," *Boston Herald*, June 11, 1904.

176   entered Quong Sing's lungs: Charlestown State Prison, Inmate Case Files.

176   "No, it is not," said Ryan: "From Rupture of Heart," *Boston Daily Globe*, June 11, 1904.

176   "We have shown the character…": "'Must Be a Motive;' Judge Bixby Argues for Ryan at Plymouth; Says Jury Can't Otherwise Find Verdict of Murder; Character Should Have Some Weight," *Boston Daily Globe*, June 11, 1904.

177   not responsible for his demise: Ibid.

177   "The question is…": Ibid.

178   "…tell the story he did": Ibid.

178   "…but of robbing him": Ibid.

178 "It is admitted by the defendant...": Ibid.

179 "...counsel as to the verdict": Ibid.

179 "...gazed steadily at the jury": "Second Degree," *Boston Daily Globe*, June 12, 1904

179 in the second degree: "Convicted and Sentenced," *Old Colony Memorial* [Plymouth, MA], June 18, 1904.

179 "I wish it'd been the chair," but later retracted his statement: Ibid.

180 back to Plymouth Jail: "Second Degree," June 12, 1904.

180 his transfer to Charlestown: "Given Life Sentence," *Boston Daily Globe*, June 16, 1904.

180 not second-degree murder: Commitment Registers, Charlestown State Prison, September 1882-December 1930, roll #2, Massachusetts Archives, Boston, MA.

180 for murdering several children: Harold Schechter, *Fiend: The Shocking True Story of America's Youngest Serial Killer* (New York: Pocket Books/Simon & Schuster, 2000).

180 the prison contained eight hundred fifty cells: Theresa Mitchell Barbo, *The Cape Cod Murder of 1899: Edwin Ray Snow's Punishment and Redemption* (Charleston, SC: The History Press, 2007), 29.

181 and five assistant watchmen: Board of Prison Commissioners, *Fourth Annual Report of the Board of Prison Commissioners of Massachusetts for the Year Ending September 30, 1904*, (Boston: Wright & Potter Printing Co., State Printers, 1905), 3-4.

181 the ninth prisoner serving a life sentence: Ibid., 9.

181 Ryan was given bread and water: Schechter, *Fiend: The Shocking True Story of America's Youngest Serial Killer*, 261.

181 in the prison shoe shop: 1910 United States Federal Census, Boston Ward 5, Suffolk County, Massachusetts, April 22, 1910, 7A.

181 fighting in the shoe shop: Charlestown State Prison, Inmate Case Files.

181 all constructed with brick, stone, and concrete. D. Hamilton Hurd, *History of Plymouth County, Massachusetts, with Biographical Sketches of Man of its Pioneers and Prominent Men*, (Philadelphia: J. W. Lewis & Company, 1884), 806.

181 adjust to the prison environment: *The Boston Medical and Surgical Journal*, Volume CLXXVI, Boston: The Boston Medical and Surgical Journal Society, Inc., 1917), 353.

181 to Charlestown on September 8, 1913: Commitment Registers, Charlestown State Prison.

182 "...insanity in order to go to Bridgewater": HS9.01/Series 292x, Charlestown State Prison, Punishment Books, volume 5, page 143; Massachusetts State Archives, Boston, MA.

182 "...very little from punishment": Charlestown State Prison, Inmate Case Files.

182 represented by Attorney Peter Maher: Commission on Economy and Efficiency, *The Commonwealth of Massachusetts; Functions, Organization and Administration of the Departments in the Executive Branch of the State Government*, (Boston: Wright & Potter Printing Company, 1914), 476.

184 to await the governor's decision: Charlestown State Prison, Inmate Case Files.

184 from the governor's office: Ibid.

184 rejected his petition for pardon: Ibid.

184 "...is interested in good reading...": Charlestown State Prison, Inmate Case Files.

185 *...Your affectionate son, C. L. Ryan*: Ibid.

186 returned to the State Prison on December 17, 1920: Commitment Registers, Charlestown State Prison.

186 assaulting an officer with a chair: HS9.01/Series 292x, Charlestown State Prison, Punishment Books, volume 6, page 370; Massachusetts State Archives, Boston, MA.

186 on August 23, 1927: Bruce Watson, *Sacco and Vanzetti: The Men, the Murders, and the Judgment of Mankind* (New York: Viking Penguin, 2007).

186 ...Love to all from Cyrus: Charlestown State Prison, Inmate Case Files.

187 "...nor anyone in particular": Ibid.

187 for the last time fifteen months later: Commitment Registers, Charlestown State Prison.

187 for more serious violations: Ibid.

187 blame others instead: Scott O. Lilienfeld and Hal Arkowitz. "What 'Psychopath' Means; It Is Not Quite What You May Think." *Scientific American*, November 28, 2007.

188 needed during his formative years: Interview with Margaret Johnson, PhD., Professor of Psychology, Bridgewater State University, Bridgewater, MA.

188 "...not an underlying cause": Town of Bridgewater, Massachusetts, Certificate of Death 143, Cyrus L. Ryan, December 4, 1962.

189 to Pine Hill Cemetery in Tewksbury: Ibid.

189 in Cornwall, Prince Edward Island: John MacPhail Collins, *MacPhail from the Isle of Mull to Prince Edward Island: Being the Genealogies of the Several Families of MacPhail on that Island* (Sarnia, Ontario: J. M. Collins, 2006), 57-3.

189   buried in Rockland: Massachusetts Vital Records, Deaths, Rockland, 1949, volume 81, page 34, certificate 28, Massachusetts Bureau of Vital Records and Statistics, Boston, MA.

189   in New Calvary Cemetery, Boston: Massachusetts Vital Records, Deaths, Boston, 1935, volume 26, page 279, certificate 11098, Massachusetts Bureau of Vital Records and Statistics, Boston, MA.

Bibliography

Foreword

Bechtel, H. Kenneth. *State Police in the United States, a Socio-Historical Analysis*. Westport, CT: Greenwood Press, 1995.

Blackstone, Sir William. *Commentaries on the Laws of England in Four Books, Book Four: of Public Wrongs*. Philadelphia: Rees Welsh & Co., 1902.

Crocker, Uriel H., and Barker, James M. *The Public Statutes of the Commonwealth of Massachusetts*. Boston: Rand, Avery and Company, 1882.

Massachusetts Civil Service Commissioners. *First Annual report of the Civil Service Commissioners of Massachusetts*. Boston: Wright & Potter Printing Company, 1885.

Massachusetts Civil Service Commissioners. *Thirteenth Annual Report of the Civil Service Commissioners of Massachusetts*. Boston: Wright & Potter Printing Company, 1897.

Powers, William F. *The One Hundred Year Vigil, the Story of the Massachusetts State Police*. Foxboro, MA: The Foxboro Company, 1965.

Rogers, Alan. *Murder and the Death Penalty in Massachusetts*. Amherst and Boston: University of Massachusetts Press, 2008.

Roth, Mitchel P. *Crime and Punishment; a History of the Criminal Justice System*," 2nd ed. Belmont, CA: Wadsworth Publishing, 2011.

Rum

Abbott, L. A. *Seven Wives and Seven Prisoners, or Experiences in the Life of a Matrimonial Monomaniac – A True Story*. New York: published for the author, 1870.

Adjutant-General of the Commonwealth of Massachusetts. *Annual Report of the Adjutant-General of the Commonwealth of Massachusetts for the year ending December 31, 1864*. Boston: Wright and Potter, State Printers, 1865.

Adjutant-General of the Commonwealth of Massachusetts. *Massachusetts Soldiers, Sailors, and Marines in the Civil War*, Volume I. Norwood, MA: Norwood Press, 1931.

Barker, Barbara, and Molyneux, Leslie J. *Images of America: Hanover.* Charleston, SC: Arcadia Publishing, 2004.

Barry, John Stetson. *A Historical Sketch of the Town of Hanover, Massachusetts: with Family Genealogies*. Boston: S. G. Drake, 1853.

Blackstone, Sir William. *Commentaries on the Laws of England in Four Books.* Philadelphia: George T. Bisel Company, 1922.

Chase, Frederic Hathaway. *Lemuel Shaw, Chief Justice of the Supreme Judicial Court, 1830 – 1860*. Boston and New York: Houghton Mifflin Co., 1918.

Clark, W. L., Marshall, W. L., and Lazell, H. B. *A Treatise on the Law of Crimes.* Chicago: Callaghan, 1952.

Cutter, William Richard, A. M. *New England Families – Genealogical and Memorial: A Record of the Achievements of Her People in the Making of Commonwealths and the Founding of a Nation - Volume II.* New York: Lewis Historical Publishing Company, 1914.

Davis, William Thomas. *History of the Judiciary of Massachusetts*. Boston: Boston Book Company, 1900.

Dix, John Ross. *Local Loiterings, and Visits in the Vicinity of Boston, by Looker On.* Boston: Redding and Company, 1846.

Driscoll, Barbara A. *The Tracks North: The Railroad Bracero Program of World War II.* Austin: University of Texas Press, Center for American Studies, 1999.

Dwelley, Jedediah, and Simmons, John F. *History of the Town of Hanover, Massachusetts: with Family Genealogies.* Hanover, MA: Town of Hanover, 1910.

225

Eliot, Samuel Atkins, A.M., D.D., ed. *Biographical History of Massachusetts, Volume II.* Boston: Massachusetts Biographical Society, 1909.

Ellis, Leonard Bolles. *History of New Bedford and its Vicinity, 1602-1892.* Syracuse, NY: D. Mason and Company, 1892.

Finkleman, Paul. *An Imperfect Union: Slavery, Federalism, and Comity.* Union, NJ: The Lawbook Exchange, Ltd., 2000.

Fisher, Charles Eben. *The Story of the Old Colony Railroad.* Taunton: By the author, 1919.

Gray, Francis Calley. *Prison Discipline in America.* Boston: Charles T. Little and James Brown, 1847.

Great Britain. Surveyor-General of Prisons *Second Report of the Surveyor-General of Prisons.* London: Printed by William Clowes and Sons, Stamford Street, for Her Majesty's Stationery Office, 1847.

Haynes, Gideon. *Pictures from Prison Life: An Historical Sketch of the Massachusetts State Prison.* Boston: Lee and Shepard, 1869.

Hedin, Robert. *The Great Machines: Poems and Songs of the American Railroad.* Iowa City: University of Iowa Press, 1966.

Hurd, D. Hamilton. *History of Bristol County Massachusetts with Biographical Sketches of many of its Pioneers and Prominent Men, Illustrated.* Philadelphia: J. W. Lewis & Co., 1883.

Lewis, O. F., PhD. *The Development of American Prisons and Prison Customs, 1776-1845.* Albany: Prison Association of New York, 1922.

Masur, Louis P. *Capital Punishment and the Transformation of American Culture, 1776-1865.* New York: Oxford University Press, 1989.

Maynard, William Barksdale. *Walden Pond: A History.* New York: Oxford University Press, Inc., 2004.

New England Historic Genealogical Society. *Memorial Biographies of the New England Historic Genealogical Society, Volume VI, 1864-1871.* Boston: Published by the Society, 1905.

O'Connor, Thomas H. *The Boston Irish: A Political History.* Canada: Little, Brown and Co., 1995.

Officer, L., and Williamson, S. *Purchasing Power of Money in the United States from 1774 to 2008.*

Prison Discipline Society. *Reports of the Prison Discipline Society – 1846-1847.* Boston: Press of T. R. Marvin, 1855.

Reno, Conrad, LL.B. *Memoirs of the Judiciary and Bar of New England for the Nineteenth Century with a History of the Judicial System of New England,* Volume III. Boston: The Century Memorial Publishing Company, 1901.

Rogers, Alan. *Murder and the Death Penalty in Massachusetts.* Amherst and Boston: University of Massachusetts Press, 2008.

Schechter, Harold. *Fiend: The Shocking True Story of America's Youngest Serial Killer.* New York: Pocket Books/Simon & Schuster, 2000.

Shannon, William V. *The American Irish: A Political and Social Portrait.* Amherst, MA: The University of Massachusetts Press, 1966.

Thacher, James. *History of the Town of Plymouth.* Boston: Marsh, Capon & Lyon, 1832.

Wadsworth, H.A. *History of Lawrence, Massachusetts, with Portraits and Biographical Sketches* Lawrence, MA: Lawrence Eagle Steam Job Printing Officer, 1880.

Wakin, Edward. *Enter the Irish-American.* Lincoln, NE: iUniverse, Inc., 2002.

A Tailor's Goose

Davis, Charles G. *Report of the Trial of Samuel M. Andrews, Indicted for the Murder of Cornelius Holmes, Before the Supreme Judicial Court of Massachusetts, December 11, 1868, Including the Rulings of the Court Upon Many Questions of Law, and a Full Statement of Authorities Upon the Subject of Transitory Insanity.* New York: Hurd and Houghton, 1869.

Davis, William Thomas. *History of the Judiciary of Massachusetts*. Boston: Boston Book Company, 1900.

Davis, William Thomas. *Bench and Bar of the Commonwealth of Massachusetts*, Volume II. Boston: Boston History Company, 1895.

Dearborn, Jeremiah Wadleigh.ed. *A History of the First Century of the Town of Parsonsfield, Maine*. Portland, ME: Brown, Thurston and Company, 1888.

Dedham Historical Society. *Dedham Historical Register*. Dedham: Dedham Historical Society, 1890 and 1893.

Evans, Colin. *Criminal Investigations: Crime Scene Investigation*. New York: Infobase Publishing, 2009.

Fisher, Charles Eben. *The Story of the Old Colony Railroad*. Taunton, MA: By the author, 1919.

Heard, Franklin Fiske. *Report of the Trial of Leavitt Alley: Indicted for the Murder of Abijah Ellis*. Boston: Little, Brown & Co., 1875.

Hurd, Duane Hamilton. *History of Norfolk County, Massachusetts with Biographical Sketches of Many of Its Pioneers and Prominent Men*. Philadelphia: J. W. Lewis and Company, 1884.

Newton, David E. *DNA Evidence and Forensic Science*. New York: Facts on File, Inc., 2008.

Norris, Curt. "The Case of the Scarlet Slipper." *True Police Cases,* June 1975 Edition.

Norris, Lowell Ames. "Evidence from a Low-Studded Attic." *Yankee Magazine*, September 1966 Edition.

Officer, L., and Williamson, S. *Purchasing Power of Money in the United States from 1774 to 2008*. Measuring Worth, 2009.

Owen, David. *Hidden Evidence, 40 True Crimes and How Forensic Science Helped Solve Them.* London: Quintet Publishing Limited, 2000.

Rexford, Nancy E. *Women's shoes in America, 1795-1930.* Kent, Ohio: Kent State University Press, c2000.

Rogers, Alan. *Murder and the Death Penalty in Massachusetts.* Amherst and Boston, University of Massachusetts Press, 2008.

Wadsworth, H. A. *History of Lawrence, Massachusetts, with Portraits and Biographical Sketches.* Lawrence, MA: Lawrence Eagle Steam Job Printing Officer, 1880.

Witthaus, R. A., and Becker, Tracy C. *Medical Jurisprudence: Forensic Medicine and Toxicology, Volume 1.* New York: William Wood & Company, 1894.

Zonderman, Jon. *Beyond the Crime Lab: the New Science of Investigation.* New York: John Wiley & Sons, Inc., New York, 1990.

A Soap Box

Bacon, Edwin M., ed. *Men of Progress: One Thousand Biographical Sketches and Portraits of Leaders in Business and Professional Life in the Commonwealth of Massachusetts.* Boston, New England Magazine, 1896.

Barbo, Theresa Mitchell. *The Cape Cod Murder of 1899: Edwin Ray Snow's Punishment and Redemption.* Charleston, SC: The History Press, 2007.

Board of Prison Commissioners. *Fourth Annual Report of the Board of Prison Commissioners of Massachusetts for the Year Ending September 30, 1904.* Boston: Wright & Potter Printing Co., State Printers, 1905.

Borden, Alanson. *Our Country and Its People; a Descriptive and Biographical Record of Bristol County Massachusetts.* Boston: The Boston History Company, 1899.

Chen, Shehong. *Reconstructing the Chinese American Experience in Lowell, Massachusetts, 1870s – 1970s, Making a Living as Laundry Men, 1876-1920.* Boston: Institute for Asian American Studies, University of Massachusetts, 2003.

Commission on Economy and Efficiency, *The Commonwealth of Massachusetts; Functions, Organization and Administration of the Departments in the Executive Branch of the State Government*. Boston: Wright & Potter Printing Company, 1914.

Cutter, William Richard, ed., *Historic Homes and Places and Genealogical and Personal Memoirs Relating to the Families of Middlesex County, Massachusetts*, Volume IV. New York: Lewis Historical Publishing Company, 1908.

Davis, Charles G. *Report of the Trial of Samuel M. Andrews indicted for the Murder of Cornelius Holmes, before the Supreme Judicial Court of Massachusetts, December 11, 1868*. New York: Hurd and Houghton, 1869.

Davis, William Thomas. *History of the Judiciary of Massachusetts*. Boston: Boston Book Company, 1900.

Eliot, Samuel Atkins, A.M., D.D. *Biographical History of Massachusetts: Biographies and Autobiographies of the Leading Men in the State*, Volume II. Boston: Massachusetts Biography Society, 1913.

Fisher, Charles Eben. *The Story of the Old Colony Railroad*. Taunton, MA: By the author, 1919.

Hurd, D. Hamilton. *History of Plymouth County, Massachusetts, with Biographical Sketches of man of its Pioneers and Prominent Men*. Philadelphia: J. W. Lewis & Company, 1884.

Hutton, Frankie, and Reed, Barbara Strauss, eds. *Outsiders in 19th Century Press History: Multicultural Perspectives*. Bowling Green, OH: Bowling Green State University Popular Press, 1995.

Metcalf, Henry Harrison, and Clintock, John Norris, eds. *The Granite Monthly: A New Hampshire Magazine devoted to History, Biography, Literature and State Progress, Volume XLI*. Concord: Granite Monthly Publishing Company, 1909.

Mullgart, Louis Christian. *All about Tobacco*. Las Vegas, NV: Epic Publishing Company, 2014.

Rogers, Allen. *Murder and the Death Penalty in Massachusetts*. Amherst and Boston: University of Massachusetts Press, 2008.

Schechter, Harold. *Fiend: The Shocking True Story of America's Youngest Serial Killer*. New York: Pocket Books/Simon & Schuster, 2000.

Yu, Renqiu. *To Save China, To Save Ourselves: The Chinese Hand Laundry Alliance of New York*. Philadelphia: Temple University Press, 1992.

Yung, Judy, Chang, Gordon H., and Lai, Him Mark, eds. *Chinese American Voices, From the Gold Rush to the Present*. Berkeley, CA: Regents of the University of California, 2006.

231